GNVQ Intermediate

Information Technology

W W Milner and Ann Montgomery-Smith

Stanley Thornes (Publishers) Ltd

First published in 1997 by:
Stanley Thornes (Publishers) Ltd
Ellenborough House
Wellington Street
Cheltenham
GL50 1YW
UK

A catalogue record for this book is available from the British Library.

97 98 99 00 01 / 10 9 8 7 6 5 4 3 2 1

ISBN 0 7487 3029 X

Typeset by Columns Design Ltd, Reading, UK
Printed and bound in Great Britain by Scotprint Ltd, Musselburgh, Scotland.

Contents

Acknowledgements

The authors and publishers are grateful to the following for permission to reproduce photographs and other material:

RS Components Ltd (pages 11 and 55) and Alan Rutherford for the cover image.

Every effort has been made to contact copyright holders, and we apologise if any have been overlooked.

Introduction
Study skills for GNVQ Intermediate IT

Understanding yourself, and why you are on the course

What is the course? Do you match up with the course?

GNVQ courses are preparation courses for work. The GNVQ in information technology is a course about using computers at work. It is not about computer games, not even educational ones. You will learn about business and industry to see how computers fit in with their needs. You will learn about the information they use as well as the technology they use to process it. Do you think this will interest you?

IT is about communication

You will be using commercial computer programs such as word processing packages, desktop publishing packages and graphics packages to communicate information. You may have grammar and spelling checks on your computer but you will need to be able to write sentences and paragraphs that make sense. You must still know enough about spelling and grammar to make choices using the spellchecker.

Computer software can be complicated to use. To understand a computer program you will have to understand help messages and to be able to read and understand manuals. Communication is an important part of this course. Are you interested in improving your communication skills?

IT is about numbers

Some graphic design and desktop publishing packages can be complicated to use. You may need to make accurate measurements, to get something exactly right. You will be using spreadsheets and other packages for numerical processing, and must understand the arithmetic and mathematics behind the processing to use them properly. Are you interested in improving your number skills?

IT is about solving problems

This is not a course where there are always right and wrong answers. You will often need to work round complications until you get something working. Do you enjoy solving problems? Are you persistent in trying to get things working? Can you try a new way to get the computer doing what you want? Can you work through computer help messages? Are you able to use computer manuals? Do you enjoy playing with computer packages to find new ways of doing things?

IT is about office skills

You will be setting up filing systems using databases. You will need to understand what you are filing and how to index the files. You will also need to be competent at other office skills such as keyboarding. Will you enjoy learning office skills?

IT is about technology

Technology changes every day. You will need to learn about more than one machine because tomorrow you will have a different one to work on. You will need to understand how computers work, so that you can set up a new computer system, and in a fast-changing field such as IT you will need to read newspapers and magazines to keep up with new products. Are you interested in reading computer magazines? Even the articles not about games? Can you remember where you read about a new product?

IT is about people

IT is for people to use. It is a tool for people to use. But people make it work. People feed it with information and people use the information coming out. Are you interested in improving your skills at working with others?

Working and studying on a vocational course

You are choosing a *vocational* course, a course preparing you for work. This is not a course for children who look on their teachers as the 'them'. This is a course for students prepared to act responsibly and to treat their studies as work. You must imagine customers waiting for your outcomes. Are you able to look on study as work? Can you make the commitment to work and study for 30 hours a week? And this means actually *working*, not dossing in a classroom rather than at home. Can you organise your own time so that you produce work on time without constant nagging? Can you organise your time so that you study regularly throughout the course, not just half the night before an assignment is handed in?

Your teachers and lecturers will help you with this, but in the end you must take responsibility for your own work. Do you think that you would like being responsible for your own work?

Where does this course lead?

Jobs in IT can be divided into three types:

1 Jobs using IT

Most jobs are of this type. They include jobs in the office, in business, in graphic art or design, in automation, in retail, banking and accounting. Most jobs nowadays use IT and an intermediate GNVQ in the subject will help you in any trainee job at this level.

2 Supporting IT users

With so many people using IT as part of their work, people are needed to help them with the IT systems. You can work in system support as a technician or by running a help desk.

Technician work includes making sure that the equipment is working correctly, that printers have paper and ink, that faults are corrected, that users can be advised on new hardware and software, being a network manager. Trainee technician work is available at this level. Running a help desk involves helping users with their IT. It involves learning the technology very thoroughly so that you can help users to work it. There are openings for help desk trainees at this level.

Some firms recruit for system support jobs at a higher level from outside the firm, but may move juniors from other areas to this type of job if they show aptitude.

3 Developing IT systems

This involves setting up a system to do a specific job. The system is developed using a suitable general purpose package such as a spreadsheet or database, or even a programming language. There are very few jobs available in systems development at intermediate level. Most firms recruit at advanced level or direct from universities, but may move juniors working in other areas to this type of job if they show aptitude.

Further education

After an intermediate GNVQ in IT you could go on to study:
- Advanced GNVQ in IT.
- Most other advanced GNVQ courses.
- Some people also go on to take advanced level GCEs (non-vocational A-levels).

After Advanced GNVQ or GCE courses have been passed, students can go on to university in appropriate subject areas.

What do you know already about IT?

What computers have you used? At school? At home? Elsewhere? What programs have you used? Commercial packages? Programming languages? Games? Anything else? Have you taken any courses in IT before? Have you any qualifications in IT?

Activity I.1

May be suitable for communications

1 In pairs, or a group of three if there is an odd number of students, interview each other. Find out the other person's personal details, what he or she knows about IT already, why they chose this course and where they see themselves in five years time.

2 Using an appropriate computer package, write a one-page article about your partner.

3 Make these pages into a wall display to introduce members of the course to each other.

Activity I.2

May be suitable for communications

In small groups, write a questionnaire suitable for interviewing staff members of the course team. Each group should interview a different staff member, produce a one-page article, and add this to the wall display.

Understanding yourself, and how you learn

Different people have different ways of learning. Some people learn best by reading, some by hearing explanations and others by trial and error. It is worth finding out which is the best method for you, then make sure that you can use that method to your best advantage. Also find ways to make it easier for you to learn.

To help you understand how you learn best, work through the questionnaire in Figure I.1. Read each of the statements carefully and tick the box that best describes your feelings about it. This is a diagnostic test to help you develop good study skills so *answer it truthfully*.

Tick box 1 if you agree fully 2 if you agree more or less 3 if you disagree more or less 4 if you disagree fully	1	2	3	4
1 I like to read	☐	☐	☐	☐
2 I learn best from books	☐	☐	☐	☐
3 If I want to find something out, I usually look it up in a book	☐	☐	☐	☐
4 I often use a book index to find what I want	☐	☐	☐	☐
5 I learn best by listening	☐	☐	☐	☐
6 I like a teacher to explain something carefully before I try to do it myself	☐	☐	☐	☐
7 If I want to find something out, I usually ask someone	☐	☐	☐	☐
8 I make notes in lessons	☐	☐	☐	☐
9 I learn best by trying things out	☐	☐	☐	☐
10 I like to try things out for myself before learning about them	☐	☐	☐	☐
11 I like to find out what all the options do on the menus of computer programs	☐	☐	☐	☐
12 I use help messages in computer programs to help me use a new program	☐	☐	☐	☐
13 I like to think through what I have learnt at the end of a day	☐	☐	☐	☐
14 I like to know what I am expected to learn during a new course	☐	☐	☐	☐
15 I like to be able to check off what I have learnt as the course goes on	☐	☐	☐	☐
16 Before I give in a piece of work, I check it	☐	☐	☐	☐
17 I like to make things work	☐	☐	☐	☐
18 I always read instructions before using anything	☐	☐	☐	☐
19 I really enjoyed school	☐	☐	☐	☐
20 I like learning new things	☐	☐	☐	☐

Figure I.1

You will have guessed by now that all 1s make you an ideal student!

We're not all ideal. If you ticked a 4, or perhaps a 3, and want some help in this area, here are some suggestions.

1 You may dislike reading because you find it difficult. If you find it difficult there may be a physical reason, such as eyesight problems or dyslexia. Ask your tutor about diagnosis and help with reading. It may not be possible to cure your problem, but there are often reading strategies which can help. Maybe you find reading boring because you read too slowly. Look in your library for a book on reading faster or reading better. Follow some of the exercises in the book to try to increase your reading speed. It is worth speeding up your reading now because it will help you for the rest of your life. You do not always need to read through a whole book – you might only need to find the relevant paragraph. If you are reading for information here is a useful strategy.

- Have the question you want to answer clearly in your mind.
- Use the index or contents page to find what you are looking for.
- Skim through the page or chapter to find the information that you want.
- Read the information carefully – but save time by not reading the rest of the page or chapter thoroughly.
- Close the book (though keep your finger in the right page) and try to recall the answer to your question straight away.
- Check with the book that you have remembered it correctly.
- Make a note of what you have found (see question 8).

2 If you learn best by hearing something, maybe it will help you to read important text out loud, or even into a tape recorder for revision. If you learn best by trying things out, try to do what you have just read about. If this is not possible then try to imagine yourself doing it in as much detail as possible. Think what you would feel, and what might go wrong.

3 Sometimes you might only find the information that you need in a book or magazine. Use strategies such as that described in 1 and 4 to help. Many reference books have now been put onto CD-ROM. Learn to use these to find information.

4 If you have difficulty using a book index, ask your tutor or librarian to explain – it will save you a lot of effort.

5 If you find it difficult to concentrate when someone is speaking to you, pretend you are a newspaper reporter and take notes. At the first opportunity, review your notes and make sure that you still understand them. You may find it helps you learn to picture in your mind what is being said, or even to draw a picture on a piece of paper. Ask questions to help with this picture.

6 This is probably because you prefer to try to work things out for yourself. Not everyone feels this way, and many students in the class want to hear the explanation. So be patient and try to picture yourself following the instructions in your head, or maybe take notes. Let others learn the way they learn best.

7 As long as you find out some other way, this is not a bad thing. But don't get to the stage where you are too proud to ask. Even if you pretend to other people that you know something that you do not really understand don't pretend to yourself.

8 Making notes can be useful if:
- your teacher does not give you handouts

- you find it helps you concentrate
- you want a permanent record, and don't want to rely on your memory. It might also be helpful to make notes of what you have read and what you have found by other means. Do *not* try to write down everything said in a lesson – write down only the main points. You might find it easiest at first to make notes immediately after, rather than during, a lesson. Make notes with a friend, and try to recall what the lesson was about as soon as it is over. If you find this difficult, ask the teacher or lecturer to summarise the lesson for you at the end. This will show you whether you are understanding correctly the points he or she is trying to make.

9   Are you nervous about trying things out? If so become braver. Young children learn by this method all the time and it is a natural way to learn (until it is trained out of you as you grow up). When learning a new computer program it is often useful to spend a little time trying out different menu options or different buttons – and you shouldn't do any damage this way. If you do the program is at fault, or you have no proper backup system. It helps to *read the messages on the screen* and you can make notes if you find it helps.

10 If you disagree with this statement, you probably agreed with statement 6. There are usually tutorials for new programs either on-line or in a manual. Use these.

11 Arrange some time to play with the menus. Decide on a target such as 'find out what one new menu item does' before starting the rest of your work on the program. Another useful strategy is to browse through a manual – this is particularly useful when you think you know the program. You may find a shortcut for something that has taken you several key presses up to now.

12 Get a friend or a tutor to help you understand how to use help messages. They become easier to use with practice and can be very useful once you start to understand them. Persevere.

13 Computers have an internal memory which they use when they are working. This memory is volatile and loses everything when the computer is switched off. To keep any work, it must be stored on backing store such as a disk. Human memory works in a similar fashion – you have a short-term memory which you use for what is happening here and now and a long-term memory for remembering what happened yesterday, the day before or last year. When you learn something it has to be transferred from short-term to long-term memory. Your brain decides what to transfer automatically, but it is worth helping it from time to time.

   You can aid this transfer by reviewing what you are learning from time to time. Useful habits can include making notes after each lesson or lecture (see 8, above), reviewing in your mind what you have learnt that day during your journey home, or immediately you reach home, reviewing at the end of each week what you have learnt that week. If you make notes as you review you are creating your brain's backup copies. This is very useful, and you should make the most of its use by storing your notes carefully in a filing drawer, a loose leaf file or on a database.

14 So you like a mystery tour? OK – just make sure you keep up with work set.

15 In a GNVQ, *you are responsible for your own learning*. Your tutor will monitor your learning, but at the end of the day it is up to you. If you cannot cope with this, then perhaps you are on the wrong course.

16 See the paragraph on assignments (below).
17 If you ticked box 4 on this statement, you should consider whether you are on the right course. Discuss this with your tutor and your parents or guardian while there is still time to change courses.
18 Just remember – *if all else fails, read the instructions!*
19 Let us hope that GNVQ, where *you* are responsible for your own learning, changes that. The course is vocational; you should treat teachers and lecturers as work supervisors. This works both ways –they should treat you as an adult, and you should behave towards them as an adult. Once you achieve this balance you will enjoy this more. Let's hope so.
20 See 17, above.

Unit specifications

Each GNVQ unit is made up of elements, for instance unit 1, Introduction to Information Technology (Intermediate level) is made up of three or four elements:

Element 1: Examine industrial and commercial information technology systems
Element 2: Examine the components of a stand-alone computer system
Element 3: Set up a stand-alone computer system to meet user requirements
Element 4: Produce an application software macro to meet user requirements

Each element is made up of a number of performance criteria which are the skills which the students must be able to demonstrate that they have. For instance Element 1.1 (element 1 of unit 1) states that a student must:

1 Describe the **benefits** and **limitations** of **commercial systems**
2 Describe the **benefits** and **limitations** of **industrial systems**
3 Explain the **features** of a selected **commercial system**
4 Explain the **features** of a selected **industrial system**

You must therefore prove that you can perform each of these criteria. To help your tutor understand what the performance criteria mean, some of the words or phrases are emboldened, and the range of meanings to these words and phrases are listed. Thus **benefits** are listed as meaning accuracy, cost, efficiency, speed, impact on environment. **Commercial systems** are listed as meaning booking systems, electronic funds transfer, electronic point of sale systems, stock control, order processing, payroll processing.

The ranges may not include every possibility, but you need to show evidence of being able to describe the benefits in terms of the listed range for all the listed commercial systems.

This book covers the GNVQ mandatory and Edexel optional units. Each chapter covers one unit. Each chapter section covers one element. The contents page is also a summary of the units. A summary of the core units (application of number and communications) is given below. If you ticked 1 in the diagnostic test for questions 14 and 15, you may like to buy your own copy of units. Ask your tutor for your examiner's address.

Assignments

On this course you must prove that you can perform certain skills. These may be practical skills or may entail demonstrating your knowledge. The assignments that you are given should provide evidence that you can perform these skills. *Always* check that you have followed instructions in the assignments *exactly* as they have been designed to give evidence of these skills. Otherwise, however beautiful the work that you produce, you will not have done what is required.

Tests

The mandatory units involve externally marked multiple choice question tests, which have a pass mark of 70%. They test your knowledge. The specifications for the tests are available from the awarding bodies and detail the topics to be questioned and how many questions will be asked on each topic. Your teachers will guide you as to what you need to know.

Each question has a choice of four answers. One is the correct answer, the others are known as distractors. Do not be distracted. The question papers are not a race. You should have enough time to answer the questions slowly and carefully.

1 Read the question. No one will press the buzzer before you, so read the whole question. Each word written in each question has a purpose; why is it there?

2 Try and give your own answer before reading the answers offered. Then look at the answers offered
   - If your answer is there mark the appropriate box.
   - If your answer is not there, is there an answer with the same meaning?
   - If you are unsure of the answer cross out the ones that are obviously wrong; if there is only one answer left then use it.
   - If you still do not know the answer, go on to the next questions. There are often groups of questions in the same knowledge area, and one of the later questions may jog your memory. You will have time to come back to this question if you do not waste time on what you don't know.

3 When you have had a first run-through and answered the questions that you are sure of, go through a second time to try the questions that you are unsure of.

4 Read the question again, carefully. What is the examiner getting at? What does the question mean? What do the answers mean?
   - If all else fails, guess. You won't lose a mark for a wrong guess and you might gain a mark for a correct guess.

Past question papers are available from the awarding bodies and your teachers will probably give you some practice tests.

Key skills

Employers have asked that vocational GNVQs make sure that all students have good skills at communications, numeracy and information technology. Students must demonstrate these key skills as well as the vocational skills.
Summary of GNVQ Key Units Level 2
Application of number
Element 1: Collect and record data
Element 2: Tackle problems
Element 3: Interpret and present data
Communications
Element 1: Take part in discussions
Element 2: Produce written material

Element 3: Use images
Element 4: Read and respond to written materials

Activity I.3

May be suitable for application of number
This activity is to find out if there are any characteristics making students more likely to choose this course than any other. In small groups, discuss your reasons for being on this course. They may be because of your interests, your existing qualifications, the job you hope to have or some other characteristics entirely such as how well you get on with other people. Choose one area of characteristics (interests, qualifications, future job, characteristic of your choice – e.g. teamworking, friends' jobs) and invent a short questionnaire (five or six questions) designed to test these characteristics. For instance, if you choose 'qualifications' you might ask:

- How many grades A–C did you get?
- What grade did you get in maths?

Give this questionnaire to the students on your course, and also to other students of the same age or stage in your educational establishment. Analyse the results, displaying them with suitable graphs.

Grading criteria and working practices

Your work will be graded according to how you carried it out (the process) and according to the quality of the work (the outcome). Each piece of work has three marks for process, one each for:

- planning your work
- seeking and handling information
- evaluation

and one mark for outcome. These are called *interim* grades and can be pass, merit or distinction.

When you have completed your portfolio of evidence (your work), you select one-third of the best marks for each process and for the outcome. The lowest mark determines your grade. To gain a distinction you must have a distinction in at least a third of your work for all four grade themes. To gain a merit you must have a merit or distinction for at least a third of all interim grades for each grade theme. You must also have passed every assignment and every test, and have evidence for all your core skills.

Planning

To gain a merit or distinction for planning, you must show evidence of having planned your actions for the assignment, and of seeing when to ask an assessor for help and for changing your plan. To help you with planning evidence you should:

- make a list at the start of each day of what you intend to achieve, how long you think it will take and what equipment you will need
- keep a diary, jotting down at the end of each day what you have achieved and how long it took
- plan the tasks needed for completing an assignment, and for group assignments plan who will undertake each task.

Whether you obtain a merit or distinction for planning will depend on the complexity of the tasks being graded.

Information seeking and handling

For a merit you will need to show that you have identified the information needed for simple tasks, and you must access and collect the information on your own. For a distinction you must be able to do this for complex tasks. Sources of information could be:

- reference books
- a library
- CD-ROM
- the Internet
- magazines and newspapers
- catalogues.

You need to plan and document your information seeking.

Evaluation

When you have finished a piece of work you should judge it against what you were asked to do. For a pass you must have done exactly what you were asked to do. You should have achieved each task set. For a merit you should show how you achieved each task set and suggest other ways that you might have achieved it. For a distinction you should also suggest how the tasks could have been performed better.

Outcome

For a merit your work must show that you have put together your knowledge, skills and understanding to achieve the tasks set. The way you completed your tasks and described them should also show that you understand language used for IT. For a distinction you must do this for hard as well as simple tasks.

You may find some of the forms given here useful.

Daily Planning Sheet/Diary

Name

Date

Time	Task	What I need	Review
Expected time for task	This could be a lecture or lesson, or could be an activity that you are carrying out on your own or in a group	Equipment, books, previously completed work, etc.	Did you complete it? Did you time it right? Does it lead to new tasks? Any other comments?

Group Planning Sheet

Assignment/Activity   Names

Date

Task	By whom	By when	Review

Individual Assignment Planning

Assignment

Name

Date

Task	Task order	When to do task	Review

Information Seeking

Name

Date

What I need to know	Where to look	Where found	Review

Evaluation of Assignment

Name

Date

I have completed the assignment criteria	I did it by	I could have improved it by
List criteria here	Explain what tasks you used to achieve each criterion	
I wish to claim PCs: List vocational and core key skill PCs here	**Assessor comments**	

Action plan for period: _____

Name
_____

Assessor comments

Student comments

Further action:

Signatures

Assessor _____   Date _____

Student _____   Date _____

Activity I.4

This activity may be completed individually or in a small group. Read through the whole activity before starting it.

A student on this course wishes to buy a stand-alone computer system to use at home to help with the work for the course. Find out a suitable system in terms of hardware and software. Submit a costed proposal for such a system using advertisements and catalogues to find the costs.

Read through the core skill units and list any performance criteria that you have demonstrated in working through this activity. Plan, carry out and evaluate the activity and submit evidence for grading themes.

Activity I.5

Describe the organisation of this course within the educational establishment. Again, read through the core skill units and list any performance criteria that you have demonstrated in working through this activity. Plan, carry out and evaluate the activity and submit evidence for grading themes.

Assignment AI.1
Explaining the course to your parents

This assignment provides evidence for the following key skills:
Application of numbers: all elements
Communications: all elements

Aims

1 To get to know each other:
  a colleagues (other students)
  b other staff (supervisors such as teachers and lecturers, technicians and administrative staff)
  c the structure of the workplace (educational establishment).
2 To get to know the course:
  a working practices
    • timetable
    • vocational skills
    • core skills
  b assessments
    • providing evidence of skills
    • providing evidence of knowledge
    • providing evidence for grading.
3 To explore presentational information technology.
4 To involve parents and guardians with the course.

Tasks

1 Read all the tasks.
2 Plan your tasks:
  a Some of these tasks will be done as the whole group, and must be planned by the whole group. This will include
    • choosing small groups, allocating work to the groups and monitoring the group work
    • planning the final display
    • organising the final display.
  b Some of these tasks will be done in a small group (two or three people), and must be planned by the small group. The groups should be made up of people who do not yet know each other, or who do not normally work with each other. Tasks will include
    • allocating work to individuals and monitoring the individual work within the group
    • arranging and carrying out interviews
    • arranging and carrying out displays
    • arranging and carrying out any other group tasks allocated.
  c Some of these tasks will be done individually, and must be planned individually. This will include
    • organising time and equipment for your own tasks
    • learning display information technology packages
    • carrying out and recording your own tasks.
  d Do all your planning on the planning sheets provided, so they can be used as evidence for your planning.

      e You will need to plan both your actions and your information seeking and you will be provided with forms for both planning actions.

      f When you have finished the assignment you will need to evaluate how well you have done, so don't forget to fill in all the sections on the planning sheets.

3 Decide, with your tutors, how you can best explain the course to your parents or guardians. This may be by inviting them to an event at the educational establishment, in which case you must decide a date, time, place and format for the event, who to invite, how to invite them. Or it may be by sending them written material, in which case you must still decide the format and date to be sent.

4 Use material from exercises to describe the people on the course and the organisation of the course and the educational establishment and display this information.

5 Prepare a display on your working practices.

6 Prepare a display on the assessment of the students on the course.

7 Prepare a display to explain the IT used for the displays.

8 Hold the event and/or print and send material.

9 Evaluate the success of this assignment as a group assignment, in small group work and in individual work.

Key skills coverage of assignments

Key skills	Assignments
Communication	
2.1	AI.1, A1.3, A3.2, A6.1, A7.1, A7.2, A7.3, A8.3
2.2	AI.1, A1.1, A1.2, A2.1, A2.2, A3.2, A3.3, A4.1, A4.2, A4.3, A5.1, A5.2, A5.3, A6.1, A7.1, A7.2, A7.3, A8.3
2.3	AI.1, A1.2, A2.1, A2.3, A3.2, A3.3, A6.1, A7.1, A7.2, A8.3
2.4	AI .1, A7.2
Information technology	
2.1	A2.1, A2.2
2.2	A2.2, A2.3, A2.4
2.3	A1.2, A2.1, A2.2, A4.1, A5.2
2.4	A1.1, A2.4, A4.3
Application of number	
2.1	AI.1, A7.2
2.2	AI.1, A2.3, A5.2, A5.3
2.3	AI.1, A7.1, A7.2, A8.3

CHAPTER 1

Introduction to IT

Element 1.1: Examine industrial and commercial IT systems
Element 1.2: Examine the components of a stand-alone computer system
Element 1.3: Set up a stand-alone computer system to meet user requirements
Element 1.4: Produce an applications software macro to meet user requirements

What is covered in this chapter

- The benefits, limitations and features of commercial IT systems
- The benefits, limitations and features of industrial IT systems
- The hardware components of stand-alone computer systems
- The software components of stand-alone computer systems
- How to connect the hardware and install software for a system
- How to produce a user macro

Items you will need in your portfolio for this unit:

- Assignment 1.1
- Assignment 1.2
- Assignment 1.3
- Assignment 1.4

Introduction

Most people would say that information technology (IT) is important to the way we live and work today, and that in order to get a good job you need a good understanding of the way IT works and how to use it.

Nearly all young people use computers at school, and many families have a computer at home. However, few people are clear about what **information systems** are. This chapter looks at the way commerce and industry make use of IT.

Activity 1.1 ───────────────────────────────

Find out some basic facts about the computing facilities your college provides.
1 Where are the computers you are allowed to use? When may you use them?
2 Are there any special security rules about using the computers, such as about the use of floppy disks?
3 What types of computers are available, and what printers? Are there any special devices, such as document scanners or modems?
4 What operating system do the computers use? (The operating system is the software which makes the computer run – many use MS DOS). Do they use Windows?

1

5 What word-processing package is normally used?
Prepare a report detailing your findings.

Element 1.1: Examine industrial and commercial IT systems

Machines are found in industrial settings (factories and industrial units) for manufacturing things like circuit boards, cars or plastic pipes. You will also find machines at home (your washing machine or central heating system, for example) and in public (pedestrian crossings, turnstiles, revolving doors in supermarkets). All of these machines must be controlled – motors or pumps must be switched on and off, heaters adjusted, lights flashed. The control can be carried out by humans (and often is), but it is often faster, cheaper and safer to use a computer system. Computer systems that control machines are known as **industrial** systems. Computers are also used in industry for other purposes, such as designing products.

The information in a bank's 'hole-in-the-wall' cash machine (properly called an 'automated teller machine' or ATM), an airline's flight booking system, the checkout at a supermarket or a mail-order company's records also need to be controlled. Before the use of computers the information would probably have been kept in folders in filing cabinets and people had to search manually for the information they needed. This was both laborious and slow. **Commercial** computer systems are designed to store, manage and retrieve data quickly and efficiently.

Activity 1.2

Which of the following are controlled by commercial systems and which by industrial systems?
- Booking a hotel room or an airline flight
- Robot paint sprayers in a car factory
- Bank cash dispensers
- Designing a road bridge
- Production of milk bottles
- Manufacture of electronic circuit boards
- Purchases using debit cards
- Managing a company payroll
- Coal mining

A supermarket's stock control system

The manager of a supermarket must keep careful control of each item in stock – if a particular item runs out the customers will be unhappy and the shop may lose trade, but if there is too much of one item there may not be space to store it all and the product could go past its 'sell by' date. It would be very difficult to keep this fine balance without the help of IT, because a supermarket may stock 10 000 or more product lines and updating the paper records of each one would be a never-ending job.

Activity 1.3

Suppose the store starts the week with 500 packets of frozen peas. During the week 260 packets are sold, and a lorry delivers a further 310 packets.

1 How many packets of peas should the store have in stock at the end of the week?
2 Can you think of ways in which more packets are lost than the 260 actually sold?
3 What actions could the manager of the store take to reduce the stock level if there are too many of a particular item? Would it be better to raise or lower the price?

Features of the stock control system

Data

The information in the system (the data) can be held in the form of numbers, text, images or sound. Data must be put into an IT system so that it can be manipulated. A supermarket's stock control system needs information in four areas:

- The product lines sold. A supermarket will sell thousands of different products, from packets of cornflakes to tins of shoe polish. For each item they need to know the numbers in stock, the selling price and the supplier of the product.
- Each sale. Every time an item is sold, the stock level goes down, and so they need data on sales. They need to know what was sold, how many, and on what date.
- Each delivery. When new supplies are delivered into the store, the stock levels increase. They need to know what was delivered, how many, and when.
- Suppliers of new stock – names, addresses, phone numbers.

Hardware

Some of the hardware in a supermarket's system, such as keyboards, screens and printers, is very standard. Other items, such as laser scanners at checkouts, are only used for particular systems. In a supermarket most product lines have a barcode which is unique to that line on the container. At each checkout a laser scanner reads the barcode. All the checkouts are connected to the store's main computer.

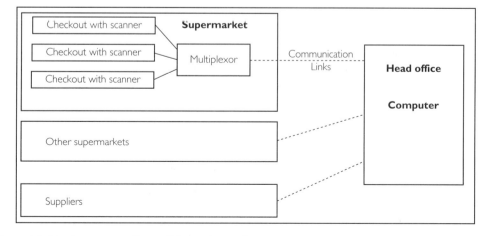

Figure 1.1 Hardware connections within a supermarket

Another uncommon piece of hardware likely to be found at a supermarket is a **multiplexor**, to which all the checkout scanners in the store are connected. The multiplexor combines the data from all the computers and scanners in the store into a single communications channel, which is connected to the main computer at head office.

Software

In a stock control system, software is needed to:

- control the input of data on sales and deliveries
- process the information
- ensure that goods are reordered at the right time so that stocks do not run out
- produce reports to management, such as showing which days of the week are the busiest.

Activity 1.4

If you were the manager of a supermarket, how would you use information on which days and times were the busiest? Think of some other reports that could be produced, and how you could use them.

Processing

Processing data involves one or more of these steps:

- the data is checked to ensure it is correct
- the data is stored for later use, retrieved for immediate use, or moved from one place to another
- some sort of mathematical process is performed, such as adding up numbers
- comparisons are made between data, and logical decisions made on the results.

The data processing involved in the supermarket's stock control system would include:

- looking up the price of each item sold from its barcode
- adding up the price of all the items scanned to give the total the customer must pay
- reducing the stock level by one for each item sold
- increasing stock levels when new stocks are delivered
- regularly comparing the actual stock levels with target levels and reordering any items that are in short supply.

People

People are essential in all information systems. Important people in a supermarket stock control system are:

- the checkout operators who deal with sales
- the staff who record deliveries of new stock
- the designers of the special equipment, such as the laser scanners, and of other parts of the system
- the engineers who maintain the hardware, carrying out repairs and replacements
- the programmers who produce the software
- the managers who use the information produced by the system to run the store.

It is essential that all of these people know what they are supposed to do, and that they are regularly retrained to keep their knowledge up to date.

Benefits of using a stock control IT system

The real benefits of using IT for stock control result from its use.

Accuracy

In processing information using pen and paper mistakes are inevitable, and happen much more often than they would if a computer system is used. The stock control of a large supermarket would be almost impossible without IT. The best that could be done would be to estimate stock levels, which is not very accurate.

Costs

Costs are reduced in many ways by using an IT-based system.
- The ability to read barcodes means that individual items don't need price labels, cutting down on the staff needed.
- Special offers can be applied at the point of sale as the computer reads the barcode, so fewer staff are needed to reprice reduced items.
- The checkout process is much faster, reducing the number of checkouts (and so number of staff) needed. This also makes more space available in the store to display items.
- Because the checkout is faster, queues are shorter.
- The shop is unlikely to run out of items and lose sales.
- Customers receive itemised receipts that they can check. Many people like this.

Environmental impact

Many people are worried about the ways we are damaging our environment – our air is polluted by vehicle exhaust fumes, farming chemicals (pesticides, fertilisers etc.) are being absorbed into other animals, and we are producing more and more plastic waste, which does not decay.

An IT stock control system in a supermarket can have some beneficial effects.
- Deliveries of new stock can be made as efficient as possible, reducing the number of lorries on the road and thus reducing air pollution.
- People can do all their shopping in one place and so will need to drive less.
- Stores don't have to carry large amounts of stock, so fewer items are likely to pass their sell-by date. Waste is therefore reduced.

Activity 1.5

Most of the benefits just described are to the advantage of the company owning the supermarket. List some ways in which these systems benefit the customer.

Review question

How does a supermarket benefit from using IT-based stock control rather than pen and paper methods?

Limitations of an IT-based system

Nothing is perfect, and there are bound to be bad aspects to all systems. You should be aware of the drawbacks, and the places where it is possible to reduce the difficulties.

Costs

Most of the costs of an IT system are involved in setting up the system – hardware must be bought, software written and staff trained to use it all. The largest costs incurred are in buying the laser scanners and training people to use them. However, once the system is in operation costs are usually small, as explained in the previous section. There are two main exceptions to this.

1 If the system is badly designed it will not work well – for example, the equipment might break down often and costs of repair could be high.
2 If a very small business rents the IT equipment, and does very little trade, they may not make enough money to cover the running expenses. An IT solution would not be right for such a business.

Security problems

The most important aspect of an IT system is information, and it is vital that the information is kept correct and available to the right people, is not lost or corrupted, and can be accessed only by the right people.

Problems that are likely with a supermarket's system are listed below.

- Data input errors may occur, for example the barcode on a frozen item might be unreadable if it is covered by frost. All barcodes include a 'check digit' to enable the scanner to detect a misread, so the frost can be wiped off and the item rescanned.
- Occasionally the laser scanners break down and that checkout must be closed, resulting in longer queues at other checkouts. Fortunately this would be a problem only at very busy times.
- Information can be lost if disks fail, or if the files are accidentally or maliciously deleted. It is extremely important that backup copies of all files are kept.

Health and safety

The law requires that the workplace is safe and healthy for the people who work there. The following general guidelines must be followed by all users of IT systems.

- People should not drink near the equipment, since spillages could cause electric shocks.
- The equipment must be checked regularly to ensure it is properly earthed.
- Power leads and signal cables must be carefully routed – if they trail across the floor, people are likely to trip over them.
- Appropriate fire extinguishers must be available in all rooms containing computer equipment.
- A person using a keyboard or mouse for hours at a time may develop repetitive strain injury – RSI – which usually takes the form of pain in the wrists,

elbows or shoulders. RSI can be prevented by taking frequent breaks, making sure the keyboard is at the correct height, and using foam wrist supports.

- Prolonged use of a VDU can produce eyestrain, headaches and pain in the neck. It is important that the VDU is at the correct level and does not reflect light from the window or ceiling lights. Anti-glare filters in front of the screen may help. Employers must provide free eye tests for workers who spend significant amounts of time using a VDU.
- It has been suggested that radiation from a VDU can cause miscarriage, and pregnant women may be advised to limit the time they spend working at a computer. Some VDUs are available which produce very low levels of radiation.
- Special safety measures must be taken when using an application involving heavy machinery moving at quite high speeds. These systems should be well tested and have 'fail safe' features.

Considerations specific to our supermarket system mostly involve checkout staff. They can suffer back and wrist strain as a result of turning to carry the items across the laser scanner, and from prolonged use of the keyboard. It is important that their seats are positioned at the correct height, and that they take frequent breaks.

Activity 1.6

Arrange a visit to a local supermarket to see how they use commercial IT systems. Take notes, collect material and ask questions to familiarise yourself with the system you are studying. You may want to ask:
- What is the purpose of the system?
- How effective is it?
- What hardware and software does it use?
- What people are involved?
- What data is processed?
- How does it save money/time?
- Does it operate more accurately than a non-IT-based system?
- Does its use affect the environment?
- How does it benefit the organisation?
- How does it benefit members of the public?
- How much did the system cost to purchase?
- Is it expensive to run?
- How are people trained to use it?
- Are there any problems with security?
- What goes wrong?
- What health and safety problems does it raise?

The people you are visiting may allow you to take photographs, audio and video recordings, and may supply you with leaflets, brochures and training manuals to help your studies.

Test questions

1 A nuclear power station uses a computerised control system. How does the system benefit people living nearby?
   a It reduces the cost of nuclear research
   b It makes efficient use of nuclear fuel
   c It allows more power to be produced
   d It continually monitors for radiation leaks

2 The journalists working on a newspaper word process articles on a network of computers. How do the computers help the journalists?
   a They speed up the production of the newspaper
   b They make the newspapers smaller
   c They cut down the amount spent on journalists' salaries
   d They control the number of newspapers produced

3 An airline uses a computer system to deal with flight bookings. Why does the airline use a computer system?
   a The computers are more adaptable
   b A larger number of airports can be used
   c To avoid booking too many seats on one flight
   d So more aircraft can be bought

4 A bank is using more computers and introducing telephone banking. Why are bank workers worried?
   a Mistakes in bank accounts will increase
   b The bank will attract fewer customers
   c Computers are expensive to install
   d Fewer bank workers will be employed

5 How will the bank's new computer system help the bank's customers?
   a Bank charges will be reduced
   b Customers do not have to go to the bank during the day
   c It will stop them going overdrawn
   d They will have more money in their accounts

6 A car manufacturer uses computer-controlled machines to make gears. Why is computer control used?
   a It allows different sizes of gears to be made
   b It works out the workers wages
   c It reduces the price of the cars
   d It means that more accurate gears can be made

7 Shoppers at a supermarket can make purchases by electronic funds transfer (EFT). How does the supermarket benefit by using EFT?
   a Fewer checkouts are needed
   b A larger range of vegetables can be sold
   c Less cash is held in the tills
   d The supermarket can control stock levels

8 A college now has computers in many classrooms. Which of the following will the college's Health and Safety Officer insist on?
   a The college is registered with the Data Protection Registrar
   b Every room with a computer must also contain an electrical fire extinguisher
   c People do not use the lifts if there is a fire
   d The students are given less homework

Element 1.2: Examine the components of a stand-alone computer system

Some computer systems are very large and expensive and high powered, while others are smaller and less powerful. Sometimes special devices are connected to computers. This element looks at the different parts of a computer, identifying what they do and why they are needed.

The most obvious parts of a computer are the **hardware** components. Computer hardware is the machinery which makes up the computer – the keyboard, printer, VDU, etc. The hardware is useless without the **software** to control it. Software means computer programs, instructions to the computer. Software items include word processing, spreadsheet and database. The software is stored on disks or microprocessor chips, so you cannot actually see it.

Stand-alone and networked systems

A **stand-alone** computer system is not connected to any other computers – it works by itself. A **networked** computer is connected to other computers.

Activity 1.7

1 Are any of the computers in your college networked? If so, find out what type of network is used and how to log on to it.
2 Are any of your college's computers on a wide area network such as the Internet?

Hardware components

The usual hardware components of a computer are shown in Figure 1.2 – you must learn what the parts are called. There are four kinds of hardware devices – input, processors, output and storage devices.

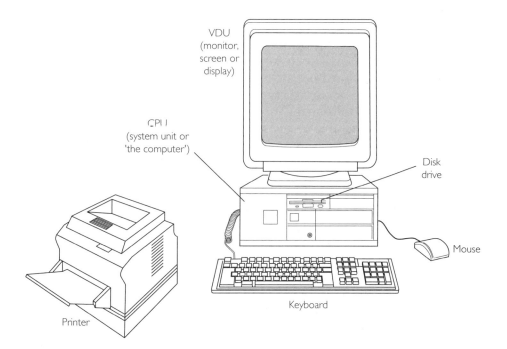

Figure 1.2 The common hardware components of a computer system

9

Input devices

Input devices, such as keyboard, mouse or barcode reader, are used to enter data into a computer. After data has been input it can be stored, retrieved, processed and outputted. This process is shown in Figure 1.3.

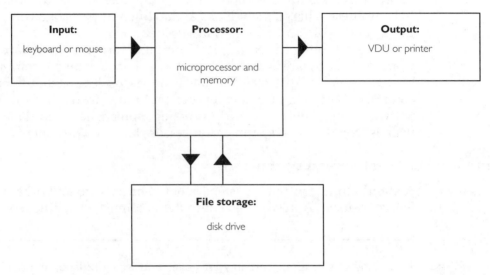

Figure 1.3 Data flow through a computer system

The choice of input devices is large. Some are manual, in the sense that a human user is needed to enter the data. Others are automatic and can collect data without a human being present – a road traffic speed camera is an example. Some devices are faster than others, some are more accurate than others – for example a barcode reader makes fewer input errors than a typist. Security is also sometimes an issue, for example with bank cheques.

The most common input device is the **keyboard**, which is used to type in text and input commands such as to save or print a file. Keyboard layout is fairly standard – you are all likely to be familiar with the 'QWERTY' layout. Because different countries have different character sets, keyboards are country-specific (a French keyboard would have keys for é and â, for example, which you must use a combination of keys for on an English keyboard).

A **mouse** is another type of input device. Underneath the mouse is a rubber ball which rolls as the mouse is moved. Sensors in the mouse detect the movement and send data to the computer, where the software moves a pointer on the screen in the same way. The mouse buttons are just switches. A **trackball** is effectively an upside-down mouse – the user rotates a ball and moves a pointer around the screen in the same way as with a mouse.

A **joystick** is mostly used for games. It has a short vertical handle which can be tilted forwards and backwards, left and right. It may have one or more buttons on it.

A **sensor** measures a physical quantity and inputs the reading into the computer. Examples include a temperature sensor in a system controlling a greenhouse, a pressure sensor used in a computer system controlling a car engine or a light sensor connected to a computer in a photographic developing system.

A **scanner** is used to input data from text, photographs, diagrams and drawings. A **barcode reader** will scan a barcode printed on something and read it

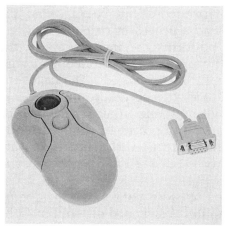

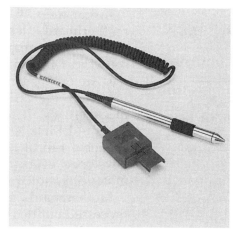

Figure 1.4 Input devices from left to right: trackball, joystick and light pen (not to scale)

into a computer. The barcode reader may be built into a supermarket checkout, but hand-held devices are also available – you may see one of these at your local library. A **graphics tablet** is a large flat panel on which you can 'draw' with a special input pen to move a cursor on the screen. The user of a **touch screen** can touch different parts of the screen to select displayed options. Touch screens are often used in public places where thousands of people might want to use the terminal, for example an information display in a museum or a bus timetable display at an airport. **Light pens** allow the user to point the pen at different parts of a screen to select an option or draw a graphic, so they are like very accurate touch screens. The use of light pens is quite rare.

An **optical mark reader** (OMR) is often used for marking examinations, where the student has to choose one of several answers by marking it with a pencil. At the bottom of a bank cheque you will see the cheque number, the account number and the bank's sort code, printed in special magnetic ink. A **magnetic ink character recognition** (MICR) is used to read in this information. Use of MICR enhances security, because the information provided by the magnetic ink is difficult to forge.

Activity 1.8

From computer magazines, gather information on keyboards. Look at articles and advertisements, and find out the different types available and how much they cost. Do the same for mice, joysticks, trackballs and sensors (you might need an electronic components catalogue for the last one). Keep the information you collect for a later assignment.

Processors

In most computers the keyboard is connected to a box called the 'base unit' or 'system unit'. This contains disk drives and the **central processing unit** or CPU.

Processing data means doing one or more of the following:
- doing arithmetic on the data, for example adding up a set of numbers
- comparing one piece of data with another – for example when the computer is searching for matching data
- storing or retrieving the data
- moving data from one place to another, such as sending e-mail.

Inside the CPU of most computers is a printed-circuit board called the **motherboard**. This contains **memory chips** and a **processor chip**. The processor is the 'engine' of the computer, and performs the instructions in the software. Different processors have different code names or numbers – examples are 68030, 486 or Pentium – and work at different speeds. The faster the processor, the faster it can process data. Processor speeds are measured in megahertz (MHz), which is a measure of how fast the electronic processor click 'ticks' – 1 MHz is one million ticks per second. The processor chips currently available run at about 100 MHz. Faster and more powerful processors are developed every couple of years. Older processors are often unable to run more recent software packages.

Motherboards also contain memory chips to store data while it is being processed but this data is lost when the computer is switched off, so it must be stored on a disk to be kept.

Other printed-circuit boards that control disk drives and printers are connected to the motherboard. A sound card to work a speaker and microphone, and fax/modem to connect to a telephone line may also be connected to the motherboard.

Output devices

An output device is used to get information out of a computer. There are many kinds of output device.

The **visual display unit**, or VDU, is the most common output device. It is also sometimes called a monitor. All modern VDUs can display graphics, and many are available in colour.

Printers come in many forms. A laser printer gives high-quality output but is expensive, while an ink-jet printer is cheaper and nearly as good. A dot-matrix printer is fast and cheap. Both black and white and colour printers are available. Printers contain toner cartridges (like those in a photocopier), ink cartridges or ribbons, which need to be replaced from time to time. Ribbons are very cheap but toner cartridges can be expensive.

A **plotter** contains a pen which draws lines on paper – this is the key difference between plotters and printers. Plotters are used by architects, engineers or anyone who wishes to produce high-quality line drawings.

All desktop computers contain a very small speaker, which can produce warning bleeps, but if the processor has a **sound card**, it can produce high-quality stereo sound. This has many uses, from enhancing games and educational programs to producing voice mail. (When sending voice mail you speak your message through a microphone into your computer, which then sends it to a distant computer. The person receiving your message can actually hear your voice.)

Storage

Storage means keeping data, perhaps for only a few minutes while you use a program, or overnight while the computer is switched off, or for many years.

Amounts of data are measured in **bytes**. One byte is needed to store one character – one letter or punctuation mark on the keyboard. That means that a word-processed document with, say, 1000 words of an average of five letters would take about 5000 bytes. Graphics need much more storage space than text. One high-resolution colour image might need several millions of bytes. It is more convenient to use bigger units:

- 1 kilobyte (kB) is about 1000 bytes

- 1 megabyte (MB) is about one million bytes
- 1 gigabyte (GB) is about one thousand million bytes

Activity 1.9

How much data can the computers at your college store:
- in memory?
- on the hard disk?
- on the network file server?

Both disk storage and memory are measured in megabytes, but they are very different things. The data held in memory is often lost when the computer is switched off, but data stored on disk is not. Hard disks usually have about a hundred times the storage capacity of memory. Memory is made of chips (electronic integrated circuits), but disks are usually magnetic media, like audio cassette tape.

Memory

There are two kinds of memory – ROM and RAM. ROM, which stands for **read-only memory**, is permanent storage – the data in it is fixed. ROM is used to hold information that the computer needs as soon as it is switched on. Data in ROM can only be read, not written in to it. RAM, which stands for **random-access memory**, can be both read and written to, so it is used for changing data, such as different programs and documents being worked on. However, when the computer is switched off, anything in RAM is lost.

Most computers have between 4 MB and 32 MB of RAM. A computer with 32 MB will work faster than one with only 4 MB because if the amount of memory is small more of the data being used has to be kept on disk, and is much slower to access than data in RAM.

Disks

The documents you produce on your computer can be stored on disks – which retain the information even after the power has been switched off. A **disk drive** is used to read and write information onto disks.

On small computers two types of disk are used – **floppy** disks and **hard** disks. Floppy disks hold one or two megabytes but hard disks can hold much more – hundreds of megabytes. The hard disk is faster and more reliable than a floppy, but can't be changed over like floppy disks can. Another type of disk is an Optical disk.

A **CD-ROM** disc can also be used to store data, but is very different from floppy and hard disks. The information is stored on a CD-ROM in the form of microscopic pits and read by reflecting a laser beam off them. A CD-ROM is normally read-only – the user can read information but can't store new information onto it. CD-ROMs are slower to access than hard disks, but have a high storage capacity – about the same as 700 floppy disks. They are used for reference material such as encyclopedias, and for supplying new software packages (see Element 1.3). It is now possible to buy 'Writeable CD-ROMs' – CD-ROMs that you can write data to.

Information can also be stored on **magnetic tape**. Large computers use tape in the form of large reels. Desktop computers sometimes use data cartridges, which contain very long loops of tape. These can be read from and written to by tape streamers, which are usually used for **backing up** – to make a copy of all the files on a hard disk so they will not be lost if the hard drive fails.

Activity 1.10

From computer magazines gather information on motherboards. Look at articles and advertisements, and find out current prices for different amounts of memory, speed and processor type. Then get prices for laser and ink-jet printers, and disk drives. What is the cheapest colour printer you can find? Keep the information you collect for a later assignment.

Software

Software is computer programs – the instructions telling the computer what to do. When the program is 'run', it is loaded into memory, and the computer carries out the instructions one after another. Programs contain many thousands of instructions. They must be tested very carefully to make sure they make the computers do the correct things.

Usually several programs work together, in a **software package**. A software package will supply you with a set of programs on disk, and a manual to tell you how to use it. Note that the plural of software is *not* 'softwares' - you can buy several software packages, but it is wrong to say 'I bought some softwares'.

There are two broad types of software – **systems** software and **applications** software.

Systems software

This software is needed simply to make the computer work – to load and save files on disk, delete (erase) files, change the names of files, move files from one disk to another and so on. Systems software is needed to control how information is displayed on the screen – to make the cursor move in response to the mouse, show icons on the screen, move windows around and so on. It also controls the computer, such as letting several programs work in the computer's memory at the same time.

Large parts of systems software are grouped in **operating systems**. Some of the operating systems currently used on small computers are MS DOS, MacOS, Windows 95, OS/2, Windows NT and UNIX. When a computer is switched on, it loads the operating system from disk into RAM and starts it running. This process is called 'boot-strapping' or **'booting'** the computer.

Modern systems software provides the user with a **graphical user interface** (or GUI). This is what the user sees (and uses) on the screen, and involves resizable movable overlapping windows with menu bars, icons representing programs, buttons, a pointer controlled by a mouse, and so on. Most people find a GUI easy to use. Examples of GUIs are found in Microsoft Windows, OS/2, X Windows in UNIX and the Macintosh's system.

Applications software

Applications software makes use of the computer hardware and systems software to solve real problems and help people do their jobs. Some application programs are general-purpose, such as word processors like Word, WordPerfect or WordStar or spreadsheets, like Excel or Lotus 123. Some applications are not so general – they are written to do just one particular job. An example for a small computer would be a package used by a dentist to keep records of patients' treatments, arrange appointments and work out charges. On a larger scale, the gas bills for several million people are prepared by an application program.

Activity 1.11

Which of the following pieces of software are systems software and which applications software?
- A hotel booking system
- A program to compress files (make them smaller so they use less space on disk)
- A graphics program such as Paintbrush or CorelDraw
- A route-finding program to help you find the best roads between two places
- A display driver, to enable the computer to show more colours and sharper images on the screen
- A database program
- A network login program that checks passwords
- A desktop publishing program such as PageMaker

Some of the best-known applications are mostly concerned with processing words, numbers and pictures. The computer may be used to perform calculations, to arrange words and pictures into complex documents or to store large amounts of similar data, such as names and addresses, in a logical way. The data might be arranged in tables, in rows and columns containing text and numbers. An example is shown in Figure 1.5. Data like this could be used to calculate people's weekly wages. Tables like this are often called **databases**.

Name	Date of birth	National Insurance Number	Hours worked this week	
John Smith	15.1.53	YX 576 123 X	35	
Alia Butt	12.12.64	FF 233 217 F	40	One row or record
Rukhsana Kauser	01.02.69	UI 955 295 G	45	
Marcus Jones	12.08.76	TI 638 893 T	21	

Figure 1.5

Other examples of processing programs are **word processors**, which process data in the form of text, and **graphics programs** (either line drawing or brush painting) where the data is in the form of visual images. If the data is mostly numbers, and lots of calculations need to be done, a **spreadsheet** is used (an example is shown in Figure 1.6).

Activity 1.12

List the spreadsheet and database packages available at your college.

Control applications are common in everyday life – for example:
- The central heating system in your house is controlled by software that turns the boiler on and off at certain times of the day.

	A	B	C	D
1		Jan	Feb	Mar
2	Petrol	14.50	12.33	21.45
3	Rent	35.00	35.00	35.00
4	Wages	350.00	350.00	350.00
5	Totals			

Figure 1.6 Formulas can be placed in a spreadsheet which will automatically calculate values

- You can select a particular wash programme on your washing machine and the controller will heat the water, wash for a certain length of time, rinse and spin.
- A robot doing welding on a car assembly line.
- A computer helps a pilot to fly, navigate and land an aircraft.

Control applications use special input devices like temperature and pressure sensors, and the output is used to switch electric motors and similar components on and off.

A third kind of application is known as **modelling**. This means setting up a mathematical version of a real system. Physical models such as a model aircraft are small versions which look just like the real thing but a mathematical model tries to work out values describing how a real system behaves. An example of this is a flight simulator, where the user sees on the VDU what the pilot would see, and the keyboard and mouse are used in the same way that the pilot would use the controls and instruments on the real aircraft. Simulators like this can be used to train pilots more cheaply and safely than in real aircraft.

Other modelling applications do not have such realistic output; they produce numbers which try to show how real systems would behave. For example traffic flow simulation is used to show the length of queues at traffic lights and other obstacles. By changing the road layouts the designers can see how the traffic flow will be affected. This type of modelling with numbers is often done on a spreadsheet.

Activity 1.13

Find examples of and prices for the following pieces of software:
- An operating system
- A file compression utility
- A programming environment
- A word processor
- A spreadsheet
- A graphics package
- A route-finding program

You will need to look through computer magazines, catalogues of office supplies companies, visit shops retailing IT equipment or telephone software suppliers.

Test questions

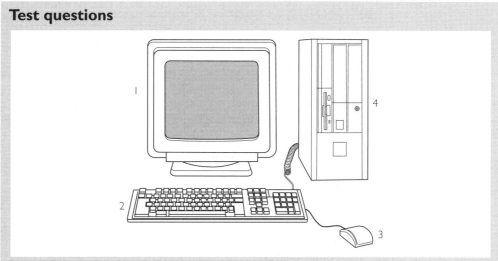

Figure 1.7 A stand-alone computer system

1 Look at Figure 1.7. What is the part labelled 1?
   a The main processor
   b The printer
   c The keyboard
   d The VDU

2 Which part of the computer is labelled 4 on Figure 1.7?
   a The printer
   b The keyboard
   c The VDU
   d The main processor

3 What is the purpose of the part labelled 4?
   a Processing and storing data
   b Manual data input
   c Data output
   d Producing hard copy output

4 Which type of storage can be removed from the computer?
   a RAM
   b The hard disk
   c A floppy disk
   d ROM

5 You are using a spreadsheet to do some calculations. Which input device is easiest to use for entering numbers?
   a Mouse
   b Mark reader
   c Card reader
   d Keyboard

6 A student is producing a newspaper in college. Which device is essential for producing the newspaper on paper?
   a Joystick
   b Scanner
   c VDU
   d Printer

7 The instructions to 'boot' a computer when it is switched on are stored in ROM. Which type of storage is ROM?
   a Temporary
   b Read and write
   c Read only
   d Hard copy

8 Which software organises the memory of the computer?
   a A word processor
   b A spreadsheet
   c A graphics package
   d An operating system

9 You use a computer system to calculate how much money your company has spent and how much profit it might make. Which software would be best for this?
   a A graphics package
   b A DTP package
   c A database system
   d A spreadsheet package

10 An architect uses a computer to produce floor plans of buildings. Which would be the best hardware components to use?
   a Mouse, tape drive, processor
   b VDU, mouse, printer
   c Printer, processor, mouse
   d Keyboard, tape drive, processor

11 A secretary uses a computer package to write business letters. Which would be the best input device?
   a Keyboard
   b Touch screen
   c Numeric keyboard
   d Graphics tablet

Element 1.3: Set up stand-alone computer systems to meet user requirements

In this element you will learn how to find out what kind of system users need, how to set it up and test it. If you were to wander around college, you would probably find a lot of people using computers and IT. The table below lists some of the uses of IT you might find in your wander.

User	Use of IT
Students	Word processing assignments
Exams officer	Receiving results from exam boards through a modem
College accountant	Working out budgets on a spreadsheet
Librarian	Entering new books into a database
Art teacher	Scanning a photograph into a computer to retouch it
Estates manager	Setting temperatures on the boiler of the heating system

Even though the computers being used are basically the same, they will differ in the amount of memory they have, the kind of monitors and the special components they are connected to. This is because different users have different needs.

Finding out users' needs

Before you can set a system up to meet the user's needs, you have to find out what the needs *are* – and unfortunately you can't just ask them, because if they don't know a lot about IT, they won't know how their job requirements can be met by technology. You need to use your skills to help people identify what they need and then match that to IT solutions.

You will probably find out what a user needs by interviewing them. The following points are important to successful interviewing.

- Make an appointment with your interviewee. He or she has their own schedule, and you must arrange a time that is convenient for both of you to do the interview.
- Tell them how long you expect the interview to take and try to meet in a place where you will both be comfortable and where neither of you will be distracted.
- Prepare yourself and list the questions you are going to ask. For example:
  - What is your job title?
  - Outline what you have to do in broad terms (not detail).
  - How does information come to you? (The user will probably not be familiar with thinking in terms of information, and you will have to help them. The finance clerk gets information on purchase order forms and invoices. The librarian gets information from students' library cards. The exams officer gets information from the exam boards through a modem.)
  - What do you have to do with the information?
  - Where does the information go?
  - Do you already use IT equipment?
  - What type of hardware do you have?
  - What software do you use?
  - Are there any problems with anything?
- Always respect the other person's privacy. You can't simply ask them anything you like, and they are entitled to refuse to answer.
- Remember, this is an interview not a questionnaire. Don't just read out your questions. You will need to explain them and adapt them to the situation and the person you are interviewing. Be prepared to follow up any unexpected answers.
- Record what you find out. You might do this by writing down the answers on paper in the form of quick notes or by taking an audio or video tape of the interview. Remember to check whether your interviewee is happy to be recorded on tape.
- Thank the person you are interviewing for their help.

Activity 1.14

Look at the table at the top of the following page and decide what sort of hardware you would expect the people listed to need.

Job	Hardware	Software
College secretary	Standard PC	Word processing, DTP
Rock musician		
Journalist		
Art teacher	Graphics document scanner	
Librarian		
Accountant		Spreadsheet

Setting up hardware

Check that the equipment is switched off and unplugged before you do anything else.

Look carefully at the plugs and sockets on the cables and the back of the computer. Usually there is no doubt about which plugs go where, because there is no choice. For 'D' type connectors (see Figure 1.8) check which way round the D goes, and make sure that the size of the plug matches the socket. Keyboard connections usually use round plugs, and the top is marked. Do *not* force plugs into sockets – if you need to use any amount of force, you've got it wrong. Many plugs have small screws or knobs at each end – tighten these up once you've pushed the plug home.

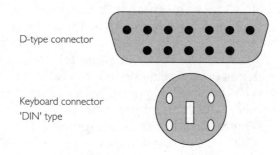

D-type connector

Keyboard connector
'DIN' type

Figure 1.8 Types of connector

Think about where the equipment will be positioned on the desk. The mouse will be at the side of the keyboard – is the user right or left handed? The VDU should not be reflecting light from a window, and should be directly in front of the user at eye level. Is there a suitable place for the paper supply to the printer?

Once you have set the equipment up, do a final check on the connections and then switch on the power – at the wall, the computer, the VDU and the printer. Make sure the computer 'boots' as expected. Don't switch the power quickly off and then on – you could damage the computer's power supply. Hard disk drives should not be subjected to sudden movement when switched on.

Activity 1.15

Watch your lecturer disconnect and reconnect a stand-alone computer. If the VDU does not work, how would you find the problem and fix it?

Installing software

Once you've set up the hardware you need to install the applications software. Software for desktop computers is usually supplied on floppy disk or CD-ROM, and to install it you must set it up on the computer's hard disk.

If you are installing a simple or old package, you will have to do all the steps in the installation yourself. These will include:

1 Create a directory. Remember, a hard disk is divided into different directories to hold different groups of files. A new package will probably go into its own directory.
2 Copy files from the floppy disk into the new directory.
3 Decompress the files. Files on floppy disk are often **compressed**, which means they are coded so they take up less space. Before they can be used, they have to be expanded back to a normal size.
4 Alter the way the system is set up. This might mean setting up new icons in graphical systems, or adding new menu items to provide access to the new software. This is called **altering the system configuration**.
5 Set options on the new software. For example, you may need to select the type of printer to be used.

Most software now comes with installation routines to do most of these tasks for you. In this case, the following may happen:

1 You may be asked to choose between options, such as which hard disk to install to, or whether to include sample documents.
2 A check is made whether there is enough hard disk space for the software.
3 Any directories needed to store files are created on the hard disk.
4 Files are uncompressed and copied to the hard disk.
5 Changes to system software set up, such as setting up icons, may be made.

The documentation supplied with the software package should give you instructions how to install it, and may include a 'Getting Started' booklet providing more installation information.

Testing systems

Once a new system has been set up and the software installed, it has to be checked to make sure everything works. There are many things that can go wrong, and you must methodically check as many aspects of the system as possible. It is important to do these checks in the correct order, or you can waste a lot of time. For example, if nothing appears on the screen, don't start worrying about the installation of software before making sure the VDU is switched on!

After the hardware has been connected, make sure the computer responds correctly to the 'power on', and that it boots properly. The computer power light should come on, and the VDU should show a normal boot sequence.

If possible, make the printer run a 'self-test' to make sure it is working. Look in the printer manual to find out how to do this.

Start the application and watch that there are no error messages.

Check the application works. You should be able to:

1 Enter data – type in some words in a word processor, numbers into a spreadsheet, create some records in a database, draw a picture in a graphics package.
2 Save the data in a disk file.
3 Quit the application, and then restart it.
4 Reload the file you just saved. Make sure you are using the re-loaded version, not the original.
5 Print it out.

If any step does not work, you must work out why and fix the problem. Take notice of any error messages that appear on the screen – they are clues to the problem.

Test questions

1 You are connecting up the hardware on a computer system. In what order should you do things?
   a Connect equipment, switch on, switch off
   b Switch off, connect equipment, switch on
   c Switch off, switch on, connect equipment
   d Connect equipment, switch off, switch on

2 You are trying to install a DTP package, but it tells you there is not enough space left on your hard disk. Which would *not* help?
   a Deleting old unwanted files on the disk
   b Telling it not to install clip art
   c Buying a larger hard disk
   d Reinstalling the package

3 You have installed the DTP package, but it does not respond to the mouse. What is the first thing you should do?
   a Buy a new mouse
   b Reinstall the DTP package
   c Reinstall the mouse driver
   d Check the mouse works with other packages on the same computer

---

Element 1.4: Produce an applications software macro to meet user requirements

What are macros?

When you are using a word processor, you probably do the same thing lots of times. For example, you probably save your document, print it out, and quit from the package. It would be useful if you could 'record' yourself doing this, and then just play it back when you want to do it again. This is what a **macro** does. A macro lets you automate something. Many applications, not just word processors, let you make use of macros. Most spreadsheets and database programs also offer macros.

With a macro you can usually
• Use the macros supplied with the package
• Make new macros by 'recording' a series of key strokes, menu selections, etc.
• Make new macros by writing them in a special 'macro language'.
• Edit (change, adapt, correct or extend) macros in the macro language.
Writing a macro is like making up a script that the computer will follow when the macro is run. Most people find it easier to make macros by recording them, and then editing them if necessary.

Activity 1.16

Use your word processor to develop a macro. It should be very simple, and produced by 'recording' yourself doing something. Don't worry at this stage whether the macro is any use to anyone – you could just record yourself typing 'Hello'.

You can use macros to carry out many useful tasks. For example:
- setting a function key to set text to a particular size and font
- saving, printing and then closing a file
- setting tabs in a word processor to a certain pattern
- go through your document, formatting the first character on each page with bold, italic, and 16-point formats
- when you open a new file automatically changing to the directory in which you normally store your files
- automatically running other applications, such as starting a spreadsheet or calculator from within a word processor
- creating special calculations in a spreadsheet.

Activity 1.17

Set up a simple macro in a spreadsheet. This could be to insert a new column at column B, but if you would like to do something different, go ahead. Check the macro works, and save it.

Uses for macros

Macros have many kinds of uses. Here are a few.
- *To replace repetitive key strokes*. For example, at the end of a letter you might always say 'Yours sincerely'. This is a lot of typing and uses the same keys every time. You could easily turn it into a macro.
- *Setting up templates*. These are often used in word processors and spread-sheets, and are slightly different from macros. A template is a whole document, set up as a starting point to modify. For example, a template for a business letter would use a certain paper size, margins and font. It would already have in it a company logo as a graphic, the company name and address and the current date. It would say 'Dear Sir ...', leave several lines blank, and then say 'Yours faithfully ...'. The user would just have to load this template and type in who it was to, and the body of the letter.
- *Setting up a spreadsheet template*. The column headings could be already set up, some text, and the formulas already in place. The user just has to enter some numbers, and the preset formulas do the calculations. A good example of this would be an invoice template.
- *Setting defaults*. A default is a 'normal' value. For example, a default page size might be A4, which means that the page size will be A4 unless you change it. Macros can be used to select suitable default values for page size, margins, fonts, etc.
- *Carrying out calculations*. This is usually done in a spreadsheet, in the form of a template, as described above. Formulas worked out and tested in advance can be placed in suitable cells. All the user has to do is enter the data and the formulas will do the calculations needed.

Activity 1.18

List as many uses of macros as possible. Keep your list for a later assignment.

Advantages of using macros

Using a macro means you can work more quickly. A macro can replace a long series of key strokes or menu selections with one button click, so it is much faster.

A macro can reduce the chances of making mistakes. If you do something 'the hard way', making all the menu selections and so on every time, there is a good chance you will make a mistake. But if you use a macro, you can thoroughly check it first, and can then be sure that it will work without error.

You can make sure the same thing is done every time, so that standard procedures are used. A good example of this is the use of letterheads for business letters. A letterhead is used at the top of business letters sent out by a company and usually has the company's logo at the top, the company's name in a particular font, and graphics, producing a distinctive and easily recognisable effect. The letterhead helps to promote the company image and can be easily set up using a macro or template.

Macros are convenient. Once it has been set up, a macro is a lot less effort to run than to do the same action the long way. Usually a macro can be invoked by a single keystroke.

Activity 1.19

List some reasons why macros are used. Keep these for a later assignment.

Macros and programming

When you develop a macro you are doing a kind of computer **programming**. Programming means writing software – setting out the sequence of steps the computer needs to do to carry out some task. The programmer must write the instructions in a special language – not in English, because computers are not intelligent enough to 'understand' English. If you look at the macro you produced in Activity 1.16, you will see the use of a **programming language**.

Differences between macros and general programming

- Macros use a very special-purpose language, but programming languages are usually fairly general purpose. Each different application has its own macro language. Programming languages such as C, Pascal or BASIC are used to write hundreds of different kinds of applications.
- Macros are only about applications – general programming is also used for systems software.
- Macros are often written by users, while software is developed by people whose career is in programming.

Macro specifications

The specification for a macro sets out clearly what the user wants the macro to do. For example, people working in an office might realise they do a certain task on a word processor very often, and decide they want a macro written to speed this up. The office people have to give the person who will write the macro detailed instructions as to what they want. This is a **user specification**.

Parts of a specification

- The applications software and version the macro is for – such as Word for Windows 2.
- The purpose of the macro.
- How the macro is be carried out – perhaps a keystroke combination such as holding down the control key while pressing 'm'.
- Uses of the macro.
- Data to be embedded in the macro, such as a company logo, a filename or a date.
- Layout styles such as margin settings.
- Tests to be used to make sure the macro works

Test questions

1 You have written a word processing macro. How does the macro *not* help users?
   a They can learn more about the software
   b It saves time
   c It is more convenient
   d It reduces errors
2 A spreadsheet macro has been set up. How will it help the people using it?
   a It is faster
   b It uses less disk space
   c It avoids viruses
   d Power failures will have no effect
3 A word processing template is set up. What might be a feature?
   a It tells the user what to write
   b It checks the spelling
   c It means there will be no punctuation errors
   d It sets the page size and margins
4 How can a macro be used to improve a spreadsheet?
   a The formulas can be set up before the spreadsheet is used
   b The data entered is sure to be correct
   c The screen resolution will be increased
   d The computer can store more data

A user is interviewed and describes a word processing macro they would like.

5 Part of the specification would *not* be:
   a The software package to be used
   b The purpose of the macro
   c The names of the users
   d The layout styles to be used
6 Part of the specification *would* be:
   a The method of executing the macro
   b How often the macro will be used
   c How long the macro took to write
   d The date by which the macro must be finished

Assignment A1.1
Examine industrial and commercial IT systems

This assignment provides evidence for Element 1.1, and is relevant to the following key skills elements:

IT 2.4: Evaluate the use of IT
Communications 2.2: Produce written material

Write a report on two commercial and two industrial systems. Your teacher will choose the systems for you, or you may be allowed some choice.

Possible commercial systems: leisure centre bookings, bank systems, travel agents, hotel reservations and mail-order companies. Within the college you might be able to look at the library dealing with the borrowing of books, the finance system, the student records system, a computerised attendance register system, or the exams entry and results system.

Possible industrial systems: traffic light control, pedestrian crossings (Pelican crossings), car assembly lines using robots, photographic developing services. Within college you might look at security video camera systems, swipe card systems controlling entrances, CAD or CAM systems. Systems at home include the washing machine or central heating system.

You may be supplied with some material but you will probably have to do some research, writing away for information or visiting industrial links.

Write a word-processed report the following headings (you can miss out the 'feature' part for one of the commercial and one of the industrial systems).

- Features
  - What is the system for?
  - Data used in the system
  - Hardware
  - Who uses the system, and what do they do?
  - Software
  - Processing
- Benefits
  - Improved accuracy
  - Reduced costs
  - Environmental benefits
- Limitations
  - Costs resulting from the system
  - Security problems such as data loss
  - Health and safety issues
  - Environmental impact

Assignment A1.2
Examine the components of a stand-alone computer system

This assignment provides evidence for Element 1.2, and also the following key skill elements:

Communications 2.2:	Produce written material
Communications 2.3:	Use images
IT 2.3:	Present information

You work for Mandrel and Chuck, an engineering firm making machine tools. Mandrel and Chuck started in 1874, and they have a very traditional approach to how things should be done. Your boss, Mr Joshua Firebrace, has heard his friends in the Chamber of Commerce talk about how useful IT is, but he is very sceptical that computers will ever amount to very much. On the other hand, he does not want a commercial advantage to pass him by. He wants you to write a 'User Guide to IT' for him so he will know a bit more about it.

The user guide must have the following sections:

- A description of hardware components and their purposes:
  - input devices (keyboard, mouse, sensor)
  - processors
  - output devices (VDU, printer, plotter, sound)
  - storage devices (RAM, ROM, disk, tape)
- A general explanation of the purposes of various software types:
  - operating systems
  - spreadsheets
  - database systems
  - control systems
  - modelling

Recommend packages for Mr Firebrace to buy, give their probable costs and list the hardware that would be needed to run them on. Your user guide should be as attractive and informative as possible, and should include drawings, photographs and diagrams in a document produced using a word processor or desktop publisher.

Assignment A1.3
Set up a stand-alone computer system to meet user requirements

This assignment provides evidence for Element 1.3, and also for the following key skill elements:

Communications 2.1:	Take part in discussions

Mr Firebrace was pleased with your last report, and he is now convinced that IT could be profitably used by Mandrel and Chuck. Now he wants you to set up a suitable system for his secretary, Mrs Peabody. There are budget limits on this – Mr Firebrace won't let you spend an unlimited amount of money – so you will be given a list of hardware and software components to choose from.

Interview the college secretary or another member of the college support staff to find out the IT needs of a secretary. Write a short report summarising the interview, describing the requirements, and giving a specification of the hardware and software needed.

Connect up the hardware you have chosen from what is provided, and install the applications software required. Your lecturer will watch you do this and complete a Record of Observation.

Test the system you have set up. Produce a printout of some data you have entered into the application package.

Assignment A1.4
Produce an applications software macro to meet user requirements

This assignment provides evidence for Element 1.4 and also for the following key skill elements:

Communication 2.2:	Produce written material
Information technology 2.2:	Process information
Information technology 2.4:	Evaluate the use of IT

Mr Firebrace liked the work you did setting up a computer for Mrs Peabody, who is getting on well using the computer, and has learnt some basic skills in using the application. To make her more efficient, the time has come to set up some macros.

- On the basis of what you found out in Assignment 1.3, draw up a specification for what the macro would do. If you are not sure, choose one of the uses of macros described in Element 1.4, such as a business letterhead.
- Produce the macro and test it. When you are sure it is correct, print it out.
- Draw up a report, which should contain:
  - An explanation of what macros are
  - A list of the advantages of using macros (use the list you compiled in Activity 1.9)
  - Some examples of tasks that can be carried out by macros (use the material you collected in Activity 1.8)
  - A review of the macro you have written, and suggestions for two more macros Mrs Peabody might find useful.

CHAPTER 2

Using IT

Element 2.1: Process commercial documents
Element 2.2: Process graphic designs
Element 2.3: Process and model numerical data
Element 2.4: Use information technology for process control

What is covered in this chapter

- Types of commercial documents
- Design and production of documents using word processing and desktop publishing
- Security of documents
- Types of graphics software and their use
- Types of computer models
- Use of numerical models and 'what-if' queries
- Process control systems – uses, components and operation
- Construction and use of a control system

Items you will need in your portfolio for this unit

- Your completed Assignment 2.1, with four documents and other notes as indicated
- Assignment 2.2
- Assignment 2.3
- Assignment 2.4

Introduction

In Chapter 1 you worked through an introduction to IT systems and looked at why they are used. This chapter will give you an opportunity to develop skills in using standard types of applications software. Word processing and desktop publishing are covered in Element 2.1, graphics software in Element 2.2, spreadsheets in Element 2.3 and process control hardware and software in Element 2.4. These skills will be developed further in the optional units.

Element 2.1: Process commercial documents

Introduction

In business lots of different documents are used to help people do their jobs. Most of these documents are still printed on paper, but an increasing number are now sent electronically, by e-mail or fax. In this element you will see the kinds of documents used and how they should be designed, produced, and handled securely. The applications software used will be mostly word processing or desktop publishing (DTP), perhaps with some graphics software.

Case Study

Documents at On-Line Graphics

On-Line Graphics is a small graphics design business, designing tee-shirts, posters and CDs. Most of their work is done using IT. They have a colour printer, but it doesn't work very well. One day Jim got very annoyed when it wouldn't work properly. He sent a memorandum to his boss Jo, asking her to buy a new printer.

Jo was reluctant to buy a new printer, since the business was small and they didn't have much money to spend. She called a meeting to discuss the problem, sending out an agenda giving the date and time of the meeting, and outlining what they were to discuss.

At the meeting someone suggested that it was possible to buy a printer combined with a colour photocopier. This was considered too expensive, but someone else said that these machines could be rented, which would save money. It was decided at the meeting that Jo would prepare a report about colour printers and photocopiers. The minutes of the meeting summarising what was said and decisions taken were circulated to everyone involved.

As a result of Jo's report, it was decided to rent a colour photocopier/printer from a local company. A business letter was sent to the company, inviting them to send a sales representative to describe and demonstrate their services.

On-Line Graphics ordered a medium-priced model. It was delivered a couple of weeks later, and at the same time they received an invoice for the printer, stating the amount they were being charged. The invoice asked them to pay within 30 days.

They were very pleased with the new printer, and it worked very well. One of the first things they did with it was to produce a newsletter, describing how On-Line Graphics was developing and the services they could provide. The newsletter was sent to all their local customers.

Activity 2.1

Table 2.1 contains the names of several document types and their descriptions, but it is mixed up. Find the correct purpose for each document type.

Table 2.1

Document	Purpose
Agenda	One to four sides giving news of what is happening in an organisation
Business letter	A formal note sent from one person to another
Invoice	Formal letter from one business to another
Memo	A formal summary of what has been discovered as a result of an investigation or research
Minutes	Shows the items to be discussed at a meeting
Newsletter	Sent when one company buys something from another – the invoice tells the purchaser what they have to pay, on credit
Report	A record of the discussions at a meeting

Activity 2.2

Try to obtain copies of actual documents used in college. You might be able to get copies of memos, meeting agendas and minutes from your course team leader. If you approach the college office they might be able to give you copies of invoices. The college marketing department will probably have business letters and newsletters.

Features for enhancing documents

Word processing and DTP software offer many different features that can be used separately or in combination to make documents more attractive. Some of these facilities are described in this section, and you will see many of them illustrated in Figure 2.1.

Page orientation
This means which way round the paper is – the choices are landscape and portrait.

Paper size
Standard size is A4. Other common sizes are letter, A3 (twice as big as A4) and A5 (half the size of A4).

Columns
Text can be set into two or more columns on one page, as in a newspaper. This makes it easier to have a lot of separate items on one page.

Fonts
A font is a particular style of letters. For example, this font is Avant Garde, while this is Times. It is sometimes a good idea to have two fonts in one document, one for titles and the other for the main text. However, having more than two fonts on a page can be very distracting and is generally not a good idea.

Font size
The size of a font is measured in points, 72 points equalling one inch. This text is in 18 point, while this is 9 point. The text most people use is 10 or 12 point.

Footers
The footer to a page can contain the page number, the date, the name of the person wrote the document, the filename used to store the document on disk – or any other information you require! The footers in this book simply contain the page numbers.

Headers
These are placed at the top of the page. Headers can contain useful information, such as section titles so that the reader can locate points in the text quickly.

Indents
An indented section of text is set in from the margins. It helps to separate a block of text and make it more distinct.

Justification
Usually all the lines of text line up at the left-hand edge. This is called left justification. If the text lines up at the right-hand edge, this is called right justification. Right justification is normally only used for the addresses at the start of a letter.

Text that lines up at both edges, as most of the text in this book does, is called fully justified. Text can also be centred. Centring is usually used for titles.

Line spacing

Text in a word-processed document is usually single-spaced, but the spacing can be varied. Double spacing gives a blank line between each line of text. This is sometimes used for a draft piece of work, which someone will check and correct or add to. The double spacing allows space to write in comments.

Margins

The text does not usually run right to the edge of a page. Blank space is left at the top, bottom, left and right of the normal text in the middle of the page. These are the margins. A header can be placed in the top margin, and a footer in the bottom margin. Some page designs have a large left or right margin to improve the appearance of the work.

Tabulation

Using tabulation you can put information into a table, with rows and columns. There are many examples of tables through this book. Tabulation can be done in two ways. The first way is to use the 'tab' key, which moves the cursor to the next tab position (you can adjust these). Another way is to insert a table into the document. This usually allows you to use more features, such as putting a border around the table. Setting up a table using the space bar to move across to the start of each column is very bad practice. You will find that the columns are not straight when you print the work out. Inserting a table or using the 'tab' key is faster and produces better results.

Activity 2.3

Make sure you know how use the facilities of the word processor that you normally use. If there are any features you are not familiar with, use the on-line help to find out how to do it.

Graphics editing

Graphics can be copied, moved, rotated and tilted – as shown in Figure 2.2.

Activity 2.4

Make sure that you can move, copy, rotate and delete images in the graphics package you usually use.

Table editing

Rows and columns can be inserted and deleted, and row heights and column widths can be changed. The data in each cell (place in the table) can be moved, copied to other cells or deleted.

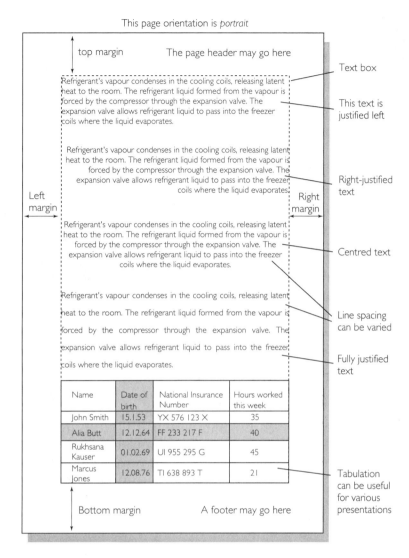

Figure 2.1 *Common features of word processing or DTP software*

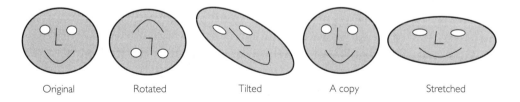

Figure 2.2

Text editing

Editing text means changing it in some way – by copying, moving, deleting or enhancing it. Text is edited in blocks. A block could be one word, a sentence or several paragraphs. The block must be selected before it can be edited.

Activity 2.5

- How do you insert a table into your word processor?
- How do you insert rows and columns into the table?
- How do you change the height of a row?
- How do you move the contents of one cell to another?
- Do you know how to move blocks of text in your word processor?

Directories and filenames

It is important to be able to find your documents after you have saved them. You should name each file you create, bearing the following points in mind.

- The operating system will have some rules about the way files can be named. In MS DOS, for example, filenames can contain no more than eight letters, with no spaces. After the filename a three letter extension shows the type of file – `.doc` for document and `.xls` for spreadsheet. Usually the application will automatically add the filename extension.
- Within these rules, you should name the file carefully to make it easier to find. This means the name should suggest which document it was. A name for the minutes of a meeting held in July 1996, for example, could be `mnsjul96`. Using your own name for your files is not a good idea – you will quickly run out of choices, and could waste a lot of time working out which file is which.

If all your files are stored together it will soon become difficult to find the one you want out of a long list. To solve this problem, disk storage space is divided into different areas, called **directories**. For example, you might create a directory for the accounts department, another for personnel, another for marketing. Usually this is still not enough, since it means all the accounts files are kept together, and this is not very organised. To solve this problem, directories can be divided into **sub-directories**. Then, for example, the orders could be kept in one sub-directory, invoices in another and so on. This makes it a lot easier to find the file you want.

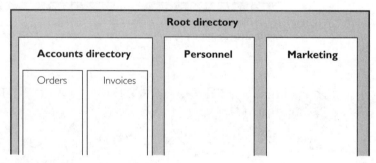

Figure 2.3 Directories and sub-directories

Activity 2.6

To help you organise your work better, create sub-directories in your file storage area (perhaps on a floppy disk or a network drive). You might decide to create a sub-directory for each unit you are studying, or one for each of your teachers. If you are not sure how to do this, ask your tutor.

Proofreading and spellchecking

Proofreading a document means checking that the spelling and punctuation are correct, that it has been copied from a source document correctly, that the graphics are in the right place, etc. It is a good idea to proofread a document before you print it out – a lot of paper can be wasted if you proofread the hard copy. However, always double-check your printed version for anything you may have missed on screen.

Most word processors have a **spellcheck** facility. A spellchecker contains a large dictionary of words, and will compare every word in your document with this dictionary. The spellchecker will query any words it can't find and suggest possible alternatives.

Security of documents

Documents need to be kept securely, both on paper and in computer systems, so they are not lost, are not changed (either maliciously or accidentally), and so they do not fall into the hands of someone who should not see them.

Backups

If you take a **backup** of your document you can go back to the last copy if you lose the file you are working on. Files can be backed up in several ways – for example, by saving two copies of a file with different filenames, preferably on different drives. One drive might be a hard drive, and the other a floppy. Many computer systems use a tape drive to make backup copies of all files, with the backup usually being done overnight when no one needs to work on the system. The tape drive makes a copy of all the files onto data cartridges. Backups should be stored at another site, otherwise a disaster such as a fire could destroy both the originals and the backup.

Saving regularly

An immediate way of ensuring a document is not lost is to regularly save your work, say every few minutes. If you don't save regularly an unforeseen disaster, such as a mains power loss, will mean all the work done since the last backup is lost. Many packages can be set up to save automatically at regular intervals, so the user does not have to remember to do it.

Source documents

Source documents are the original documents from which data was obtained and entered into the computer. For example, in a mail-order company, customers would send in orders through the post, on order forms. The orders would be entered into the computer. If the original order forms have been kept, the information can always be re-entered if the computer system fails.

Data protection

Many business documents contain personal information about people. In this case the business must be registered with the Data Protection Registrar, and care must be taken not to disclose any of the information to people who are not authorised to see it. One way to help with this is to use a system of **passwords** and **user names**, or IDs. The user ID lets the computer know who the user claims to be and the password is intended to prove it. When users log on to a network, they nearly always need to enter their user ID and password before they are allowed access to information.

Copyright

Much of the material on a computer system is subject to copyright laws. This applies to almost all software packages. When you buy a package, you buy a licence to use the software on one computer – or perhaps a network pack to use on, say, 20 machines. Making copies to use on further machines is illegal. Some data is also copyrighted – for example many on-line news services, and some graphics images.

Preventing theft

Computer equipment is often stolen. Theft-prevention measures include physically bolting down the computers to the desks, and using surveillance equipment such as closed-circuit TV – video cameras. A big problem caused by theft is that all the files on disk are also lost. This is another good reason for taking regular backups.

Activity 2.7

Check out the security at a computer site you are familiar with – perhaps the college network, or your home computer. Copy and complete the following table:

Precaution	Yes/no	Details/comments
Backups made?		
Backups stored off-site?		
Applications do autosave?		
Source documents kept?		
Registered with the Data Protection Registrar?		
Antitheft devices used? ·		
Passwords used?		
All software properly licensed?		

Develop this into a short report on security at the site, and recommend ways of improving it.

Document specifications and templates

A **document specification** is a 'set of rules' about the format of a document, covering page size and orientation, fonts used, headers and footers, margins, justification, etc. A company might use the same document specification for all its documents in order to develop a 'corporate image.'

Many applications help the user to be consistent about document specifications by using **templates**. A template is set up by preparing a document containing what is required for the specification, and then saving it as a template. Any new documents can be based on this template, saving a lot of work. Templates were mentioned in Element 1.4.

A common example of a template is the cover page for a document to be faxed. This would probably have the company logo, telephone and fax numbers, date and time, and spaces to write in who the fax is to and who it came from. Using a template like this saves a lot of time.

Document checklist

When you review a document design, perhaps to improve it, you will find the following checklist helpful.
- Is the page big enough to be seen? Does it need to be a standard size?
- Is the page the best way round?
- Would columns improve the layout?

- Do the fonts used give the correct 'feel' for the document (casual or authoritative)? Are too many fonts used?
- Is the text big enough to be read easily? Is it too large, wasting space?
- Are headers and footers used effectively?
- Do the margins make the page look well balanced and attractive?
- Are graphics used? If they are, are they well placed and a suitable size?
- Would tables help?
- Are bold, italic, underlining, centring used well?

The use of these features will depend on the kind of document. The document must be designed to do the job it is intended for. For example, it must be possible to read a wall poster quickly, at a distance – it should attract attention. This means the paper and font size must be large, graphics should be used, and there should not be too much text. The font could be very unusual to 'grab' attention. On the other hand, a newsletter would benefit from using a standard page size like A4. A font size of 10 or 12 points would allow a lot of text to be placed on one page, and columns might help to organise the items. A small company logo might be appropriate, with headings in bold or underlined. The font should be sensible to carry a feeling of reliability.

Test questions

1 A management meeting was held last Tuesday, and the secretary has a record of the discussion and the decisions taken. This document is:
   a A report
   b A memorandum
   c Minutes
   d An agenda

2 A mail-order company sends a parcel containing several items to a customer. It then sends the customer a document listing the items, their prices, the total, and requesting payment. This document is:
   a A newsletter
   b An invoice
   c A memo
   d A business letter

3 Which diagram in Figure 2.4 shows a portrait orientation without columns?

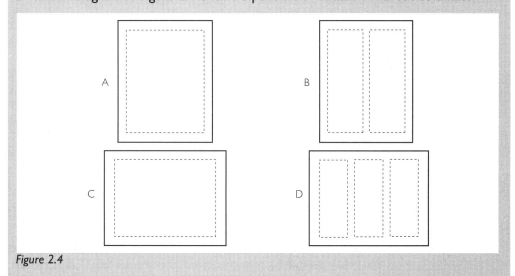

Figure 2.4

4 Look at Figure 2.5. You are given picture 1 and you need to produce picture 2. Which is the quickest way to do this?

a Reflect 1
b Stretch 1 then copy it
c Copy 1 then rotate it
d Draw 2

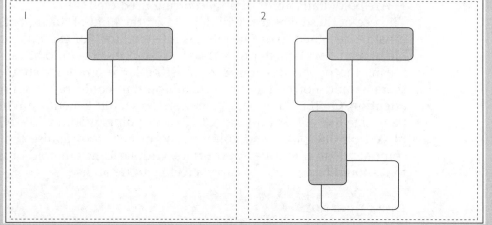

Figure 2.5

5 The following table contains a mistake – the fourth row starting 'Modem' should not be there

Item	Price
Computer	£790
VDU	£210
Modem	£110
Keyboard	£19

What is the quickest way to correct this?

a Retype the table without that row
b Retype the fourth column to contain the data 'Keyboard £19' and then delete the keyboard row
c Delete the fourth row
d Resize the fourth row

7 When should you proofread a long document?

a After you have printed it out
b About every 10 minutes
c Before you print it out
d Never

Element 2.2: Process graphic designs

Introduction

Images are useful ways of communicating in many different situations. A diagram makes it easier to explain how the tracks and sectors are arranged on a disk. A bar chart could be used to show sales of computers month by month through the year. Pictures can be used to illustrate a restaurant menu and make it more attractive. A talk to a group can be made more lively and easier to follow if it is accompanied by a series of slides projected on a screen. An engineering drawing might be the basis for actually making a gearbox for a car. Applications software is available which makes it easy even for non-artistic people to produce good images.

Design specification

A design specification is a set of 'rules' according to which a graphic will be created. If the graphic is being produced by a professional, then the specification is decided upon by the customer for whom the graphic is going to be produced.

Purpose

This is just what the graphic is for. It might be a wedding invitation, an advertisement for a CD, a diagram showing how a printer works, a map showing people how to get to a college.

Content

This is what will be in the design. It might be facts (like the date of the wedding) or images (like a company logo).

Dimensions

This is the size of the graphic. If the graphic is to fit a single sheet of paper this is likely to be a standard size such as A4 or A3. If it is an illustration in a newspaper, the size might be given as so many millimetres wide and so many high, so that it will fit into a page design. An engineering drawing will be made to a certain scale. There is a certain tolerance, or range of sizes, acceptable. It is impossible to manufacture something to an exact size. If the item is within the tolerance range the pieces will fit together, but not if the item is a long way from its intended size.

Graphic type

Another part of a design specification is the type of graphic it is to be.

Bitmaps A bitmap graphic is made of a grid of dots, called pixels or picture elements. The graphic in Figure 2.6 shows the individual pixels in a picture.

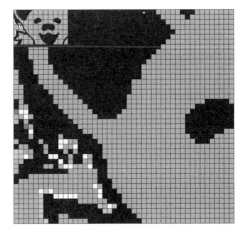

Figure 2.6 A bitmap graphic. The picture is shown in the top left-hand corner, and the rest shows this 'zoomed' to see the individual pixels

Bitmap graphics are usually used in software which does on a computer what an artist does on canvas with a brush (not with a pencil). This means that areas are 'painted' in solid areas of colour, perhaps with a lot of detail and shading. These types of packages can usually 'import' photographs, and 'scan' in other pictures from paper.

Vector graphics

Vector graphics are made of simple objects like straight lines and circles. Figure 2.7 shows a vector graphic. Packages that produce vector graphics do on a computer what an artist (or draughtsman) does with a pencil (not a brush). It produces a line drawing rather than a painting.

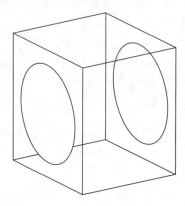

Figure 2.7 A vector graphic

Vector graphics are most often used for engineering drawings and computer-aided design (CAD), for architects' drawings, electronic circuit diagrams, etc.

Charts Charts can be prepared from sets of numbers, usually by spreadsheets and specialist graphics packages. Some word processors can also produce charts. Different kinds of charts are possible – the most common are pie, bar and line charts. These could be two- or three-dimensional.

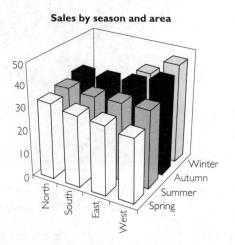

Figure 2.8 A three-dimensional bar chart prepared in a spreadsheet

Presentation software

When you are giving a talk to an audience you can prepare a set of slides to show using presentation software.

Presentation software lets you prepare a series of pictures, usually containing some graphic images, a small amount of text and some charts. These are shown in sequence throughout the talk, usually by connecting the VDU output to a projector so that the pictures can be shown on a large screen. Different effects can be used to change between slides, such as fades or wipes. One slide can be changed to the next by the click of the mouse, or after a preset time. The software also allows the user to prepare a set of written notes that accompany the talk – these 'handouts' should help the audience follow the talk.

Activity 2.8

Identify which of the packages you use are able to produce bitmaps, vector graphics, charts or presentations. Complete the table.

Type of software	Package name(s)
Bitmap (brush painting)	
Vector (pencil drawing)	
Charting	
Presentation graphics	

Image attributes

The different 'measurements' of an image are called its **attributes**. For example, an image could be in black and white or in colour. It could be 5 cm, or 3 cm × 6 cm. The areas of colour might be shaded or not.

An image in black and white (or monochrome) uses less storage space than the same image in colour, and if it is to be printed on a printer which does not produce colour, a monochrome graphic may be better. The different colours of a colour image will usually be printed as shades of grey on a monochrome printer, but this is not always required. Colour images can contain only a limited number of different colours – usually 16, 64 or 256. The set of colours in the image is called its **palette**. The image saved on disk will also contain palette information, so that the colours in the palette best represent those present in the real scene.

Page attributes

The page has different attributes from the image that is printed on it. Page attributes were discussed in Element 2.1. The software will usually warn you if you try to print an image on paper smaller than the image. Most printers cannot print right to the edge of the page, and the page margin settings should take this into account.

Graphic components

Graphics are usually drawn using a mouse. The mouse pointer is used to click on a graphics 'tool' to select the graphic component to be produced, and the component is drawn by clicking and dragging with the mouse.

Lines

Straight lines are drawn by 'rubber banding', which is dragging from one end of the line to the other. Curves are produced in a similar way, dragging from the start to the end and then dragging the amount of 'bend' needed. Freehand line drawing allows the user to drag the mouse over any path, which turns into a line.

The width of lines can be altered. Line width is usually measured in points, just as text. Line 'style' means whether the line is continuous or broken in some pattern – 'dash-dot-dot' is shown in the example in Figure 2.9.

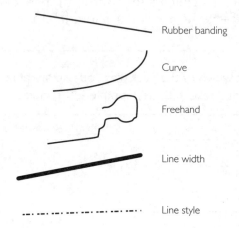

Figure 2.9 Line drawing tools

Shapes

You can draw many shapes with a graphics package, including circles, rectangles, polygons and ellipses. Examples of these are shown in Figure 2.10.

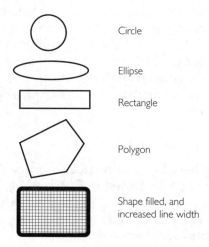

Figure 2.10 Common shapes

These shapes may be filled, in which case they will hide another object underneath them, or not filled. The width and style of the boundary lines can be altered.

Text

Text can be included in graphics and the fonts, sizes and styles, such as bold, italic and underlined, altered as required.

Colour areas and spray

As you can see in Figure 2.11, areas can be given a number of special effects – for example, an air-brush style can be used, the area painted with brushes of different shapes and sizes, and filled with colour patterns.

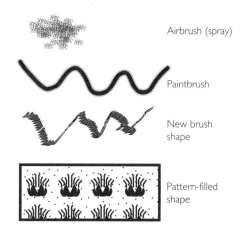

Airbrush (spray)

Paintbrush

New brush
shape

Pattern-filled
shape

Figure 2.11

Review questions

1 What are:
   • bitmap graphics
   • vector graphics
   • image attributes
   • page attributes?
2 What are:
   • rubber banding
   • free-hand line drawing
   • polygons
   • ellipses?
3 What is the usual unit of measurement of line width?
4 What is meant by 'line style'?

Test questions

1 You have been asked to draw an electrical circuit diagram on a computer. Which
   would be the best type of graphics to use?
   a Bitmap
   b Slide show
   c Vector
   d Charting

The notice in Figure 2.12 has been produced on a computer.

Figure 2.12

2 Which feature of a graphics package would have been used to produce the lettering?
a Paint brush
b Spray can
c Filled shape
d Text tool

3 Which line tool would have been used to draw the bar across the picture of the camera?
a Rubber banding
b Curve
c Freehand
d Line style

4 Which one of the following is *not* a page attribute?
a Margin settings
b Paper size
c Landscape or portrait orientation
d Number of colours

5 Which one of the following is *not* a shape?
a Vector
b Rectangle
c Polygon
d Ellipse

Element 2.3: Process and model numerical data

Introduction

The purpose of modelling is to be able to predict a result, in the form of numbers. This is useful because it enables you to plan so you can obtain the result you want. For example, you might be running a restaurant. Many things will affect how much profit you make – how many people you can seat at one time, how long they occupy a table for, the price of the meals, how much you pay for the ingredients, how much you pay your staff. A model of the process would let you see how much profit you would make by changing some of the features – for example, if you employed fewer people, or had more tables, or charged more for the meals.

Models are usually not exact, but even approximate answers are useful. Because modelling involves a lot of arithmetic calculations, spreadsheets are often used. Other applications, such as database systems and process control software, can also be used for modelling, but not usually as effectively as a spreadsheet.

Computer models

Computer models are software that act like 'real' systems. There are two types of models: **prediction models**, which are used to forecast what would happen in a real system, and **gaming models** such as flight simulators, car driving games and adventure games

Basic spreadsheet ideas

Spreadsheets are grids made up of rows and columns, as shown in Figure 2.13. The places in the grid that contain data are called cells, and are referred to by their column and row numbers – cell B3 is shown in Figure 2.13. This is like the x and y co-ordinates on a graph.

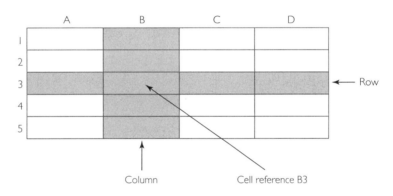

Figure 2.13 Rows and columns in a spreadsheet

A typical spreadsheet is shown in Figure 2.14. It shows the money spent on various items for each month for the first quarter of the year. It also shows totals for each month and each item. These cells contain two types of data – numbers (in cell B3 and others) and characters (in A3 and so on). Cells can contain a third data type, formulae.

1	A	B	C	D	E
2		Jan	Feb	Mar	Totals
3	Rates	£23.56	£23.56	£23.56	£70.68
4	Petrol	£34.55	£31.46	£22.99	£89.00
5	Wages	£48.50	£48.50	£48.50	£145.50
6	Electricity	£16.50	£18.99	£21.22	£56.71
7	Totals	£123.11	£122.51	£116.27	£361.89

Figure 2.14 An example of a typical spreadsheet

Cell B7 contains the total for January. The computer has calculated this because this cell contains a formula (in Excel, the formula would be =B3+B4+B5+B6). Carrying out numerical calculations is the main purpose of a spreadsheet.

Activity 2.9

Set up the spreadsheet shown in Figure 2.14 on your computer. You may need some help in entering the formulae. Save the spreadsheet for use in later activities.

Review questions

1 What is the difference between a row and a column?
2 Give an example of a cell reference.
3 What kinds of information can you put in a cell?

Spreadsheet layouts and formatting

The layout of a spreadsheet can be changed easily. The width of a column can be altered if it is not wide enough to contain a piece of text. The height of rows may also be changed.

It is also possible to alter the format of the numbers in the spreadsheet. For example, if the number represents an amount of money, then 24.55 will display correctly, but 24.50 will usually be shown as 24.5. By changing the format of the numbers, so that they always show two decimal places, all the numbers are presented in the same way. You can choose date formats. The default is usually the American format (month/day/year order), but it is possible to change this to the British day/month/year. Text can be left justified, right justified or centred (see Element 2.1).

You should be able to set titles on the spreadsheet, so that when it is printed out the titles will appear at the top of each page.

Usually the spreadsheet will display the amount calculated by a formula – not the formula itself. However, if you want the formulae themselves shown, you can do this by another kind of formatting.

Activity 2.10

Check you know the answers to the following questions for the spreadsheet you normally use. If you do not know, find out by using on-line help. Try these out on the spreadsheet you saved in Activity 2.9.

1 How do you change column widths and row heights?
2 How do you change text alignment (justification)?
3 How do you change date formats?
4 How do you change the number of decimal places shown?
5 How do you set print titles?
6 How do you display formulas rather than values?

Recalculation

Because the numbers in a spreadsheet are usually connected by formulas, altering one number will mean recalculating the whole spreadsheet. Recalculation is handled in two ways.

- Usually it is done automatically. If any cell in the spreadsheet is altered, the software goes through all cells, row by row and column by column, and recalculates the new values for any formulas. The advantage of this is that all the spreadsheet values are correct all the time. The disadvantage is that if the spreadsheet is very large there may be an annoying delay waiting for the recalculation every time any number is changed.
- The alternative is manual re-calculation – new values are worked out only when the user makes it happen, by pressing a function key or some other command. This method is not commonly used.

Activity 2.11

On the spreadsheet you usually use, how do you stop automatic recalculation and switch to manual? If you do not know already, use on-line help to find out. Try some recalculation on the spreadsheet from Activity 2.9. What command do you have to use to make the spreadsheet recalculate when it is manual mode?

Functions

In the spreadsheet you prepared in Activity 2.9, you used the formula =B3+B4+B5+B6 to add up a column of numbers. If there had been 20 numbers to add up the formula would have been extremely long, =B3+B4+B5+B6…B23. This difficulty can be overcome by using the **sum function** in the formula. In Excel this would give the formula =sum(A3:A23).

Some of the functions in a spreadsheet are like the functions you find on a calculator, such as square root and cosine. Others work on a block of numbers, such as the sum function. Functions that work on blocks of numbers are **average**, **maximum** and **minimum**. The exact way you use these functions will vary from one spreadsheet package to another, and you need to use the on-line help for details on how to do it in your software.

Activity 2.12

Mr Brown is an IT lecturer, and he keeps a record of his student assessments in a spreadsheet, as shown in Figure 2.15.

	A	B	C	D	E	F	G
1	Name	Marks					Totals
2	John	7	33	77	8		125
3	Jane	29	41	32	99		201
4	Julie	38	22	59	92		211
5	Joe	89	60	34	33		216
6	Jaspinder	90	31	78	75		274
7	Jock	65	39	4	40		148
8						Maximum	274
9	Average	53.00	37.67	47.33	57.83	Minimum	125

Figure 2.15

This shows the marks that six students obtained in four assessments (marks out of 100). Column G contains the totals for each student, and the maximum and minimum values. The average marks for each assessment are also included, so that Mr Brown can see which tasks were easier than others.

Keeping records like this has several advantages over keeping them in an ordinary markbook. It is easy to make a copy of the spreadsheet file as a backup, but a markbook can be lost. If a new student joins the class it takes little effort to add a new row. For meetings, such as parents' evening, he can print out the spreadsheet to make it easy to refer to. Most importantly, having the computer do all the calculations saves a lot of time.

Set up a spreadsheet like the one in Figure 2.15. In cells B9 to E9 use a formula using the average function. In G2 to G7 put in a formula using the sum function. In G8 use the maximum function, and in G9 the minimum function.

Activity 2.13

The Greasy Spoon Cafe
Celia Sniff is planning to open a cafe, and she is working out whether she will make a profit. She thinks people will spend about half an hour at a meal, and thinks that about half the tables are likely to be occupied. She plans to be open for 8 hours a day, and to pay the waiters £3.50 an hour. She thinks that the food will cost her about half what she can sell the meals for. She puts these numbers into a spreadsheet, as shown in Figure 2.16.

- Celia thinks that a waiter can cover five seats, so the number of waiters in row 10 is the number of seats divided by 5.

	A	B	C	D	E	F	G	H
1	**Restaurant costs**							
2								
3	Seats	0	5	10	15	20	25	30
4	Time in restaurant	0.5	0.5	0.5	0.5	0.5	0.5	0.5
5	Occupancy	0.5	0.5	0.5	0.5	0.5	0.5	0.5
6	Open time per day	8	8	8	8	8	8	8
7	Price per meal	£4.50	£4.50	£4.50	£4.50	£4.50	£4.50	£4.50
8	Food cost	0.5	0.5	0.5	0.5	0.5	0.5	0.5
9	Waiters pay per hour	£3.50	£3.50	£3.50	£3.50	£3.50	£3.50	£3.50
10	Waiters	0	1	2	3	4	5	6
11	Meals per day	0	40	80	120	160	200	240
12	Profit per meal	£2.25	£2.25	£2.25	£2.25	£2.25	£2.25	£2.25
13	Meal income	£0.00	£90.00	£180.00	£270.00	£360.00	£450.00	£540.00
14	Wage cost	£0.00	£28.00	£56.00	£84.00	£112.00	£140.00	£168.00
15	Rent and rates	£130.00	£130.00	£130.00	£130.00	£130.00	£130.00	£130.00
16	Profit	−£130.00	−£68.00	−£6.00	£56.00	£118.00	£180.00	£242.00
17		Loss	Loss	Loss	Profit	Profit	Profit	Profit

Figure 2.16

- The number of meals per day shown in row 11 is calculated by dividing the opening time by the time taken for one meal, multiplying it by the number of seats, and multiplying that by the occupancy rate.
- The profit per meal is the meal cost times the cost of the food.
- The meal income is the number of meals times the profit per meal.
- The wage cost is the pay per hour, times the hours open per day, times the number of waiters.
- The rent and rates are fixed, at £130 per day.
- The profit is the income from meals, less the wages cost and the rent and rates.

In row 17 is an '**if formula**', which gives a different value depending on whether a condition is true or false. For example, row 17 shows 'Loss' or 'Profit' depending on whether the number in row 16 is less than or greater than 0. In Excel the formula for this would be =if(B16>0,'Profit','Loss')

Set this spreadsheet up for yourself. How many seats does Celia need to fit in to make a profit? In fact she finds she can only get 10 seats in the cafe. What price should she make the meals to make a profit with 10 seats?

Activity 2.14

The Cardboard Box Company

The Cardboard Box Company manufactures cardboard boxes. They make the boxes by taking a square of cardboard, cutting parts out of the corners and folding it up – as shown in Figure 2.17. The company wants to predict the biggest volume of box they can manufacture from a given square of cardboard.

They start with a piece of cardboard and cut out a square at each corner. The four side flaps are then folded up to form the sides of the box. If the cuts are big more height is produced, but the box has a small base. If the cut-outs are small the base is

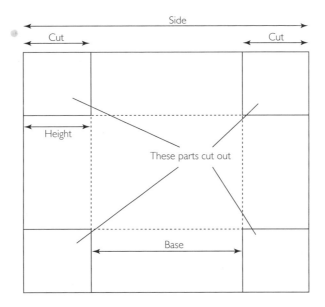

Figure 2.17

big, but the box is not very high. What will make the box with the biggest volume? A spreadsheet can be used to work this out, as shown in Figure 2.18.

	A	B	C	D	E
	Side	Cut	Height	Base side	Volume
1					
2	1	0	0	1	0.0000
3	1	0.02	0.02	0.96	0.0184
4	1	0.04	0.04	0.92	0.0339
5	1	0.06	0.06	0.88	0.0465
6	1	0.08	0.08	0.84	0.0564
7	1	0.1	0.1	0.8	0.0640
8	1	0.12	0.12	0.76	0.0693
9	1	0.14	0.14	0.72	0.0726
10	1	0.16	0.16	0.68	0.0740
11	1	0.18	0.18	0.64	0.0737
12	1	0.2	0.2	0.6	0.0720
13	1	0.22	0.22	0.56	0.0690
14	1	0.24	0.24	0.52	0.0649
15	1	0.26	0.26	0.48	0.0599
16	1	0.28	0.28	0.44	0.0542
17	1	0.3	0.3	0.4	0.0480
18	1	0.32	0.32	0.36	0.0415

Figure 2.18

This spreadsheet is for a square with sides of 1 metre.
- Column A is the size of the original square, 1.
- Column B is the size of the cut, trying different values starting at 0 and increasing by 2 cm each time.
- Column C is the height of the box this produces – this is the same as the cut in column B.
- Column D is the size of the base. This is the original square less twice the cut-out, so the formula for this is =A2–2*C2
- Column E gives the volume, the base squared times the height. The formula for this would be =C2*D2*D2

From the values in column E, it can be seen that the biggest volume is obtained with a cut-out of about 16 cm.

1 Set up a spreadsheet with these formulas and see if you can get the same answer.
2 What would the result be if you started with a square of cardboard which is 50 cm across?

Test questions

I Which type of model lets a person try to estimate what will happen in the future?

  a Predictive

  b Financial

  c Gaming

  d Reality

Questions 2 to 7 relate to the information given in Figure 2.19.

	A	B	C	D	E	F	G	H
I						% OF	PRICE	
2	**CARS**				QTR	TOTAL	PER	VALUE
3	MANUFAC	JAN	FEB	MAR	SALES	SALES	CAR	SOLD
4	FORD	25	9	24	58	37.17949	8500	493000
5	VAUXHALL	23	7	14	44	28.20513	7900	347600
6	NISSAN	12	3	6	21	13.46154	9210	193410
7	TOYOTA	3	14	16	33	21.15385	6900	227700
8								
9								
10					156			1261710

Figure 2.19

2 Which cell format would be most appropriate for columns G and H?

  a Date

  b Scientific

  c Percentage

  d Currency

3 Which cell contains the main title?

  a E3

  b A2

  c H10

  d G1

4 How would you ensure that the contents of cell A3 are shown as MANUFAC-TURER?

  a Reduce the width of column D

  b Delete column B

  c Increase the width of column A

  d Reduce the width of column E

5 Which cell calculates the total number of FORDs sold in the quarter?

  a C3

  b B4

  c E4

  d A1

6 Which cell calculates the total value of cars sold in the quarter?

  a H4

  b H10

  c E10

  d G7

7 Which cell contains the formula =E5*G5?

  a E5

  b F5

  c G5

  d H5

Element 2.4: Use information technology for process control

Introduction

Computers and IT are used in many organisations to 'control', to help managers make decisions and run their business. **Process control** is different. In process control, a real process is controlled automatically by IT. An example is a market gardening company that grows tomatoes in big greenhouses – the temperature, humidity, light levels and watering must be just right if the plants are to grow well, and this is controlled by computers.

Activity 2.15

Which of the following are examples of process control?

- A turnstile at a library exit which only opens if a book has been borrowed properly, not stolen.
- Producing mail-merged advertising 'fliers' to market a product.
- Charging fines for library books that have been returned late.
- Deciding whether to raise the price of a product.
- Controlling the lights and gates at a railway crossing.
- Making sure the temperature in an office building is correct.
- Sending invoices to customers.
- A burglar alarm system.
- Printing receipts at a supermarket checkout.
- Freezing peas after harvest, rejecting peas that are too big.

Example – automatic room lights

A good example of the use of process control is in switching on the lights when a person enters a room. This is becoming more common in offices, and can save electricity costs. The lights switch on if a person enters a room, stay on until they leave, then switch off by themselves. This only happens if the normal daylight is not bright enough, and if the overall system is switched on.

Figure 2.20 shows what hardware would be needed in such a system. There would be three input devices – a simple switch to enable the whole system, a light sensor to measure whether the daylight was insufficient, and a proximity sensor which would detect the presence of people in the room. These would be connected to a processor which would control the output device, switching the lights on or off.

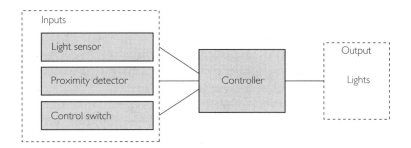

Figure 2.20

The processor would follow a control procedure as shown in the flowchart in Figure 2.21. This would switch on the lights only if the system was turned on, if there were people in the room and if the daylight was not bright enough. It then waits 10 minutes, and checks again.

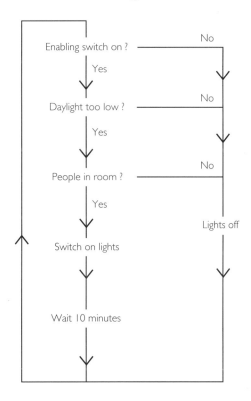

Figure 2.21

Uses of process control

There are four kinds of uses of process control:
* *Environmental control.* This means controlling the environment either inside or outside a building. A central heating system in a house is an example of this – if the temperature is too high, the heating is switched off until it cools down too far, when it switches on again. The system may also be timed, so that there is no heating at certain times of day or night. The greenhouse system already mentioned is an example of environmental control.

- *Production control.* In production control IT is being used to control manufacturing. An example is a steel rolling mill, where very hot ingots of steel are rolled under pressure into other shapes. The temperature of the steel, the pressure on it, and the rate at which it rolls along must all be kept within certain limits. Another example is a chemical plant, where chemicals are heated together at the correct temperature.
- *Quality control.* Quality control systems usually involve checking that items being manufactured are within acceptable limits. For example, breakfast cereal packets must be filled to the correct weight, and rejected if they are under or over the limit. Another example is in the manufacture of electric light bulbs – the finished bulbs are switched on, and a check is made that they work and give out the correct amount of light.
- *Security systems.* An example of this is a swipe card entry system. People who are authorised to go through a door use a swipe card to prove their identity: the door will then open to let them in. Intruders, who don't have a swipe card, cannot enter. The use of magnetic tags on clothes in clothes shops is another example – if the tag has not been removed an alarm will be set off as the clothes are taken out of the shop.

Activity 2.16

Decide which of the following are environmental, production, quality or security uses of IT.
- A turnstile at a library exit which opens only if a book has been borrowed properly – not stolen.
- Robot welder on a car assembly line.
- Controlling the lights and gates at a railway crossing.
- Making sure the temperature in an office building is correct.
- A burglar alarm system.
- Making printed circuit boards under computer control.
- Freezing peas after harvest, rejecting peas that are too big.
- Automatic room lights.
- Domestic central heating.
- Car alarm.

Keep this work for a later assignment.

Components of process control systems

Sensors

The input peripherals on a standard office PC are the keyboard and mouse, but in process control other input devices are used. A **contact sensor** detects when an object makes contact – an example is a pressure mat, used in front of automatic doors which open as people approach and tread on the mat. A **heat sensor** that turns the temperature into an electrical signal which goes into the computer would be used in a greenhouse. A **light sensor** does the same for light levels. A **proximity sensor** is like a contact sensor, but measures when an object is near (not actually touching). A proximity sensor might be used in a burglar alarm system. A **sound sensor** is a microphone –

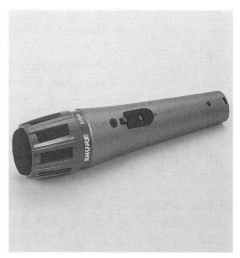

Figure 2.22 Examples of input sensors: light sensitive switch, proximity sensor and microphone (not to scale)

sound signals are picked up and converted into an electrical signal, which goes into the computer.

Processors

Input sensors are connected to a **processor**, which runs a program to control the process. The processor might be the CPU of a general-purpose PC. However, in many situations – such as the control of the operation of a dish-washer – a PC is not suitable. In cases like this a microprocessor chip and memory are used as the processor.

Control procedure

The control procedure is the program that the processor runs. These programs are described under 'Stages in process control'.

Output devices

The usual output peripherals on a PC are a VDU and printer, but in process control other devices are also used. The computer might be made to switch a heater on and off, to control temperature. Traffic lights could be used as output devices to control traffic. Robot arms have electric motors at their 'joints', and switching the motors on and off, forward and backward makes the arms move. Other possible output devices are speakers, pumps and valves.

Connecting devices

Special connecting devices are sometimes needed in process control to connect input and output devices to a processor. These are needed to
- protect the processor from unexpectedly high voltages which might damage it from the input device – effectively a fuse
- change a signal into a digital form that the processor can use
- add power to the signal – for example, a computer cannot supply enough power for a heater by itself, so the computer closes a switch providing a high current.

Activity 2.17

Write notes on the process control components available at your college:

- The sensors
- The output devices
- The processors
- The connecting devices

Keep this work for a later assignment.

Review questions

1 List four kinds of uses of process control
2 Describe four sensors
3 Describe two output devices
4 Why are interconnecting devices needed?

Stages in process control

A control procedure has three stages:
- *sense* conditions through input sensors
- in the processor, *compare* the signal with acceptable limits
- *adjust* output accordingly.

The program for a domestic central heating system works like this. Repeat the following:
- Is it too hot?
  - if so, switch off the radiators
- Is it too cold?
  - if so, switch on the radiators

In this way the temperature in the house is kept within required limits. This could be thought of as a loop, as shown in Figure 2.23. The signal (in this case the temperature) goes into the processor through the input device. The processor decides if the signal is within limits, and if not it sends a signal to the output device, to switch it on or off. This affects the surroundings (in this case warming or cooling), and this **feeds back** into the system

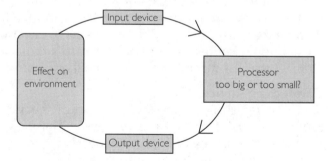

Figure 2.23 A feedback loop

Activity 2.18

In a computerised greenhouse a system might be used to water the plants automatically. In this situation, what would the three stages be? Keep your answer for Assignment 2.4.

The central heating system is an example of **negative feedback**. It is negative because the output opposes the input – i.e.

- too hot? make it cooler
- too cold? make it warmer

Almost all process control situations use negative feedback, because positive feedback produces unstable systems. Imagine a plant irrigation system that controls the water supply to crops in a field. If **positive feedback** were used, then if the field was wet (perhaps because of a shower of rain) the pumps would be switched on and more water would be supplied. As long as the field is wet, more and more water would be pumped, producing a flood! The correct system would use negative feedback – if there is too little water, more is supplied.

Activity 2.19

Imagine you are driving a car through a town centre. A good way to control the speed of the car is to say:

- Am I going too fast? Then slow down
- Going too slow? Speed up.

Is this negative or positive feedback? What would happen if you tried to drive a car using positive feedback?

System specifications and reviews

To complete this Element you must be able to review the performance of a system and suggest improvements to its specification. To see what this means we will look at greenhouse control as an example.

A system specification has five parts:

- purpose
- control limits
- response time
- sensors
- type of feedback.

The *purpose* of a system simply describes what the system is for. The purpose of a greenhouse control system might be to keep the temperature inside a greenhouse within specified limits – not too hot and not too cold. The *control limits* of a system are the upper and lower limits of the values the sensors measure. The control limits of our greenhouse might be that the temperature must be no less than 16°C and no more than 30°C. If the temperature drops below 16°C the computer will switch the heater on to heat the greenhouse up, if it is above 30°C the computer will act to cool the greenhouse down. The *response time* is a measure of how quickly the system can act. It would not matter much if the temperature inside a greenhouse was wrong for a few seconds – a reasonable response time for this system would be an hour. A variety of *sensors* can be used – contact, heat, light, proximity, sound. The greenhouse system we are looking at needs a heat sensor. *Feedback* can be positive or negative. If the temperature in our greenhouse falls the heater must switch on to raise the temperature – negative feedback.

Improving a specification

When you set up a system, you need to see how well it works, identify any problems and improve the specification to overcome the problems. You might find that the plants in your greenhouse die, even though the temperature is correct, because there was no watering system. You might decide from this that the purpose is not right, since it should control watering as well as temperature. You might also find that the plants are dying of cold because the response time is too long – they might not be able to stand the cold for an hour. To overcome this you might choose to change the response time to 10 minutes and use a more powerful heater.

Test questions

1 A process control system is used as a car alarm. If someone tries to move the car without a key, an alarm sounds. Which type of control is this?

  a Production

  b Environment

  c Quality

  d Security

2 The system in Figure 2.24 sends only capped bottles to be packed. What type of control is this system?

  a Environmental

  b Production

  c Quality

  d Security

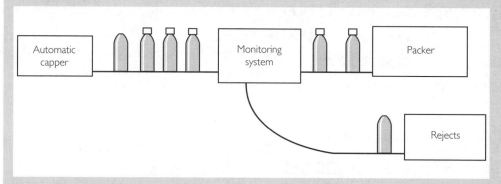

Figure 2.24

Questions 3 to 7 relate to the following information:

SquidgyBots make shower lotions. Before the shower lotion is bottled a green dye is added. Adding the dye is an automatic process controlled by a computer.

3 Which of these is an input to the system?

  a The shower gel

  b The gel ingredients

  c The detected shade of green

  d The gel's scent

4 Which of the following is an output from the system?

  a The amount of dye needed

  b The required shade of green

  c Bottles of shower lotion

  d The type of dye needed

5 Name a component of the colour control system:
  a The colour detector
  b A conveyor belt
  c Empty bottles
  d The shower lotion
6 Which type of sensor will detect the colour of the shower lotion?
  a Contact
  b Sound
  c Heat
  d Light
7 What controls the colour added to the shower gel?
  a The colour detector
  b The computer program
  c The number of bottles of gel
  d The gel ingredients
8 A central heating system uses this type of sensor:
  a Sound
  b Temperature
  c Light
  d Proximity
9 A pedestrian road crossing must warn deaf people when it is safe to cross. The component that will be different for deaf people is:
  a The car detectors buried in the road
  b The output device
  c The interconnecting devices
  d The control program

Assignment A2.1

This assignment provides portfolio evidence for Element 2.1, and also the following key skill elements:

Communication 2.2:	Produce written material
Communication 2.3:	Use images
Information Technology 2.3:	Present information

1 Develop your work from Activity 2.1 to write a short report on different document types. Include the table, and make up an example of these documents being used.
2 Create a template for a fax. Find a suitable piece of clip art for the company logo, and use it in the fax. Use the template to send a fax message. Include the fax in your portfolio.
3 Write a report (at least three pages, part in two columns) on how to use the features described in Element 2.1 on your usual word processor or DTP package. The report should be written according to a specification.

a Consider the following specification:

Page size: Letter
Font size: 8 point
Font: Courier
Columns: Three columns
Headings   Normal text
Footers: None

Write an improved specification.

b   Write your report, using your improved specification.

4 Figure 2.25 shows a poster advertising a night-club. Comment on the design, then do your own version.

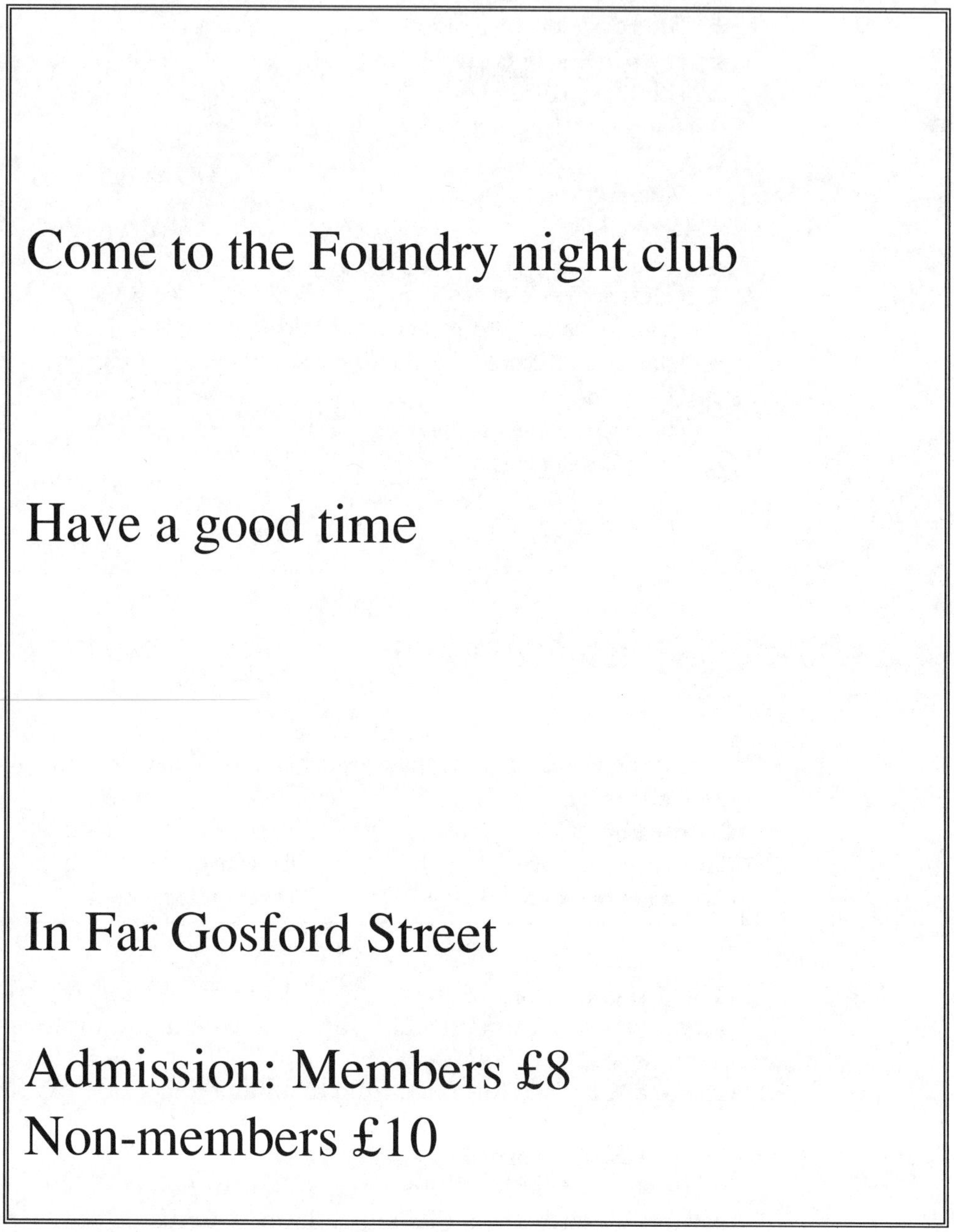

Come to the Foundry night club

Have a good time

In Far Gosford Street

Admission: Members £8
Non-members £10

Figure 2.25

Assignment A2.2

This assignment provides the portfolio evidence for Element 2.2, and also the following key skills:

Communication 2.2:	Produce written material
Communication 2.3:	Use images
Information Technology 2.1:	Prepare information
Information Technology 2.2:	Process information
Information Technology 2.3:	Present information

1 You are going to produce a user manual for the graphics software at your college, according to the following specification. If there are several packages available at your college, you need only do this for one of them.

Purpose:	A guide to the graphics packages at your college, intended to help a user to use them.
Content:	The guide should start with a list of the packages available, and what type they are. It should go on to explain how the user can produce graphic components as described in this element, with examples.
Dimensions:	A4 paper.
Graphics type:	Bitmap or vector as appropriate.

After you have completed the manual, you must compare the result with the specification, and make suggestions as to how it could be improved.

2 Use a presentation package to produce a slide show according to the following specification:

Purpose and content: choose from one of the following.

Topic	Contents
My favourite football team	Current players, ground, management, playing strip, history
A country	Where it is, population, large cities, religions, local recipes, climate, government
My family	Who they are (scan in photos), what they do, where they live, why they are annoying
Cars and driving	Car controls, automatic and manual, Highway Code, how to pass the driving test
The Internet	What it is, how it works, what you can do with it, what you need to access it
Another topic	As agreed with your lecturer

Graphics Type:	Presentation (slide show)

After you have completed your presentation, compare it with the specification, and suggest how it could be improved.

Assignment A2.3

This assignment provides the portfolio evidence for Element 2.3, and also the following key skills:

Application of Number 2.2:	Tackle problems
Information Technology 2.2:	Process information

1 Give an example of the use of a computer model for prediction, and one example of a computer game.
2 Jerry Harcia has just set up a small company called GDPC, which assembles and sells PCs. Jerry wants to get an idea of how many PCs she needs to sell every month to make a profit. She works this out on a spreadsheet, like this:

	1	2	3	4	5	6	7	8
A	Number made	0	10	20	30	40	50	60
B	Fixed cost							
C	Variable cost							
D								
E	Income							
F	Net profit							

a Set up a spreadsheet like this.
b Every month Jerry has to pay wages, rent and heating. These come to £5000 a month. Put this fixed cost across row B.
c Each PC costs £450 to make. Obviously the cost of making PCs depends on how many are made – these are called variable costs. The formula to work this out, in cell C2, is =A2*450. Put this in, and copy it across Row C.
d Jerry plans to sell the PCs for £650. This means the income from sales is the number sold times 650, so the formula in cell E2 is =A2*650. Put this in, and copy it across row E.
e The net profit is the INCOME minus the FIXED COST minus the VARIABLE COST. Put suitable formulas across row F. As you work through the following questions, print out the spreadsheet.
f About how many PCs does Jerry need to sell a month to make a profit?
g Alter the spreadsheet to get a more accurate value.
h Competition forces Jerry to drop the selling price to £600. How many does she need to sell now to make a profit?
i The company might move to newer premises, which would raise the fixed costs to £6000 a month. How many computers would Jerry need to sell at £600 then?
j Give cell references for cells containing text, numbers and formulae.

Assignment A2.4

This assignment provides portfolio evidence for Element 2.4, and also the following key skill elements:

Communication 2.2:	Produce written material
Information Technology 2.2:	Process information
Information Technology 2.4:	Evaluate the use of IT

1 Put together your work from Activities 2.20, 2.21 and 2.22.
2 Your tutor will give you a specification for a control system which you must produce using college equipment. You must select suitable components for this, and once it is working, obtain printouts to prove it.
3 Review the performance of the system and suggest ways of improving it.

CHAPTER 3

Organisations and IT

Element 3.1: Examine the flow of information in organisations
Element 3.2: Describe data handling systems
Element 3.3: Use information technology for a data handling activity
Element 3.4: Examine safety and security issues

What is covered in this chapter

- Types of organisations
- Functions of organisations
- Types of information
- Information flow
- Types of data handling systems
- Health and safety of information technology users
- Obligations of information technology users
- Investigating data handling systems
- Creating databases
- Using databases
- Checking data for accuracy
- Checking the security of a data-handling system

Resources you will need for your Organisations and Information Technology file:
- Your written answers to the activities in this chapter
- Your written answers to the review questions at the end of the chapter
- Completed Assignments A3.1, A3.2, A3.3 and A3.4

Introduction

When we work with other people, we need to agree on how to work together. We need to organise our way of working. If we organise ourselves with a formal structure, then we have created an **organisation**. On the whole, the world is run by organisations. Governments and businesses are all types of organisation. An organisation consists of lots of people working together for a common purpose. Any business, company, club, school, college, factory or similar establishment is an organisation.

This chapter looks at types of organisations and how they are organised, the information they use, how this information is handled and the technology used in handling it. It also studies safety, security and legal aspects of IT in organisations.

To help you understand this very important aspect of IT, you will need to investigate and describe a real information handling system, and also set up and use a small system yourself.

Organisations involve people working together

Element 3.1: Examine the flow of information in organisations

Types of organisation

Public service organisations

These are normally run by central or local government or by groups of people appointed by the government. They are paid for mainly through taxation and their main aim is to provide a service. Public service organisations include health services, educational establishments, the armed forces, the police, the inland revenue, customs and excise, law courts, prisons and the fire brigade.

Activity 3.1

This may produce evidence for communications element 2.4.

1 Working in small groups, find and list books which tell you about local and national organisations.
2 Use these books to list name, address, telephone number and main purpose of some local public service organisations (they may be branches of national organisations). There should be two such organisations per group member. Show how you found the information in your list – whether you already knew the organisation or whether you found it in your references.
3 One or more of the group members should have contact with one of the organisations from the list – because they have used the service, know someone who works there, or work there themselves.
   a Name the organisation
   b Describe your connection with the organisation
   c Give the name and position of a contact you have in the organisation.
Keep this information – you will need it in Assignment 3.1.

Commercial organisations

Commercial organisations have selling as their main activity: selling goods (e.g. shops, wholesalers, mail order firms), selling services (e.g. firms of accountants, insurance companies, bus companies, drain cleaners) or selling goods and services (e.g. garages, hairdressers, marinas).

Activity 3.2

This may produce evidence for communications element 2.4.

1 Work in the same groups as you did for Activity 3.1.
2 Use the reference works you used in Activity 3.1 to list name, address, telephone number and main purpose of some local commercial organisations (they may be branches of national or international organisations) – two for each group member.

Show how you found this information in your list.
3 Choose an organisation that one or more people in your group has contact with and
   a Name the organisation
   b Describe your connection
   c Name a contact in the organisation who might let you study the organisation.
Keep this information – you will need it for Assignment 3.1.

Industrial organisations

These mainly make things. For example: manufacturing products (e.g. cars, shoes, computers, pond equipment), processing raw materials (e.g. farmers grow food for eating or for further processing before it is eaten; steelworks turn iron ore into steel which is then used by manufacturing companies; chemical works create plastics and chemicals used in manufacturing; electricity works create electrical energy from gas, oil, coal or atomic materials) and construction (e.g. builders, civil engineers, shipbuilders).

Activity 3.3

May produce evidence for communications elements 2.2 and 2.4.
1 Working in the same groups, and using the same references, list the name, address, telephone number and main purpose of some local commercial organisations (they may be branches of national or international organisations) – again, each group member should list two. Describe how you found this information.
2 Choose an organisation that one or more people in your group has contact with and
   a Name the organisation
   b Describe your connection
   c Name a contact in the organisation who might let you study the organisation.
3 Write, but do not send, letters to named contacts in the three organisations you have listed asking if you can visit their organisation and investigate their information handling. The letter should explain who you are and what you require, should suggest suitable dates and times for a visit, but allow the organisation a choice.

Review questions

1 What is the prime function of
   a a commercial organisation
   b an industrial organisation
   c a public service organisation?
2 Which of the following organisatisations are commercial, which industrial and which public service?
   a a comprehensive school
   b a travel agent
   c a fish farm
   d a bus company
   e a bank.

Functions of an organisation and types of information used

The **functions** of an organisation may be divided into **external functions** and **internal functions**. Two main external functions of an organisation are dealing with customers and dealing with suppliers. These are closely linked to the internal functions of selling (to customers) and purchasing (from suppliers). One of the chief functions of an organisation is to look after its customers.

Dealing with customers

Customers need information from the organisation and the organisation needs information from and about the customer. A customer sends in an order for goods or services. An order is an official request for goods or services and should contain the word *order*. Often organisations provide special *order forms*, which customers can use for their orders. The organisation provides the goods or services and sends the customer an invoice. This is an official form telling the customer what is owed for the goods and services detailed on it. It should contain the word *invoice* and it should be dated. Customers are usually expected to pay when they receive the invoice, although regular customers may have a special agreement about when to pay – perhaps once a month. If the organisation does not know the customer they might ask for payment with the order.

Case Study

Charlwood Play Equipment

Charlwood Play Equipment makes fold-flat climbing frames and Wendy houses for nursery schools and preschool playgroups. The company prints order forms in advertisements for their products. Customers fill in these forms and send them to the company, with payment. Charlwood Play Equipment makes the toys to order, and sends them to the customer together with an invoice.

The information used by the Charlwood Play Equipment sales system can be shown on a document flow table:

	From	Document	To
1	Customer	Order form	Charlwood Play Equipment
2	Charlwood Play Equipment	Invoice	Customer

It can also be shown as a data flow diagram like the one in Figure 3.1.

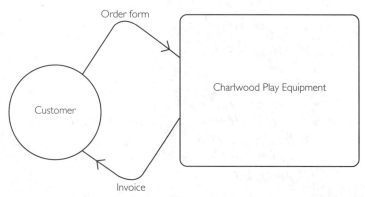

Figure 3.1 Outline data flow diagram for Charlwood Play Equipment sales system. The main organisation is shown as a box. Functions are shown as circles or ellipses. The flow of data is shown by lines and arrows

Activity 3.4

1 Last time you bought something, what information did you give the shop, and what information did the shop give you?
2 Suppose you want to go to Edinburgh by public transport. Name one organisation with whom you would need to exchange information. What information would you

need from them? What information would they need from you? Show this in an information table and as a data flow diagram,

3   A medical centre sends out appointment cards to all women who have reached the age of 50 and who have not had a cervical smear test within the last two years. What information do they need to store about the patients to be able to do this?

Dealing with suppliers

The suppliers to an organisation sell it goods and services. The organisation will need information about the suppliers and what they supply. They will also need to give information to the supplier about what they require. The organisation then acts as a customer to the supplier, so the types of document used in the supply function will also be orders and invoices.

Activity 3.5

Discuss in class what goods and services your school or college needs in order to run the GNVQ course in IT. Produce a table showing:
1   goods or services required
2   supplier or type of supplier
3   information required from supplier
4   information required by supplier.

Internal functions

There are a number of functions within organisations. Often each function has its own department.

Finance The finance function of an organisation deals with all its money matters, including making sure that
- customers pay their bills
- suppliers are paid
- employees are paid
- taxes are paid.

Examples of financial information:
- *Company accounts* – these show how the company makes and spends its money.
- *Customer statements* – tell customers what they have bought and paid for over a period of time.
- *Payroll* – what the organisation pays its staff.

Activity 3.6

May produce evidence for communications element 2.4.
Collect some financial information. You will find information about company accounts in the financial sections of newspapers. A customer statement is sent to anyone who uses a credit card and anyone who has a job should have an example of a pay slip. Explain the items written on these financial documents (you may wish to black out the names on personal items).

Operations This is the day-to-day running of an organisation. Operational functions include

- administration – organising the staff to do the tasks required by setting up work rotas, making sure people understand what they should be doing, checking that people are working properly
- transport, which includes despatching and delivering goods
- computer services, which keep computers, networks and programs running and keep good **backups**
- personnel, which hires and fires staff and looks after their welfare
- the production department, which keeps machinery running and in good repair
- the stores makes sure there are sufficient supplies to keep the work force busy
- design plans the product and how to make it
- record-keeping – in public service organisations, where it is important to keep records on people (such as patients in health care, students in education, clients in social services) the records must be correct and up-to-date, but also confidential and used only by appropriate people.

Examples of **operations information**:

- *Delivery notes* – tell the people in the despatch department what to pack and where to send it.
- *Stock control sheets* are used for counting stock on the shelves.
- *Design drawings* – in a factory these tell the people making a product what it should be like and how to make it.
- *Student records* enable a school or college to follow the progress of its students.

Activity 3.7

May produce evidence for communications elements 2.1 and 2.3.

1 Find a document containing operational information – it may be something you use in a part-time job, an operational document connected with your educational establishment or something provided by a friend or relative.
2 Describe the document to the rest of the class. Your description should include:
   a the organisation and type of organisation the document comes from
   b the name of the document
   c the function in the organisation that sends the document
   d the function which receives the document
   d what the document looks like
   e the data items that appear on the document.
3 Illustrate your description with a drawing (or photograph) that is large enough for the class to see (you could use an overhead projector or other visual aid to do this).

Sales The sales function deals with all aspects of sales, such as:

- receiving orders from customers
- providing goods to customers
- sending invoices to customers with the goods.

Case Study

More on Charlwood Play Equipment

When selling to state nursery schools Charlwood Play Equipment send the goods before they are paid for. A delivery note is sent, which contains the information shown below.

- Name and address of Charlwood Play Equipment and its VAT number
- Name and address of customer
- Date of order
- Invoice number (= delivery note number)
- Invoice date (= delivery note date)
- List of goods being sent

An invoice is sent separately from the delivery note. The invoice holds the same information as the delivery note with the addition of the prices for the goods sent, cost of post and packing, VAT and total cost. (A delivery note is often simply a copy of the invoice with the prices blacked out.)

At the end of each month the company sends the customer a statement listing

- money still owing from last month (if any)
- any invoices sent during the course of the month
- payments made during the month
- total still owing.

A document flow table can be drawn showing this information.

	From	Document	To
1	Customer	Order form	
2		Job card	
3		Customer	
4		Completed job card (with goods)	
5		Delivery note (with goods)	Customer
6		Completed job card	
7		Invoice	Customer
8		Copy of invoice	
9		Statement	Customer

A data flow diagram showing this information is given in Figure 3.2.

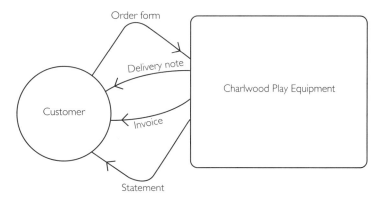

Figure 3.2 Outline data flow diagram of Charlwood Play Equipment's sales system

Activity 3.8

1 Redraw Figure 3.2 to show that the customer has paid and add a line to the information flow table to show the payment.
2 Collect some order forms from advertisements, and some invoices from goods that you or your friends have bought.
3 Charlwood Play Equipment makes three types of climbing frame and two types of Wendy house. Design for them
   a an order form
   b an invoice
   c a delivery note
   d a statement.

Within Charlwood Play Equipment information must flow between different functions so there must be internal as well as external communications. You can see a complete document flow table showing internal as well as external flow of information below.

	Outside From	Charlwood Play Equipment From	Document	To	Outside To
1	Customer		Order form	Sales department	
2		Sales department	Job card	Factory	
3		Sales department	Delivery note	Dispatch	
4		Factory	Completed job card (with goods)	Dispatch	
5		Dispatch	Delivery note (with goods)		Customer
6		Dispatch	Completed job card	Sales	
7		Sales	Invoice		Customer
8		Sales	Copy of invoice	Finance	
9	Customer		Payment	Finance	
10		Finance	Statement		Customer

Activity 3.9

The data flow diagram in Figure 3.3 shows the sales system for Charlwood Play Equipment. Copy this diagram, adding the information flow lines and labelling them with the name of the document.

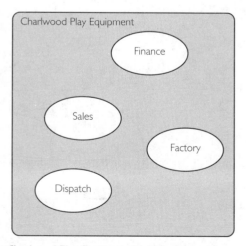

Figure 3.3 Detailed data flow diagram for Charlwood Play Equipment's sales system

Purchasing The purchasing function deals with all aspects of purchasing, such as:
- obtaining catalogues, prices and terms of business from suppliers
- sending orders to suppliers
- checking goods from suppliers against the packing notes and a copy of the original order
- checking invoices from suppliers against goods received and original orders
- passing invoices to be paid to the finance function.

Activity 3.10

May produce evidence for communications element 2.3.
1 Collect a copy of all the documents used in your college's purchasing system. Make sure that you know who sends each document and who receives it.
2 Use these documents to create a document flow table and data flow chart for the purchasing system at your educational establishment.

Note that sales and purchasing information both use invoices and orders. The difference is that the purchasing department sends out orders and receives invoices, while the sales department sends out invoices and receives orders.

Review questions

1 List two items of information that
   a a salesperson will need from the *designer* of new toys about a new toy
   b the *manager* of a supermarket needs from the main sales office before Christmas
   c a *payroll clerk* must be given by a *factory foreman* in order to calculate the month's wages
   d your *tutor* must have from *Edexel* about the mandatory tests.
2 Match the people italicised in Question 1 with the functions below:
   a customer
   b supplier
   c finance
   d operations
   e purchasing
   f sales.
3 A supervisor in a factory has to deal with a number of forms. What type of information (operations, sales or purchase) is each of the following?
   a An order form for raw materials used in the factory
   b An order form for products made in the factory
   c A rota detailing shift work for the next month
   d An invoice for new overalls
   e Drawings of new products to be made
4 Look at the organisation shown in Figure 3.4. Which department
   a keeps the company accounts
   b finds new customers
   c runs the factory
   d pays the workers?

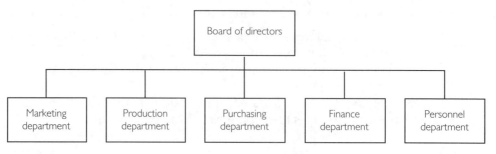

Figure 3.4

Activity 3.11 ─────────────────────────────────────

May produce evidence for communications element 2.2. Work in the same group as for Activities 3.1, 3.2 and 3.3.

> Hartford Marina is in an old gravel pit which has been turned into an artificial lake. There are mooring places around the lake which boat owners can rent. There is also a shop and a workshop for boat repairs.
>
> You know by sight the woman who runs the shop in Hartford Marina. You do not know her name, but have found out that she is also the assistant manager of the marina. You have decided to use Hartford Marina for an assignment to:
> • describe internal and external functions of an organisation
> • describe types of information used in the organisation and
> • produce a diagram to show the flow of information between functions.
> Functions should include internal functions (finance, operations, purchasing and sales) and external functions (customers and suppliers). Types of information should include operations information, purchase information (invoices, orders) and sales information (invoices, orders).

1 Write a letter to the assistant manager asking if you can interview her for your assignment.
2 Plan a questionnaire to use when you interview her. You will need to ask for:
   a a brief description of the organisation
   b a list of the functions of the organisation (you may find it helpful to list the functions that you need to include)
   c the types of information the organisation uses.
3 You will need to ask the assistant manager to help you to draw an information chart and data flow diagram for the marina. Write a short explanation of what these are and give an example of each.
4 Write a letter thanking the assistant manager for the information, and asking if you can come again if you want to do a further investigation.

Test questions

1 Which of these is an industrial organisation?
   a A coal mine
   b A health authority
   c A supermarket
   d A DIY shop

2 What is the main function of the chief buyer in a fashion shop?
   a Finance
   b Operations
   c Purchasing
   d Sales

3 What is the main function of a designer of new products?
   a Finance
   b Operations
   c Purchasing
   d Sales

4 A successful pop group hires four people to run their gigs for them. Which of these people will perform an external function?
   a Chief Accountant
   b Transport Manager
   c Chief Electrician
   d Marketing Manager

Questions 5–8 relate to Figure 3.5.

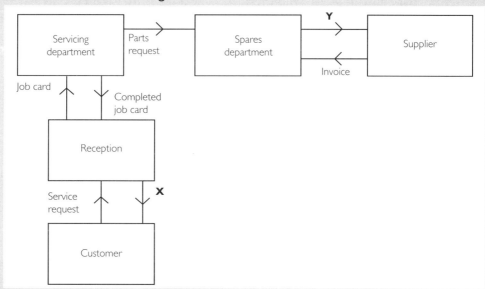

Figure 3.5 Information flow in a garage when a customer has a car serviced

5 What type of information does the job card give?
   a Operations information
   b Purchase order
   c Sales invoice
   d Sales order

6 What type of information is represented by Y?

  a Operations information

  b Purchase order

  c Sales invoice

  d Sales order

7 What information flows from reception to the customer (X)?

  a Purchase invoice

  b Purchase order

  c Sales invoice

  d Sales order

8 In order to bill the customer correctly, reception needs to know the sales price of any spare parts used in the service. How is this information likely to flow?

  a From the servicing department to the spares department

  b From the spares department to reception

  c From reception to the spares department

  d From the supplier to reception

Element 3.2: Describe data handling systems

In this element you will learn about various types of data-handling systems. Most of the functions you learnt about in Element 3.1 involve processing types of data. Every time information moves from one function to another in an organisation and data-handling system is involved.

Methods of processing data

There are two ways of processing data

- **Batch processing.** In batch processing all the data is collected together with the programs needed for a particular job or series of jobs, then the job (or series of jobs) is run all in one go. A computer can be used to do the processing without any human interaction. Batch programs are often run at night when no one else wants to use the computer. You must very careful when writing a batch program that it will not break down if some of the data is faulty. The program must be written to test all the data before use and if it finds any faulty data to skip to the next batch, leaving a message for the user reporting the faulty data.

A batch program: washing – soap powder – washing machine – ready to go!

A transaction process: wash each glass as soon as it has been used

- **Transaction processing** involves dealing with each new piece of information immediately. This is sometimes known as 'immediate' or 'real-time' data processing. The program running the transaction process must also test for faulty data and refuse to process it. Unlike the batch process, it will stop processing until the faulty data has been corrected.

Advantages of batch processing
- Processes can be carried out when the computer is otherwise unused.
- Processes can be carried out without human intervention.

Disadvantages of batch processing
- All processing must wait for a set time.
- Errors cannot be corrected during processing.

Advantages of transaction processing
- Transactions are carried out straight away so that the user does not have to wait.
- Errors can be corrected immediately.

Disadvantages of transaction processing
It is necessary to make sure that every user has up-to-date information, so there has to be a system to be sure that if one user is using particular data, others must wait to use this data until the first user has finished. This is called **record locking** and is explained further later.

Review questions

Here are some computer users describing what they do. For each, decide whether they are using a batch process or a transaction process.

1 'I do the accounts for the garage round the corner. They put all the invoices coming in and copies of invoices going out on my desk. I go in three afternoons a week and enter them all into the accounting program.'

2 'I work in the stores at the garage. When new goods come in I enter our order number on the computer and the details of the order appear on screen. I check it against the goods that have come in and use the mouse to tell the computer system which goods have arrived. The computer automatically updates the stock inventory and tells me where the goods should be stored.'

3 'All files at the office are barcoded. As we receive a file we read the barcode with our personal reader. When we finish with a file we make sure the next person to use it reads the barcode. Thay way the computer keeps constant track of all the files.'

Why have IT data handling systems?

Look at Figure 3.6. You have probably seen a sign like this before. You have probably heard stories and may even yourself have suffered from computer error, if only supermarket revolving doors that suddenly stop. However, when properly programmed and fed with correct data, computers handle data more accurately, more quickly and more cheaply than humans can, and they are used for this reason. Computers are used to provide accurate, fast and cheap data at the point of use and to provide management with information to help them make decisions.

Although a computer system provides cheaper data in the long term, it is

MISTAKES ARE
HUMAN

TO REALLY
SCREW IT UP

YOU NEED A
COMPUTER

Figure 3.6

expensive to set up initially. A computer system should be set up for a reason, which probably will include meeting one or more of the following objectives:

- Accuracy of information. Management and staff should be able to obtain accurate and up-to-date information whenever they need it. Using a manual system, they would have to look back through large quantities of invoices and other paperwork and the information they find could be out of date. Transferring figures from one report to another by hand can involve miscopying and miscalculation of data. The computer will get its sums right, and will copy data accurately.
- Speed of obtaining information. If the information is on the computer, it should be available instantly. Similar information in a filing cabinet can take some time to find. Calculations and moving information from one file to another should be almost instantaneous.
- Cost of obtaining information should go down with the speed of obtaining it. In a system where everyone likely to need information has a computer on their desk, each user can look it up when they need it. Information can be obtained from anywhere in the world for the cost of a local telephone call using the Internet.
- Obtaining information to support decision making. Figures can be moved into balance sheets and forecasts quickly, so managers don't have to guess what is happening. It is also possible to model what is likely to happen without having to actually try things out.

Review questions

The main objectives of a data handling system are:

a accuracy
b cost
c speed
d to support decision making.

Match each of the following data handling features of a supermarket to its main objective.

1 Barcode reader at the checkout
2 Reward card
3 On-line debit and credit card check
4 Scales at the checkout

Data input

It is worth going to a lot of trouble to make sure that the correct data, and *only* the correct data, is entered into a computer system. It must therefore be checked at the **data source** and during **data capture**.

Activity 3.12

Find out the meaning of the acronym GIGO.

Review questions

A dental practice uses all the following computer systems.
1 A booking system
2 A payroll system
3 An ordering system
4 An invoicing system
5 A stock control system
6 Personal records.

Match the following activities to the systems above.
a Filing information about treating a patient.
b Making an appointment for a patient to see a dentist
c Booking out items used for the treatment of patients from the medical store
d Buying items for the medical store
e Billing a patient for treatment
f Paying the dental nurse

Data sources

Where are you going to get the data for the computer system? There are several possible sources.

Electronic files

If the data comes from electronic files it should have been checked when it was first entered into the computer system, and you should be able to assume that the data is accurate. It is possible for the data in electronic files to be corrupted, but modern software will generally pick this up and give you an error message such as 'File corrupted' rather than continue using bad data. Files should be backed up at regular intervals – so that if data is corrupted the correct information can be retrieved from the backup.

Barcodes

Barcodes can be automatically read into the system using a barcode reader. Again, the data will probably be read in correctly unless the barcode reader is faulty – in which case it is unlikely to read the barcode at all.

Figure 3.7 A barcode

Barcodes store information about the barcoded item. A number of standard international codes are used in supermarkets and other retail stores, although organisations can invent their own. A series of printed bars translate into digits (these are usually also printed so that humans as well as machines can read the code). A typical retail code will contain two digits to code the country of origin, five digits to code the manufacturer, five digits to code the item and a single check digit to **validate** the code.

The codes must be stored in the computer reading the barcodes so that they can be decoded. Barcode readers are usually able to read the code right-way up, upside-down and at most angles in between, and do not require high quality printing. This makes them useful for fast automatic data entry. However, they can be used only for simple codes and are really only used for reference numbers.

Barcodes are typically used in retail stores or in libraries. The DHSS uses barcodes on document files that are passed between departments, so that they can be traced quickly, and factories sometimes barcode work in progress so that its route through the factory can be traced.

Documents

Documents, such as filled in forms, must be entered into the system by someone using a keyboard. They should always be checked by eye for obvious errors and omissions before they are keyed in. Someone entering large numbers of documents should take care to enter the information correctly. Two methods of checking such data are **verification** and **control totals**, which are explained below.

People

A customer may place an order by phone. If he or she does this, and if the method of processing is transaction processing, the computer operator can usually read data from the screen and check it with the customer. The computer operator in this case is also likely to know about what is being entered, rather than simply be entering large quantities of 'meaningless' data, and will pick up errors as they go along.

Checking that data is input correctly

Any system is only as useful as the data put into it. It is therefore important to check that data is correctly transferred from the original source and that the original source data makes sense. Data is more likely to be input incorrectly when the method of input is not automatic – in other words when a person is doing the inputting usually using a keyboard. If it is very important that data is entered correctly it is better to use either electronic files or barcodes.

Verification

Computer operators entering large quantities of data from forms or questionnaires, such as from insurance forms or from market research interviews, do so in a batch process. Two operators key in the same data, and the computer checks that the information put in by both operators is the same. If both are the same, the system assumes that the data has been input as it was written on the form. This is called **verifying** the data.

Control totals

Another method used when entering large quantities of apparently meaningless data is for the operator to add up manually one field for batches of 100 forms. The computer also adds up this field and the total is checked after entry of all forms. This is also how software checks for corruption of data files.

Validation

Automatic data entry, verification and control totals all help to ensure that the data being entered is the data provided for entry but does nothing to check that the original data is valid, sensible data. For instance if someone has claimed that they were born on 35 May 1956 and the data has been keyed in correctly then the date 35 May 1956 will be accepted by the system. Various **validation** checks are carried out by the software during input to ensure that the data is valid. These include:

- type checks
- size checks
- range checks
- check digits.

Type checks

Two types of data can be input into the system: numerical or character data.

- If the input is numerical only valid numbers can be entered. The check can be further broken down into:
  - integer (whole number only)
  - real number (allowing decimal points)
  - dates (allowing valid dates in the form DDMMYY – i.e. two digits for the day of the month, two digits for the month and two digits for the year, or other standard form)
  - time (allowing valid time usually in the form HHMMSS – hours, minutes, seconds)
  - some systems allow numerical values to be entered in the form of a simple sum, such as 60*5.3 (* means 'multiply').
- Characters can often be checked further into:
  - alphabetic characters only in certain positions
  - numeric characters only in certain positions
  - either alphabetic or numeric but no symbols in certain positions
  - only certain characters are allowed in certain positions.
  - lower case characters are sometimes seen as identical to capitals, and sometimes seen as different.

Size, or length, checks

This checks the number of characters being input. It checks for maximum length, or for both maximum and minimum length of input.

Range checks

There are two types of range checks:

- Minimum and maximum values. With numeric fields, this can check whether the numbers are within a given range. A number can be checked against a maximum and minimum value, and a date or time can be checked against an earliest or latest value. These checks can be fairly complex allowing, for example, different start and stop times for different dates.
- List or file checks. Inputs can be checked against a list of allowed inputs, or even against whether the input is already on file.

Check digits

These are used on reference numbers where a fairly long number is being input. It would be quite easy to enter an incorrect digit, or to transpose two digits. The check digit is an extra digit calculated from the original reference number and may be added at the end or the beginning of the original number. When the reference number is input, the system carries out the calculation to make sure that the number is valid. If it comes up with a different check digit the data has not been input correctly.

Example 1: The Modulus 11 check digit used on book catalogue numbers All books are given an International Standard Book Number (ISBN). Look at the back of any book to see, for example ISBN 0 19 281209 2. To check the number, multiply the digits by 10, 9, 8, 7, 6, 5, 4, 3, 2, 1 in turn, then add the numbers together. The final number should divide exactly by 11 – if it doesn't the number is not valid.

10	×	0	=	0
9	×	1	=	9
8	×	9	=	72
7	×	2	=	14
6	×	8	=	48
5	×	1	=	5
4	×	2	=	8
3	×	0	=	0
2	×	9	=	18
1	×	2	=	2
				176
Divide by 11:		=		16, no remainder – number valid

Example 2: Credit card check Treat alternate digits differently. Either copy them across, or double the number and if the result is in double figures, add the digits.

Add together all the new digits obtained. For a card number to be valid, the total should be divisible by 10. Here is an example, for the credit card number 6314–7400–0417–0033–863.

6			=	6	6
3	×	2	=	6	6
4			=	4	4
1	×	2	=	2	2
7			=	7	7
4	×	2	=	4	4
0			=	0	0
0	×	2	=	0	0
0			=	0	0
4	×	2	=	8	8
1			=	1	1
7	×	2	=	14	5
0			=	0	0
0	×	2	=	0	0
3			=	3	3
3	×	2	=	6	
8			=	8	8
6	×	2	=	12	3
3			=	3	3
					70

Final number divisible by 10, therefore card number is valid.

Activity 3.13

May produce evidence for application of number element 2.2.

Test some ISBNs and some credit card numbers for validity. Invent some numbers for yourself to test for an invalid number.

Data capture

Data capture describes the process of entering the numbers into the system. There are a number of **data capture** devices:

- barcode reader
- keyboard
- magnetic character reader
- mouse
- sensor.

Barcode reader

A barcode reader shines a light beam over the barcode. The light is reflected back from the white bars onto a photoelectric cell, and is absorbed by the black bars. The reader may be a little like a pen, which must be moved along the bar as though drawing a line through the bars. At supermarket checkouts, where customers can become very impatient if the reader can't read the barcode quickly, a laser light scans the barcode several times to produce more reliable readings. If the reader picks up a valid reading it will beep, telling the operator that a reading has been taken.

Keyboard or keypad

With these the operator inputs data manually. Keyboards have a complete range of alphabetic and numeric characters as well as a selection of symbols and function keys.

The alphabetic, numeric and symbolic characters are standard for the language being used and the keyboard should *always* be set up for the correct language on new equipment. Each language has a different character set – some languages require accents on their letters (é or ü for example) or the signs for money may be different (£ or $ perhaps).

Function keys allow one keypress to perform a particular task. Sometimes function keys are labelled – for instance 'backspace', 'end', 'insert' – or sometimes they are just labelled F1, F2, F10.

Keypads have only a small range of keys. Numeric keypads have digits only, possibly also some arithmetic symbols. Keypads also have some function keys, even if only a 'clear' button.

Many IT installations that rely on automatic data entry also have keypads that can be used in case something goes wrong with the automatic data entry.

Magnetic reader

This reads data from magnetic media such as disk or tape. Many information technology systems use small lengths of magnetic tape instead of bar codes for storing data as the magnetic tape can be more versatile.

Small strips of magnetic tape stuck to cardboard or paper are used to identify products instead of barcodes in some shops. Small strips of tape are stuck to plastic cards to produce

- financial cards, such as credit, debit and shopping cards because they can store data about the cardholder
- security keys – the magnetic strip is read at a door or gate and if the card is valid allows the user to open the gate. Information about the card is stored in the system, so if a card is lost the system can be alerted and the card invalidated.

Mouse

A mouse is often used in conjunction with a keyboard to enter data. It allows the user to move the cursor position faster than using keys on the keyboard. A ball under the mouse rolls round as the mouse is moved over a surface. Sensors inside the mouse sense this movement and software in the computer converts the movement into movement of the cursor. The mouse also has one or more buttons which can be pressed, and the 'click' is converted to some action by the software. The speed of 'clicking' can affect the action, so a mouse and its software can be used in a fairly sophisticated way.

Different makes of mouse use different types of sensor and different types and numbers of buttons, so it is important to use the correct software for the mouse type. The software usually allows the user to customise the mouse movement by changing the speed at which the cursor moves or changing the use of the mouse buttons.

Sensor

Data can also be captured by sensors. There are sensors inside a mouse, and other sensors in IT systems are used in

- control systems such as those managing air conditioning, washing machines or fire sprinklers
- retail shops – scales may be used at the cashpoint to capture data
- security systems which use heat, movement or sound sensors
- aids for the disabled – pressure, voice recognition or even small electrical impulses generated by a person's nerves may be used to control an aid.

Review questions

1 List three automatic methods of data capture and give an example of a data source for each.
2 Name two devices that are used for manual data input and give a data source for each.
3 List five types of processes used in data handling systems.

Activity 3.14

May produce evidence for communications element 2.2 and 2.3.

Imagine you are a market research interviewer and must ask the question 'What data capture devices do you use?' Obtain pictures of the data capture devices listed above from computer magazines, hardware catalogues or other written matter and use them to create a small leaflet that you could use to help people understand the question and recognise any devices they have.

Data processing

Data processing is carrying out processes on the data. For example:
- performing arithmetic calculations, such as totalling a bill, calculating pay and tax
- searching a file for a data item, such as a customer's address on an invoice
- selecting items of information from many on a file – for instance a weekly stock control batch process which lists all stock items where stocks have fallen below a set level
- sorting data, for instance a report on customers who owe a firm money might be printed out in order of age of debt, size of debt, or even in order of whose customer they are so the correct salesperson is given the information before visiting them again
- validating data on data capture.

Activity 3.15

A customer in a supermarket bought for the family dinner:
- a cabbage
- 1 kg of potatoes
- a ready-wrapped and priced joint of meat
- seven yoghurts from a display labelled 'BUY FIVE AND GET ONE FREE!!'

The customer paid with a debit card.

1 Describe the data capture methods that were probably used at the checkout.
2 Describe the processes involved in producing the bill.

Types of data handling systems

Several systems will be studied in this section:
- booking systems
- payroll systems
- ordering systems
- invoicing systems
- stock control
- personal records.

Booking systems

Booking systems are used for holiday booking, theatre booking, airline booking – your college might have a computer system for booking students on to a course. These are usually transaction processes, where bookings are made as soon as payment is made.

The systems flowchart showing how such a system in a travel agent's works is given in Figure 3.8. The holiday database is a computer file containing details of all the holidays available from the company and can be used directly by all the travel agents that have a direct line to the holiday company's computer. The travel agent will obtain the latest information about the holidays available, which should prevent two different customers simultaneously booking the same holiday.

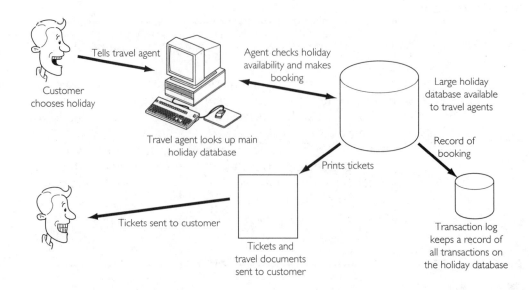

Figure 3.8 System flowchart showing a transaction processing holiday booking system

Record locking

If a customer at one travel agent wants a particular holiday the travel agent will open the computer record for that holiday, and can see how many bookings are still available. The record is then 'locked' so that no one else can use it until the agent has finished. Any other travel agent wanting to book the same holiday will have to wait until the first agent has finished – this prevents both agents booking the same holiday at once.

Booking systems need a lot of disk space. If a flight goes from London to New York every day at 9.00 a.m., say, with room for 360 people, then it is necessary to be able to store the booked places for every day separately.

Activity 3.16

Work as part of a group.

A group of you are thinking of running a cybercafe. You have five computers connected to the Internet and you rent out each machine at £2.50 an hour. Tea, coffee and food are extra. People can book a computer up to a week in advance for a set time or come in and pay for a vacant machine.

Invent a paper-based booking scheme that would work. Invent some test data, and use it to demonstrate how the booking system would work.

Payroll systems

Payroll systems are used to pay staff. They must be run at regular intervals – once a week or once a month, depending on when people are paid – so it is convenient to use a batch processing method. A company's payroll computer file will have to contain information needed to calculate the pay for each member of staff in the company. The information needed for each worker includes:

- payroll number
- name
- department
- details of bank account (if salary is paid straight into the person's bank account)
- national insurance number
- salary scale
- agreements about overtime and bonuses
- tax code (for working out income tax)
- information about pension payments in a company scheme
- information about other stoppages from the pay (e.g. savings scheme, union dues)
- the amount of pay earned so far during this tax year (pay-to-date)
- the amount of tax paid so far during this tax year (tax-to-date)

This information is stored in a file called the **master file** for the payroll system. It is stored permanently by the company and is updated regularly. To calculate the pay for the current pay period the system also keeps a temporary file called a **transaction file**. This stores data about the pay period, such as the hours of overtime worked or information about sickness, together with the payroll number of the worker. This payroll number is used to tie the data from the transaction file to the data in the master file.

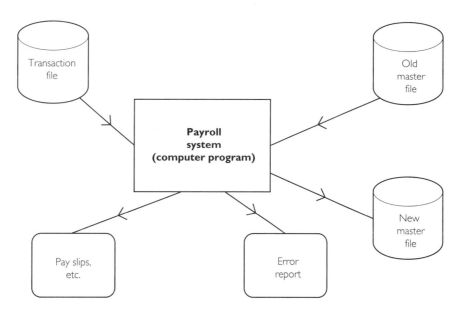

Figure 3.9 System flowchart for a batch payroll system

Every record in the master file of the payroll system is processed in turn. This means that every member of the organisation is paid. For each record in the master file, the payroll number must be checked and the appropriate records found on the transaction file. This is often done by setting up the transaction file with one record for each member of staff, and sorting it into payroll number order before running the payroll program. The is known as **pre-processing**, and the batch process may include this pre-process before running the payroll program.

Each record of the master file is processed with the corresponding record on the transaction file. Each record of the master file stores the payroll information needed for one employee and was up to date the last time that employee was paid. This is processed together with the record on the transaction for this employee which holds information about the employee since last pay day. The payroll number for that employee is on the master file record and on the transaction file record, so they can be matched.

Pay slips are produced, together with any other information needed for making the payments, such as

- the cash that must be fetched from the bank (if staff are paid in cash)
- ready printed cheques or giros (for staff paid by cheque or giro)
- instructions to the organisation's bank (for staff paid by bank credit transfer).

If the transaction file contains faulty data, for instance if the payroll number is incorrect or the number of hours worked seem improbably high, this is printed onto an error report and the data is checked manually after the batch process has finished.

A new master file is produced containing the updated master records ready for the next batch payroll process. The old master file and the transaction file are kept as backups in case the current master file is damaged. This will be explained in more detail in Element 3.4.

Case Study

Charlwood Play Equipment's payroll system
All the staff are paid monthly, on the last Friday of the month, by bank credit transfer. They are paid the basic wage for the previous four (or sometimes five) weeks. Overtime and bonuses are paid up to the Friday before, as the information for the current week is not yet on the computer.

The factory staff are paid by the hour for a 37.5 hour week, 08.00–12.30 and 13.30–16.30, Monday to Friday. Hours worked above 37.5 hours count as overtime and are paid at 1.5 times the hourly rate (evenings and Saturdays) or twice the hourly rate (Sundays). They receive a bonus of £10 per week for every week they have been punctual. Time sheets for each worker are filled in for the previous week by the foreman, who sends them to the personnel department every Monday morning. The personnel department is responsible for the payroll.

Activity 3.17

May produce evidence for application of number element 2.2.

1 Because a foreman had written the payroll numbers badly the entry clerk in the personnel department had mistyped a 5 as an 8, and the time sheets in Figure 3.10 were not processed for two of the workers. Calculate the gross pay (i.e. the amount due including basic rate, overtime rate and bonuses, before stoppages) for workers 5021 and 5022.

Week Ending Sun 26 Jan 1997	am		pm	
Employee No: 5021				
Mon	8.30	12.30	1.30	4.30
Tue	8.30	12.30	1.30	4.30
Wed	8.30	12.30	1.30	4.30
Thu	8.30	12.30	1.30	4.30
Fri	8.30	12.30	1.30	4.30
Sat				
Sun				
Hours worked				
Rate of pay				
Gross pay				
Income tax				
National Ins.				
Net pay				
Pay to date				

Week Ending Sun 26 Jan 1997	am		pm	
Employee No: 5022				
Mon	9.00	12.30	1.30	4.30
Tue	8.45	12.30	1.30	4.30
Wed	8.45	12.30	1.30	4.30
Thu	8.30	12.30	1.30	5.30
Fri	8.30	12.30	1.30	4.30
Sat				
Sun				
Hours worked				
Rate of pay				
Gross pay				
Income tax				
National Ins.				
Net pay				
Pay to date				

Week Ending Sun 2 Feb 1997	am		pm	
Employee No: 5021				
Mon	8.30	12.30	1.30	4.30
Tue	8.30	12.30	1.30	4.30
Wed	8.30	12.30	1.30	4.30
Thu	8.30	12.30	1.30	4.30
Fri	8.30	12.30	1.30	4.30
Sat				
Sun				
Hours worked				
Rate of pay				
Gross pay				
Income tax				
National Ins.				
Net pay				
Pay to date				

Week Ending Sun 2 Feb 1997	am		pm	
Employee No: 5022				
Mon	8.30	12.30	1.30	4.30
Tue	8.30	12.30	1.30	4.30
Wed	8.30	12.30	1.30	4.30
Thu	8.30	12.30	1.30	4.30
Fri	8.30	12.30	1.30	4.30
Sat				
Sun				
Hours worked				
Rate of pay				
Gross pay				
Income tax				
National Ins.				
Net pay				
Pay to date				

Week Ending Sun 9 Feb 1997	am		pm	
Employee No: 5021				
Mon	8.30	12.30	1.30	5.30
Tue	8.30	12.30	1.30	5.30
Wed	8.30	12.30	1.30	6.00
Thu	8.30	12.30	1.30	6.00
Fri	8.30	12.30	1.30	4.30
Sat	8.30	1.00		
Sun				
Hours worked				
Rate of pay				
Gross pay				
Income tax				
National Ins.				
Net pay				
Pay to date				

Week Ending Sun 9 Feb 1997	am		pm	
Employee No: 5022				
Mon	8.30	12.30	1.30	4.30
Tue	8.30	12.30	1.30	4.30
Wed	8.30	12.30	1.30	4.30
Thu	8.30	12.30	1.30	4.30
Fri	8.30	12.30	1.30	4.30
Sat				
Sun				
Hours worked				
Rate of pay				
Gross pay				
Income tax				
National Ins.				
Net pay				
Pay to date				

Week Ending Sun 16 Feb 1997	am		pm	
Employee No: 5021				
Mon	8.30	12.30	1.30	4.30
Tue	8.30	12.30	1.30	4.30
Wed	8.30	12.30	1.30	4.30
Thu	8.30	12.30	1.30	5.00
Fri	8.30	12.30	1.30	6.00
Sat	8.30	2.30		
Sun	9.00	12.00		
Hours worked				
Rate of pay				
Gross pay				
Income tax				
National Ins.				
Net pay				
Pay to date				

Week Ending Sun 16 Feb 1997	am		pm	
Employee No: 5022				
Mon	8.45	12.30	1.30	3.00
Tue				
Wed	9.00	12.30	1.30	4.30
Thu	8.30	12.30	1.30	4.30
Fri	8.30	12.30	1.30	4.30
Sat				
Sun				
Hours worked				
Rate of pay				
Gross pay				
Income tax				
National Ins.				
Net pay				
Pay to date				

Figure 3.10

2 What advantages would you see in having a computerised rather than a manual payroll?

3 Which of the following processes did you use when answering Question 1?

   a calculating

   b searching

   c selecting

   d sorting.

Ordering systems

Ordering systems are used by organisations to deal with orders from their customers.

Case Study

Cyprio's ordering system

Figure 3.11 The Cyprio logo

Cyprio manufactures pond equipment. The company started by making filter systems, but now make and sell filters, water clarifiers, pipes, hoses, pumps, fountains, etc. They have around 350 different products ranging in price from £1 to £500. They sell all over the world, mainly to garden centres and other centres who sell the equipment on to smaller customers. Most of the customers therefore have quite large and complicated orders.

Cyprio have a computerised transaction order processing system which has a number of advantages:

- Information about customers and stock levels is accurate and up-to-date at all times.
- They do not have to waste time searching through filing cabinets for information or ringing up the warehouse for information. One clerk can run the system, rather than several. Salespeople can key in orders themselves, the system files it all correctly and makes sure that the correct paperwork goes to stores, the factory and finance. This makes the system very cost-effective.
- The company's turnaround is rapid, so customers are not kept waiting for products.
- The managers can obtain accurate information whenever they need it to make decisions on future strategy.

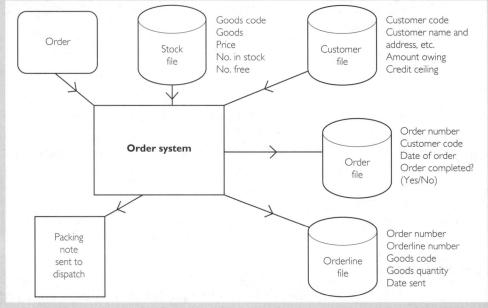

Figure 3.12 The Cyprio ordering system

Data sources and methods of data capture

The orders are received either in written form or by telephone – the source of the order data is either a document or a person. The document is usually an order form, although sometimes it is a letter. In both cases the data is entered into the system using a keyboard and mouse. The data is entered onto a screen which looks similar to the order form, so is easy to use. The order clerk receiving telephone orders uses the screen order form as a questionnaire.

Other data, such as information about existing customers and information about the goods in stock come from existing electronic files on the system.

Queries from customers can be checked from the electronic files Order and Orderline.

Data processing

Data entry

The data is validated as it is entered into the computer system. The details of an existing customer will be checked against their file, which will have been found by searching by customer code or customer name. A new customer who does not send payment with the order will be checked for credit rating to make sure that they pay their bills. They will be entered onto the computer once their credit rating has been checked. The details of new customers ordering by phone and paying with the order (by credit card) will be read and spelled back to them for manual checking (verification).

The code number of each item will be checked against its description. This is done by searching for the goods code and selecting the appropriate record from the goods file to display on the screen. If the code number does not exist or if the code number on a written order does not match the goods description the order will be queried.

The value of each line on the order will be calculated at input and read back to customers ordering by telephone for their agreement. The total value of the order will be calculated and validated against the customer's credit limit, read out to and verified by telephone customers.

Data storage

The order number (calculated by the ordering program), the customer code and the date of the order (provided by the computer) are stored on the order file together with a note that the order has not yet been completed. This last field will be changed to 'yes' when all the goods have been sent off.

Each line of the order form – each separate item ordered – is stored in a different electronic file (the Orderline file). Each Orderline is stored with
- the order number, so that the Orderline can be traced to the correct order
- an Orderline number, so that each Orderline can be separately identified
- the goods code – this allows the computer to get the information from the goods file about the description and price, so these do not need to be stored again on the Orderline
- the quantity of these goods
- the date the goods are sent, which is set at 0/0/0 and is changed by the invoicing system when the goods are dispatched.

Data output

The number of items free to be dispatched is subtracted from the 'number free' field in the goods file. If there is a waiting list the number free may be negative. The number in stock is only altered when the goods are actually sent off, so that an accurate picture of the goods in stock is available. Two copies of a packing note are printed and sent to the dispatch department.

Activity 3.18

1 Which objectives of a system does the Cyprio ordering system meet?
2 What data sources does the Cyprio ordering system use?
3 What methods of data capture does the Cyprio ordering system use?

Invoicing system

An invoicing system organises the payments for goods sold if the goods have not been paid for in advance or at the time of order.

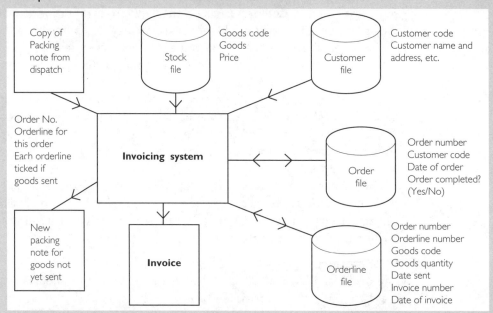

Figure 3.13 Cyprio invoicing system

The packing note sent to dispatch by the ordering system is in two parts. As the package is made up the items are ticked on the dispatch note and the ticks go through to both copies. The top copy is put in the package and sent off. The second copy is sent to the finance department for invoicing.

A new invoice is created. The invoicing system gives it a new invoice number and date. The order number from the packing note is typed in and the order file is searched for the order. The customer number is found from the selected order and the customer's name and address is found by searching the customer file.

The Orderline file is searched for Orderlines from this order, and the date that the goods were sent inserted into selected records on the Orderline file together with the invoice number and invoice date. The invoice is printed with all goods ordered. If goods have not been sent as they were not in stock, a message is printed on the invoice apologising for the delay. The invoice is then sent to the customer. If all the orders have been sent off the order record is updated as complete.

If all the Orderlines have not been sent off a new packing note with the goods still to be sent is sent to the dispatch department, who will keep it till the goods are again in stock.

As the goods are sent, the number in stock is altered.

Most of the data in this system can be captured just with the mouse, apart from entering the order number – clicks from the mouse emulate the ticks on the packing note. All the data is already on electronic files. Four files are read and three files are updated automatically.

Activity 3.19

Find an order form for a mail-order catalogue.
1 Fill in the form as though you are ordering some items. Comment on how easy, or otherwise, it is to fill in the form. How would you have designed this form?
2 Design an invoice from the firm for the goods that you 'bought'.
3 Design a packing note for the goods that you 'bought'.

Stock control

Stock control systems are used in warehouses, shops, libraries and other organisations that hold items in stock. They are used to check how many of each item are stored, and often also where they are stored. Whenever items are bought or sold the stock control system is updated so that the stock levels are always known.

Some stock control systems also have an automatic reordering facility so that when stock levels fall below a certain amount the user is told to order more of these items.

Activity 3.20

May produce evidence for application of number elements 2.1 and 2.2.

Student Hardware Ltd is planning to go round local schools and colleges selling small items of stationery – notebooks, pens, computer disks, etc. – to students from vans.
1 List 12 items you think they should sell.
2 Price the items.
3 Estimate how many of these items students are likely to buy
  a each week
  b each term.
You may need to do some market research.
4 Design a way of storing the items safely in the back of a small van. You may need to measure the boot of a small van, or car. Name or number the different storage areas and draw a plan to show what is stored in each area and how many of these items should be stored. Make sure that the storage areas are appropriate for the items to be stored.
5 Design a stock control sheet for the van drivers to use.

Personal records

A company might hold personal records of their employees for a number of reasons. Personal records may include:

- names, addresses and telephone numbers so that the employee or their family can be contacted in emergencies
- financial details for the payroll
- qualifications and training details so that an employee can be considered for different jobs or promotion
- family details so that children of employees can be invited to a Christmas party
- medical details so that the company nurse can help with health problems.

Personal information should be guarded carefully and only authorised personnel allowed access to it. An employee may be happy for the company nurse to know about any medication they may need, but may not want their colleagues or boss to know. Privacy of information is important enough for laws to be made about it. These will be discussed in element 3.4.

Activity 3.21

Class discussion

1 Think about the forms that you or your parents have had to fill in for your educational establishment. What information does your educational establishment have about you?
2 What do you think that they do with this information?
3 Who else do you think holds personal information about you, and what information do you think it is? (Do you have a doctor? Do you belong to any club? Do you get junk mail?)

Activity 3.22

You have been asked to do a survey of 100 companies to find out the type of data handling systems they use and the method of processing each system uses.

1 Design a form that allows the respondents simply to tick a box for each type of data handling system that they have.
2 For each system, they must choose between batch processing and transaction processing.
3 Write brief descriptions of the types of data handling systems and the types of processing methods. Send these descriptions with the form to help the recipients fill it in.

Test questions

1 A mail-order company has a number of computer systems in place. Which is most likely to be a batch process?
  a Customer invoicing
  b Customer telephone ordering
  c Stock control
  d Monthly updating of personnel records
2 Which of the following is most likely to be a transaction process in a theatre?
  a Selling tickets for shows

   b Paying staff

   c Ordering bar supplies

   d Paying suppliers

3 A journalist uses a computerised information system rather than a library to look up information for a story he is writing. Why?

   a The information is more accurate

   b It is cheaper

   c It is faster

   d There is more to choose from

4 Supermarkets encourage customers to use money-back cards. Why?

   a It makes billing more accurate

   b It is cheaper for the supermarket

   c It is faster at the check-outs

   d It gives supermarkets information to support decision-making

5 What is the most common method that libraries use to keep track of their books?

   a Barcodes

   b Documents

   c Interviewing borrowers

   d Questionnaires to borrowers

6 Many charities buy information of likely donors from other charities. Which is the most convenient way to receive the information?

   a Barcoded cards

   b Paper lists of donors

   c Electronic files

   d Verbal lists

7 Employees in a certain company were given plastic swipe cards to allow them into the building. Which data capture device was inside the swipe machine?

   a A keyboard

   b A magnetic strip reader

   c A mouse

   d A heat sensor

8 A secretary exits a word-processing package by choosing Exit from a pull-down menu. Which data capture device has he used?

   a A bar-code reader

   b A magnetic strip reader

   c A mouse

   d A heat sensor

9 A secretary is asked to make a correction to a letter before sending it out. What process does she use to get it back onto the screen?

   a Calculating

   b Searching

   c Sorting

   d Validating

10 A calculation is performed on a barcode to make sure that the barcode reader has read it correctly. What process is used for this?

   a Searching

   b Selecting

   c Sorting

   d Validating

Element 3.3: Use IT for a data handling activity

Data files

If we store information for future use we want to store it in such a way that we can easily find it again when we need it. A storage system can help us find the information we need in two important ways:
- by storing it in an order we can recognise, such as alphabetical order
- by keeping it in a format that we can use.

File format

Information retrieval systems that you may have used include:
- a telephone directory
- a dictionary
- a library card index, microfiche reader or computer retrieval system
- the help menu in a computer program.

If you want to find one piece of information from the system – perhaps you want to look up one word in a dictionary – it is helpful if all similar information is stored in the same format. For example, in a dictionary each entry might the following format:
- word to be defined
- part of speech (whether it's a noun, verb, adjective, adverb or preposition)
- how to pronounce the word
- main meaning of the word
- other meanings.

Activity 3.23

1 What format is used for an entry in
  a a telephone directory
  b the information about library books in your library system at school or college?
2 Look up the advertisements pages for second-hand cars in your local paper. Is the same information given for all cars? If you were keeping a file on second-hand cars, what format would you use?

Terms used in data files

The data about each object on a data file:
- one entry in the telephone directory
- the entry for each word in a dictionary
- the information about one library book in your library file
- the information about one car in your file

is called a **record**.

Each record is made up of a number of **fields**, each of which give one piece of information about or one **attribute** of the object on record, and which together make up the format of the record.

A collection of similar records stored together on computer is called a **data file**. If the same format is used for all the records in the file, the file format is the same as the record format.

Figure 3.14 shows my Christmas and Birthday Present card file. I store information here about the presents my friends and relations like best. Each card holds a record for one person. There are four fields in each record – name, address, birthday and favourite present.

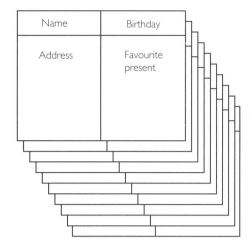

Figure 3.14

One of the fields in the record should be designated as the **key field**. This field must have a unique value – each key field in a file must be different. The key field is the reference field for this file and is used by the software package when it cross-references between files. There is usually an obvious key field for a file. The file in Figure 3.14 uses the name as the key field, but as I have two friends called Chris, I had to call them Chris E and Chris P to make the key fields unique. If I had hundreds of friends called Chris, I might number them to get a unique key field.

When we set up a data file on computer, we need to use some sort of filing software, usually database software. A **database** allows several related data files to be stored together and data to be cross-indexed between the files. Some database packages use the word **table** instead of file.

Setting up a computer data table or data file using database software

1 Decide what record format, file format or table format you are going to use – that is, the fields you want.
2 Decide each field type. You must decide how you are going to process the data items stored on computer, as different types of data item can be processed differently. The basic field types available are:
   • **number fields** – you will need numbers if you want to do any calculations, or if you want to sort into numerical order
   • **character fields** are used for alphabetical data, and for sorting in alphabetical order. Numbers in character format will be sorted as though the digits 0–9 are letters of the alphabet – the characters 100 will appear before 12.
   • **date or time fields** are useful if you want to sort in date order or do arithmetic on dates such as adding 30 days to a date
   • your database package may allow further field types – check it out.
3 Decide on the number of decimal places you will allow in a number field.
4 Decide on the length of each field – how many spaces the field will take up.
5 Choose the key field – this is the field which identifies the record uniquely. No two key fields should be the same. For a car database, for instance, you could use the number plate for the key field. A telephone directory might need a multiple key field, such as surname followed by first name, as there will be more than one Smith. You might need to use three items or more in this sort of database – such as surname, first name and address – because there could be several William Smiths. Multiple key fields are all parts of the **primary key**. If you can't think of any other primary key, simply number the records (the software will probably do this automatically).

File name:					
Record format					
Key field	Name	Type	Decimal places	Size	Validation
	Record size:				
Estimated no. of records		File size			

Figure 3.15 You might find a form like this useful for designing a database table. In the column headed Key field, you mark the primary key field with a number 1. If the primary key is made up of several fields (as in the telephone example), number them 1, 2, 3, etc. in order of use as the primary key.

Secondary keys are key fields from other database files or tables which are also fields in the field column in this table. They can be marked with an asterisk. Data can be selected and sorted through these fields, but the data will not be unique. Secondary keys are sometimes set up purely to select data, when they are called **index keys**. Most database packages will automatically set up an index when required. This slows down the search, but is still fast enough for most purposes.

Activity 3.24

Creating a database

A local car dealer wishes to computerise records for their car sales.
1 Find out how to create a table in your database package.
2 Open a database called SHOWROOM
3 Design the table structure for a table called CAR, with fields for make of car, model, body type, price, registration code, colour, extras, mileage. You could use car registration number as the key field, or simply number each car as it comes into the car showroom.

4 Create the table and print out the record structure.
5 Enter the following data:
- Fiat Punto 55S, £5995, M, metallic red, two owners, 14 000
- VW Polo 1.3 GT, 3-door coupe, £5495, L, white, one owner, 39 000
- Renault Clio 1.2 RN, 3-door hatchback, £5495, K, metallic blue, sun roof, 21 000
- VW Polo 1.3 CL, £3995, J, white, 47 000.

6 Find records for at least 20 more cars from the advertisements in your local paper and enter the details in your database.
7 Print out all the details of all the cars.
8 Close the database.

Activity 3.25

Editing and searching a database

1 Re-open your SHOWROOM database.
2 Alter the price of the VW Polo 1.3 GT with 39 000 miles on the clock from £5495 to £5450.
3 Delete the J registered VW Polo 1.3 CL selling for £3995.
4 Add a Vauxhall Astra 1.4 litre, pillar box red, H reg, with alarm, £3200.
5 Find another 20 cars from your local paper and add their details.
6 Print out the database.
7 Print out all details in reverse order of price.
8 Print out makes and models of cars in order of age of car.
9 Print out all details of all Volkswagens in price order.
10 Print out details on age, colour and price of all cars of any Ford Sierras, in price order.
11 Print out details of model, age and price for all red cars.
12 Print out all details for all cars costing between £5000 and £6000, in ascending price order.
13 Print out details, other than make and colour, for all white Renaults under £4000.
14 Print out all the details for the VW Polo, the price of which you altered from £5495 to £5450.
15 Print out the total value of the stock in the database.

Activity 3.26

Reporting from a database

1 Deduct 10% from the price of the three most expensive cars and print out the details again.
2 Set up reports to print:
  a all details for all cars for sale, in descending order of price
  b makes and models of cars in order of age
  c all details of all cars of any particular make in price order
  d age, colour and price of all cars of any particular make and model, in price order
  e model, age and price of all cars of any particular colour (e.g. red).
3 Write instructions on how to obtain the required reports.

What is a database?

When organisations first used computers, each computer application used separate data files. For example, the purchasing function would have a file of current stock, which contained information about suppliers and purchase prices and which they updated whenever new stock was delivered. The sales function would also have a file of current stock, which held information on selling prices and which they updated whenever something was sold. The two stock files shared a lot of data, and they would have to update stock levels from each other's transactions. This meant that a lot of data was held on disk in several places, which is wasteful of disk space.

Even worse, at any one time there would have been more than one version of the data, and no-one could be sure which, if any, was correct. As the technology improved, on-line hardware and more complicated programs became available. Databases began to allow all the company's data to be stored on-line at once.

The tables on a database must be carefully designed to keep repetition of data to a minimum. The database software must include security systems so that database users can only access the data they need.

Tables are 'joined' through their key fields. A database can therefore be defined as 'a data store containing one or more related tables of data together with a database management system which manages data access'.

Database software, such as Dbase, Access, DataEase or FileMaker, allows a database to be set up and managed. Database software is often just called 'a database'.

Databases with more than one table

When you decide to store information about several different kinds of objects, the data will have quite different formats and will need to be stored in different tables with different formats.

Activity 3.27

Creating a second database table

A car company wishes to use its computer for keeping track of its sales staff, many of whom work part time. They are paid a flat rate per day, depending on the rate they have negotiated with the owner of the car showroom, plus a commission which is a percentage of the selling price of the car.

1 Create a table called SALESPERSON to store details of the sales people. You might need to shorten the table name, depending on the package you are using. Create fields for salesperson's name, address, telephone number, daily rate and percentage commission. If you want to list people in alphabetical order of surname, which is usual, you will have to use separate fields for surname and forename. You could then use a double primary key using surname as the first part and forename as the second part. This allows you to have more than one salesperson with the same surname – it is possible to have several parts to a primary key. Another way to get a unique primary key is to use a reference number unique to each person. A common way of creating unique personal numbers is to make up a reference up of three letters (the first three letters of that person's surname) and three digits (001, 002, 003, etc. up to 999).

2 Whatever you choose, set up a suitable primary key.

3 Create the table in your existing database.

4 Enter three or four names and rates for sales staff.

Relationships between tables

Once you have more than one table in a database, you can decide whether the two tables are related. This is done in a common-sense way by looking at the objects about which you are storing data.

'What is the relationship between the cars and the salespeople?'
'Salespeople sell cars'

The relationship is *selling*.

A relationship works in two directions. For example, in the direction Salesperson → Car the relationship is 'a salesperson sells a car'. In the other direction (Salesperson ← Car) it is 'a car is sold by a salesperson'. We can draw a picture of this (Figure 3.16).

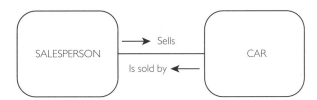

Figure 3.16

Relationships between tables on a database can be
- 1–1 (one-to-one)
- 1–N (one-to-many):
- N–1 (many-to-one) or
- N–N (many-to-many)

('many' can be strictly interpreted as meaning 0 or more).

The answer to the question 'Does one salesperson sell many cars?' is (we hope) yes, but the answer to 'Is one car sold by more than one salesperson?' is (again, we hope) no. This looks like a 1–N relationship between the salesperson and the car or a N–1 relationship between the car and the salesperson – they're the same. This relationship can be shown in Figure 3.17.

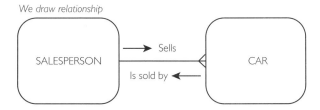

Figure 3.17

We join two tables in a database through a common field so we need a field which is in both the SALESPERSON table and the CAR table. We take the key from the '1' side of the relationship and add it to the 'many' side.

Activity 3.28

Joining database tables

1 Add a field in the CAR table you prepared in Activity 3.24 that is identical in name, type, length and range to the key field of the SALESPERSON table you created in Activity 3.27. Some database packages will automatically match everything once you give two fields the same name. Others allow joins, where fields have different names. When you create the join you will find out how your package works. This field becomes a secondary key in the CAR table as it is a primary key in a related table.

2 Join the two tables through the shared key. You will have to use the manual or on-line help to find out how to do this.

3 Set up the join as a one-to-many join in the correct direction if your database allows.

4 Add another field to your CAR table for date of sale and, since the selling price is not always the same as the asking price, add another field for selling price. Make the asking price a default for this field. (A **default** is the value that will be given if nothing is entered). You may also like to make today's date the default value for the date sold.

5 'Sell' a few cars by entering the salesperson, selling date and selling price to the appropriate CAR fields.

6 Print out a report listing the value and selling date of cars sold by each salesperson.

7 Set up a report to print out the makes, models and selling prices of all cars sold this month.

Using joined tables for reports

Once you have joined two tables, you should be able to print out reports including information from both. Since CAR–SALESPERSON is a many-to-one relation, each car points to only one seller. Through the join you should be able to amend the report you have just prepared in Activity 3.28 to include the name of the person who sold it.

You do this by setting up a **view** of the database (most databases use this term). A view is a table made from existing tables which contains the fields you need for your report. Once you have created this view you can treat it as if it is a real database table. You can also set up fields which are calculated from other fields.

Activity 3.29

Reports on more than one table

1 Set up a view called SALES which contains the following fields:
- car's key field
- make   (from CAR table)
- model   (from CAR table)
- selling price   (from CAR table)
- salesperson's key field
- name   (from SALESPERSON table)
- commission rate   (from SALESPERSON table)
- commission   (calculated field)

2 Set up and print out a report giving all the details in the SALES table.

3 Set up and print out a report giving all the details in the SALES table for last month, sorted by salesperson.

4 Set up and print out a report giving names of salespeople and commission earned last month.

More tables

There is no limit to the number of tables that you can have in a database. If the car showroom owner wants to calculate the pay of the sales staff a record must also be kept of the days each person works. We need another table called WORKDAY containing this information:

- salesperson key
- date worked

and a primary key.

The tables SALESPERSON and WORKDAY are related, as shown in Figure 3.18, or we could draw a diagram of all three tables (Figure 3.19).

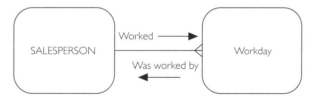

Figure 3.18

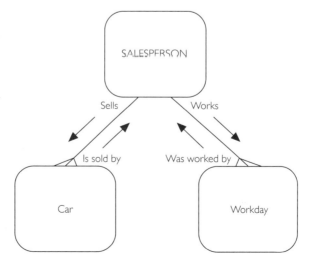

Figure 3.19

Activity 3.30

Creating, joining and reporting on a new table in the database

1 Create the table WORKDAY and join it to the table SALESPERSON using the correct relationship.
2 Enter a few days worked by the sales people
3 Set up a view by joining WORKDAY and SALESPERSON so that you can set up a report and print out the basic pay for each salesperson last month.

Test questions

1 A company stores data about its suppliers on a database. Where is the information about one supplier stored?
   a In a record
   b In a field
   c In a table
   d In a relationship

Questions 2–5 relate to the database shown in Figure 3.20.

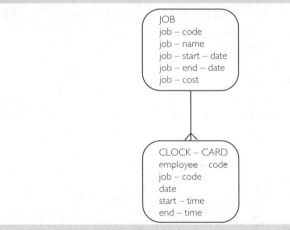

Figure 3.20 A database used by an engineering company to track the cost of their work by monitoring the time employees spend on a job

2 Which field must contain numeric data?
   a job_code
   b job_name
   c job_start_date
   d job_cost
3 Which field cannot be stored as numeric data?
   a job_code
   b job_name
   c employee_code
   d start_time
4 Which is a primary key in CLOCK_CARD?
   a employee_code
   b job_code
   c date
   d start_time
5 Which is a secondary key in CLOCK_CARD?
   a employee_code
   b job_code
   c date
   d start_time

Element 3.4: Examine safety and security issues

Accuracy checks

It is extremely important to make sure that data input into a computer is accurate, otherwise the information coming out of the computer cannot possibly be correct. All data should be validated as far as possible on input. Check back to page 79 to remind yourself how this is done.

Activity 3.31

Database validations

1 Find out what validation procedures are possible on your database software.
2 Fill in the validation column on your file design forms for your SHOWROOM database and for Assignment A3.3.
3 Implement the validations using your database software.
4 Design a test plan to check that the validations work. This will involve writing down correct and incorrect data which should test all your validations and explaining what should happen for the incorrect data. A sample test form is given in Figure 3.21.
5 Test the validations.

Test Plan for Table DOCKET			
Data item	Data entry	Expected result	Actual result
Van number	1	Accepts it	
	7	Beep	
	X	Beep	
Date	Today	Accepts it	
	27/10/1965	Redo from start	
etc.			

Figure 3.21 Test plan for table DOCKET (see Assignment A3.3). The last column should hold a tick if the validation works to plan, or brief notes of what does happen

Making a test plan can be tedious, because you have to try to think of every possible, and unlikely, data entry. A successful test is one that finds a fault. As people hate finding faults in their own work, you might like to test someone else's work, and let them test yours.

Validation can only check whether data is believable or likely, not whether the data has been entered as written on the data capture document – verification checks the accuracy of data entry (page 78 tells you more about this). However, it is not always practical for two people to enter the data. Next best is for the operator to read the entry against the original after it's been keyed in (see page 89). It helps if the operator enters a key field for the computer to show other data from the record of which this is the primary key, and check this.

Activity 3.32

Suggest one or more places in Assignment A3.3 where verification can be used. How could it be implemented?

Even though data has been validated and verified, it may still produce meaningless output. Examples of input information should always be checked for meaning. This is known as **testing for correctness**.

Review questions

1 What is the difference between verification, validation and correctness?
2 Give an example of each of the following:
   a a range check
   b a type check.

Security of data

It is important to keep data secure so that it is not lost, corrupted or made available to unauthorised users.

Securing data against loss and corruption

A number of simple precautions will help to keep your data secure.

- Back up your data regularly. Taking regular backups should be built into any working procedures for computer users and you *must* set aside time to do this. Backups can be on floppy disk if the amount of data is small, or to tape if the amount of data is large.
- Keep one set of backups in a secure and safe place on the premises so that if the data in use is corrupted it can be replaced quickly.
- Keep a second set of backups in a secure and safe place in another building. This means that if there is a fire or other disaster on the premises you still have a backup.

Activity 3.33

Find out from the computer technician or computer manager in your school or college what their rules are to prevent data loss and data corruption.

Securing data against unauthorised use

Stopping people you don't want to see your data from having access to it is also a matter of a few straightforward precautions.

- Keep the computer equipment in a locked place to discourage unauthorised users gaining access.
- Put passwords on computer systems and on software and data within the system. *Never* tell anyone else your password. Do not choose an obvious password (like your name) – these are easily guessed. Change your password frequently.
- Companies can make employees sign a non-disclosure agreement where the employees agree not to tell anyone about company software and data. Government offices and companies working for government agencies can also make employees sign the Official Secrets Act, which makes it a criminal offence to tell anyone about the work they are doing.

- Both computer programs and company data come under **copyright** law, so someone can own the rights to a program *and* the data. Breaking copyright by giving someone else the software or data is illegal.

Activity 3.34

May produce evidence for communications element 2.4.

Find out from your computer technician or computer manager what their rules are to prevent unauthorised use of data. How does the Data Protection Act affect your educational establishment?

Review questions

Explain the following terms as they apply to software security:
1 Regular saving
2 Backup
3 Non-disclosure agreement
4 Password
5 Copyright

Health and safety for computer users

The employer must guard against stress at work. In computing 'stress' includes:
- eye strain – regular computer users must have document holders to hold data being input at the correct distance and angle and employees working on screen for long periods are entitled to eye tests paid for by their employer
- repetitive strain injury – the risks of this can be reduced by making sure to use adjustable chairs and foot rests, appropriate aids such as arm and hand rests and by taking frequent breaks from data input.

The employer must also guard against putting employees into hazardous situations due to electrical faults, fire hazards, obstruction in the work place and radiation from VDU screens.

Activity 3.35

Find out from your computer technician, or computer manager, or union representative in your college or school how the management protect computer users.

Obligations of computer users

All computer users are legally obliged to do the following:
- Keep data confidential.
- Obey UK and EU copyright laws.
- Use uncensored materials responsibly.
- Be responsible about private material.
- Do not steal hardware or software.
- Check computer for viruses. Check all new disks that are used for viruses. Make sure that there are no viruses on disks that are given to other people.
- Obey UK and EU data protection laws. These include the need to register if

you are storing data about private individuals, and the rights of private individuals to see and correct any data stored about them on computer.

- Organisations must also obey UK and EU health and safety legislation to protect the workforce.

Test questions

An electricity company has issued all their meter readers with hand-held computers for the readings.

1 The name and address of the customer appears on the screen, and the meter reader must check with the person at that address that it is the correct place. What is this type of accuracy check called?

   a Range check

   b Type check

   c Verification

   d Correctness

2 Two numbers appear on the screen, and the meter reader must enter the correct meter reading. If the meter reading falls outside the two numbers shown, the person at that address must sign a form saying that the reading is correct. What is this type of accuracy check called?

   a Range check

   b Type check

   c Verification

   d Correctness

3 A customer pays with a credit card at a supermarket checkout. When the card is swiped through the machine it is checked automatically as being a legal credit card. What is this check known as?

   a Verification

   b Legitimisation

   c Digitisation

   d Validation

4 What stops you losing the work you have done today if there is a power failure?

   a Having your own password

   b Owning the copyright

   c Saving your work regularly

   d Non-disclosure agreement

5 What stops other people messing up your work?

   a Having your own password

   b Owning the copyright

   c Saving your work regularly

   d Non-disclosure agreement

6 Some computer users use foam rubber wrist rests. What does this help to guard against?

   a Eye strain

   b Repetitive strain injury

   c Radiation

   d Electric shock

7 Which of these is most likely to be a fire hazard in a computer room?

   a Sun reflecting off computer screens onto printer paper

   b Heads crashing onto fast-turning inflammable disks

    c Mouse cables being chewed through by mice

    d Mains cables running unprotected across the floor

8 A lawyer keeps information about his clients on computer. Which of the following is he legally obliged to do?

    a Keep the data for at least five years

    b Make sure no one else can access the data

    c Allow the police access to the data

    d Keep paper copies of the data as well

9 You give your friend a copy of a program that you have bought so that you can both use it at once. Which *best* describes the legal position?

    a This is legal provided you do not photocopy the manual

    b This is legal provided it is for study purposes only

    c This breaks the copyright act and is illegal

    d This is only legal if no money changes hands

Assignment A3.1
Examine the flow of information in a real organisation

This assignment provides coverage for Element 3.1.

1 Choose and agree with your tutor an organisation to investigate.
2 Write a letter to arrange an interview.
3 Plan the interview:
    a plan the questions – you will need sufficient information to provide a report
    b plan explanations for the questions.
4 Carry out the interview.
5 Produce a report on the organisation, containing
    a a chart showing internal and external functions
    b a list and description of types of information used
    c a document flow chart
    d a data flow diagram of the organisation.
6 Write to thank your informant, suggesting that you would like to investigate one of their systems at a later date.

Assignment A3.2
Investigate a data handling system

This assignment provides evidence for Element 3.2 and also for the following key skill elements:

Communication 2.1	Take part in discussions
Communication 2.2	Produce written material.

1 Choose and agree with your tutor a handling system to investigate.
2 Arrange the investigation.

3 Design a questionnaire to find out
  a the method of processing and the type of data handling system used
  b the system's objectives
  c the data sources
  d the methods of data capture
  e the processes applied to the data.
4 Carry out the investigation.
5 Produce a report of the investigation describing:
  a methods of processing and types of data handling systems
  b the objectives of your chosen system
  c at least two data sources for your chosen system
  d at least one method of data capture
  e processes applied to data, including examples of calculating, searching, selecting, sorting and validating.

Assignment A3.3
Create and use a database

This assignment provides evidence for Element 3.3 and also for the following key skill element:
Communication 2.2:   Produce written material

You are going to set up a database system for Student Hardware Ltd (the company mentioned in Activity 3.20). The materials being sold are stored in a warehouse. Twelve different type of goods have already been decided on. Each van can store a maximum quantity of these goods. All vans are identical. Every morning a van driver is given a box containing 12 clear plastic bags and a £10 float. Each bag contains enough of one type of item to take the quantity of goods in the van to the maximum number. They are also given a sales docket, which looks like the one in Figure 3.22. The boxes at the top have already been completed.

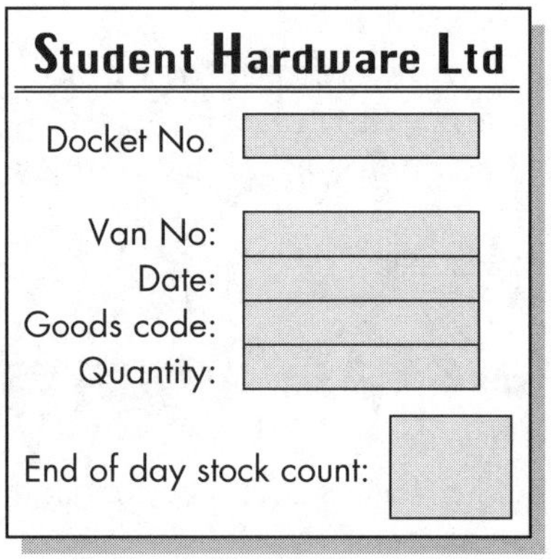

Student Hardware Ltd

Docket No.

Van No:
Date:
Goods code:
Quantity:

End of day stock count:

Figure 3.22

The driver takes the goods and spends the day selling. At the end of the day, the driver fills in the stock count on each docket and returns all the dockets and the money collected. The warehouseman enters the information from the dockets into the database, which prints out a report for each van:

- number of each type of goods sold
- amount of money that should have been collected for these goods
- total amount that should have been collected.

It also prints out the dockets for the next day.

1 Create a database for Student Hardware Ltd.
2 Design and create a table for the GOODS that you are selling. For each type of item you will need fields giving goods code (key field), goods description, cost price, sales price, maximum number that fit a van (you decided this in Activity 3.20 – assume the vans are identical).
3 Enter data into the table.
4 Design and create another table called DOCKETS.
5 The business started with only two vans, so enter data for the first day of sales. You will need the maximum number of goods for all dockets. The dates will all be the same.
6 Set up a report, or set of reports, to print out the dockets and print them. (The dockets need not be the same shape as the one shown if this is not convenient for your printer, but they should contain the same information, plus space for the van driver's stock count.)
7 Fill in the end-of-day stock count.
8 Enter the end-of-day stock count data.
9 Set up a to enable you to print out the report for each van. Set up and print the report.
10 Set up a view which will enable you to print tomorrow's dockets. Set up a report for at least one docket and print it out.
11 Write a manual telling the warehouse manager how to use the system.

Assignment A3.4
Safety and security issues

This assignment provides evidence for Element 3.4.

Add appendices to the manual you prepared in Assignment A3.3 to describe
1 Health and safety issues for users of IT.
2 The obligations of IT users.

CHAPTER 4

Communications and IT

Element 4.1: Describe electronic communications
Element 4.2: Use an electronic communication system
Element 4.3: Examine computer networks
Element 4.4: Use a computer network

What is covered in this chapter

- Types of electronic communication systems
- Technical terms such as baud rate, flow control and duplex
- Practical experience of sending data electronically
- Security issues
- Types of local and wide area networks
- Practice use of networks

For your portfolio for this unit you will need Assignments A4.1, A4.2, A4.3 and A4.4

Introduction

Small computers have been in use for nearly 20 years, but the most exciting recent developments have been made in communication of data. Mobile phones, fax machines, satellite and cable TV, the Internet and now digital TV have affected the lives of many people. This chapter discusses how IT has affected our lives.

Element 4.1: Describe electronic communication systems

Electronic communication systems

A very wide range of types of electronic communication systems is used today. These can be grouped under the following headings:
- broadcast systems
- telephone
- facsimile
- networks.

Broadcast systems
'Broadcast' means 'sent out over a wide area'. Examples of broadcast systems include TV entertainment programmes (both terrestrial and satellite) and mobile phones. Terrestrial (ground-based) TV signals are sent out by aerials on powerful radio transmitters, and are received by the aerials connected to television sets. Satellite TV signals are sent up to a satellite, which then transmits them back to dish aerials on Earth. There are networks of transmitting and

110

receiving aerials across the country for mobile phones. These aerials have a short range, but are organised into 'cells', and a phone will use the aerial in the cell it is in. Other broadcast systems include marine and aircraft control, police communications and radio broadcasts.

Some broadcast systems are video (moving pictures and sound – e.g. television), others are audio (sound) only – such as mobile phones and radio.

Telephone

Telephone systems have been in use for over 100 years, normally for person-to-person audio transmissions. Today, in addition, computers can transmit data to one another using telephone lines. A **modem** converts the digital signals from one computer to a form that can be sent down the telephone line. When the signal reaches the receiving modem, the signal is converted back to digital form for the second computer to understand.

Facsimile

Facsimile transmissions are usually called **fax**. Documents, drawings and photos can be sent all over the world by feeding the paper into a fax machine and transmitting a copy. Many computers now contain **fax/modem cards**, which allow material produced on computer (word processed documents, spreadsheets, graphics) to be faxed directly from the computer, without printing them out first.

Activity 4.1

Sometimes you have a choice between telephoning a person and faxing them. When is it better to phone? When is it better to fax?

Networks

Networks are communication systems that connect computers together. The most familiar type is a local area network (**LAN**). In a LAN the computers in a room or building are connected. Your college probably has a LAN, and you probably use it a lot.

In a wide area network (a **WAN**) systems are connected together over larger distances, perhaps across a city, a country or even across continents. A **public WAN** connects computers from several organisations and many individuals. The best-known example of this is the Internet, which interconnects many companies and individuals across the world. A **private WAN** connects computers only within one company, or closely related organisations. Several private WANs across the UK connect nearby colleges. Private WANs are often connected over **leased lines** – a communications line which the user rents, for their exclusive use, from the telephone company.

Activity 4.2

Use the following table to show which type of communication system is which.

	Video broadcast	Audio broadcast	LAN	Public WAN	Private WAN
The Internet					
Police car radio					
Local FM radio					
Mobile phone					
Network of bank cash dispensers					
College computer network					

Protocols

If you had a Spanish pen-friend and you wrote to them in English, which they cannot understand, they might justifiably be annoyed. Before you started corresponding you would have to agree what language you would write in, choosing one you could both understand – you would have to agree on the protocol you would use.

In communications, a **protocol** is an agreement between sender and receiver detailing the set of rules they will use when communicating. If you send a message in way that doesn't obey the protocol, the receiver will probably find it incomprehensible.

Computer data is made of patterns of ones and zeroes – such as 01011101. Each 1 or 0 is called a **bit** (from *binary* dig*it*). The different bits are produced by different voltages – a 0 by 0 volts, a 1 bit by 5 volts. Figure 4.1 shows what happens if the data is sent down a line, one bit after another.

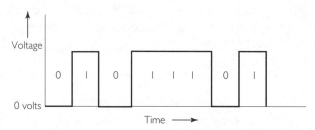

Figure 4.1   What happens to the voltage when sending data a bit at a time

The number of bits sent down a line per second is known as the **baud rate**. Common rates in use at the moment are 9600 or 14 400 bits per second. At a low baud rate it takes a long time to transmit data. If the baud rate is higher large files, such as graphics, can be sent more quickly.

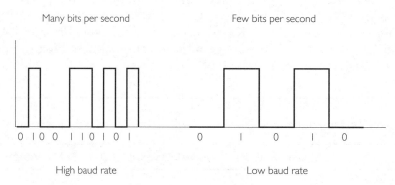

Figure 4.2   High and low baud rates

Parity checking

There is always a chance that some data will be lost when it is being transmitted, and if just one bit is changed – from a 1 to a 0, for instance – or lost, the message will be garbled. Changes might be caused by interference – on a voice phone call you will often hear crackles, and the data goes down the same lines – which can change the bits around. A way of checking whether the data has been sent correctly is known as **parity checking**.

Parity checking works like this. The data is sent in groups of seven bits, plus an extra digit that the system generates. If a group contains an odd number of 1s, the system will send another 1, to make the total number even. If the number of 1s is already even it sends a 0 so the total is still even. For example:

Data bits	Odd or even?	Parity bit	Group sent
0011 011	4, so even	0	0011 011**0**
1111 111	7, so odd	1	1111 111**1**
1100 000	2, so even	0	1100 000**0**

This is known as even parity, and means that the number of 1s in each group of eight digits received should be even. If the receiving system receives an odd number, there has been a problem in transmission.

Activity 4.3

1 What should be the parity bit for the following data bits?
   a 0000111
   b 0111110
2 If you receive 00001110, has the data been transmitted correctly?
3 Has there been an error in transmitting 11000000?

Data bits and stop bits

When agreeing on the rules about what will be sent (agreeing the protocol) there are a lot of choices to be made. For example:

- The data is sent in groups of bits – do you send seven data bits, or eight? (i.e. do you use a parity bit or not?)
- Do you choose to use even parity or odd parity (where the number of 1 bits must be odd)?

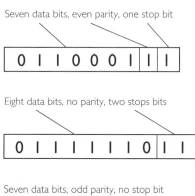

Figure 4.3 Possible combinations of data for transmission

- Are you going to include a 'stop' bit at the end of the group? A stop bit is a 1 bit, and is used to confirm the end of the group to the receiver – sometimes there is no stop bit.

Unless both the transmitter and the receiver agree on how the data is going to be sent parity bits are going to be mistaken for data bits or stop bits and many problems will be caused. The communication software that controls a modem must be given this information so that both parties can understand each other.

Flow control

If you have to write notes during a talk you may find it difficult to keep up with the speaker and might have to ask them to wait for you to catch up. This is called **flow control**.

Flow control in IT works in a similar way. The sender sends data on one wire and when the receiver can't deal with any more data, it sends a signal on a second wire (called the flow control wire) asking to sender to wait. When the receiver is ready to continue, it sends another signal on the flow control wire, and the sender sends more data.

Figure 4.4 shows protocols being set up in Terminal in Windows 3.1.

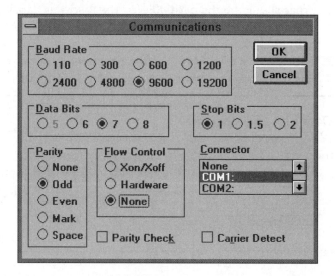

Figure 4.4 Setting up protocols. The modem has been set for a baud rate of 9600, there will be seven data bits, one stop bit, odd parity, and no flow control

Terminal emulation

In the past it was common for large computers (not PCs) to be connected to many users at once. Each user had a **terminal** – a keyboard and screen – but no CPU. Many terminals were connected to the same CPU and communications software was written to use these terminals. Some of these terminals were very simple, only being able to show lines of text and then scroll up, like on a printer. Some screens could display text at any position on the screen, by moving the cursor to certain x and y co-ordinates. Other terminals could display text and graphic blocks in colour. Because very large numbers of these terminals were used, they became standards for how the screen would be used.

Now PCs will 'emulate' terminals – that is they will mimic these old terminals, and pretend to be the same as they are. Figure 4.5 shows terminal emulation being selected in the Terminal program in Windows 3.1.

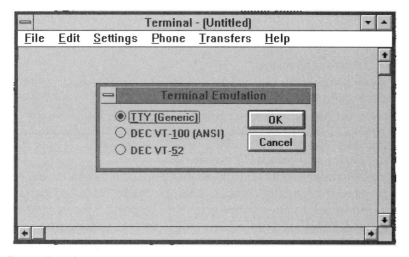

Figure 4.5 Terminal emulation

Activity 4.4

Make some notes on the following topics:
- baud rate
- data bits
- flow control
- parity
- stop bits
- terminal emulation.

You will need these notes for Assignment A4.1.

Modes of communication

The mode of communication describes in a general way how the communication takes place.

Duplex and simplex

You can receive broadcasts with a television set, but a television does not send out anything – the communication is one-way, not two-way. TV broadcasting is an example of **simplex transmission**.

Duplex transmission is two-way communication – messages can be sent in both directions at the same time. Voice phone is duplex, because each person can talk to the other.

Half duplex is two-way communication, but the two parties cannot communicate at the same time. Fax is effectively half duplex, since you can send faxes between any pair of machines, but you cannot send and receive at the same time. If you receive a fax and want to reply, you have to dial the sender.

Activity 4.5

Which of the following are simplex, which duplex and which half duplex?
- television
- voice phone
- fax
- mobile phone
- the Internet
- air-traffic control
- police radio
- local FM radio
- a LAN.

Serial and parallel transmission

If data is sent over long distances (such as via a modem on a telephone line) it is sent on a single cable. This means the bits have to be sent one after another, in series, as shown in Figures 4.1 and 4.2. This is called **serial transmission**.

If more cables are available, several bits can be sent at the same time. The cables inside a PC, and connecting a PC to some printers, are ribbon cables. A ribbon cable is a wide flat cable with many wires and each wire is able to carry bits at the same time as the others. If there are eight wires, then eight bits can be sent side by side. This is called **parallel transmission**.

Because serial transmission uses just one wire, it is much cheaper and so is used over long distances. Parallel transmission is faster, because many bits can be sent together.

Activity 4.6

Make your own notes on simplex, duplex, half duplex, serial and parallel communication modes. Keep these notes for Assignment A4.1.

Case study

College payroll

Hightown College employs about 200 staff – about 100 teaching staff and 15 support staff who work in Reception, Finance, Technical Support and so on. These people are paid monthly and the amount does not usually change. The rest of the staff are cleaners, stewards and caretakers, who are paid by the hour, and so their monthly wages vary according to the hours they work.

The college uses the city council's payroll services to do their monthly payroll. The city council takes all the college's data and calculates the wages due, sends payslips to the college to be given to staff, and sends information to the banks so that the correct amount of money is paid into employees' accounts.

Each month the college transmits the following information electronically:
- details of new staff just starting
- any changes to existing staff, such as promotions and a new rate of pay
- the hours worked by the people who are paid hourly
- details of any people who have reached the end of their contract.

The college's PC is connected to a modem, and each week the person sending the information dials up the city council's modem, which is connected to a mainframe. The user has to enter a password, and then the mainframe disconnects and calls the college back – this makes sure that an authorised person is dialling in, not an outsider trying to hack from home. The user can then enter all the information required.

Activity 4.7

What are the advantages to Hightown College of using a modem for communication over:
- the letter post
- the telephone
- fax?

Test questions

1 Satellite TV is an example of an electronic communications system. What type of electronic communications system is satellite TV?
   a Video broadcast
   b Private wide area network
   c Public wide area network
   d Local area network
2 A communication system is used to send one-to-many audio messages. Which communication system?
   a Facsimile
   b Local area network
   c Telephone
   d Radio broadcast
3 What happens if you use a higher baud rate?
   a You can tell if there is a transmission error
   b It will take longer to send a message
   c It will be quicker to send a message
   d Hackers cannot intercept your message
4 What happens if you use a parity check?
   a You can tell if there is a transmission error
   b It will take longer to send a message
   c It will be quicker to send a message
   d Hackers cannot intercept your message
5 A printer accepts data from a CPU eight bits at a time. Which type of communication does the printer use?
   a Simplex
   b Parity
   c Serial
   d Parallel

6 Fax allows two people to send documents to each other, but not at the same time. Which of the following type of communication does the fax use?
  a Simplex
  b Duplex
  c Half duplex
  d Parallel

7 You have a computer with a modem and want to access the Internet. The communications software is set to use even parity. What is the point of this?
  a To ensure compatibility between hardware
  b To prevent hacking into your computer system
  c So that phone lines can be leased
  d To avoid errors in transmission

8 Which of the following allows the receiver to tell the sender to wait until it is ready to receive more data?
  a Baud rate
  b Data bits
  c Flow control
  d The telephone number

Element 4.2: Use an electronic communication system

Introduction

This element is about setting up and using communication systems.

Electronic systems

A common arrangement for an electronic communication system is to use a PC connected to the telephone network through a modem. This is shown in Figure 4.6.

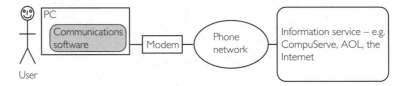

Figure 4.6

The PC must be running a communications software package. This will control the modem, allowing the setting of protocols, and probably stores a list of telephone numbers of different services to be dialled.

The telephone network was originally set up to transmit audio (voice) signals of limited quality, and is not suitable for carrying digital computer signals. A modem is needed to translate the digital information from a computer into a form suitable for transmission along a phone line. It also does the reverse job – at the receiving end it converts phone signals into digital signals.

Some modems are in a box separate from the rest of the CPU (they are **external**), and a row of lights on the front show the user what is happening. **Internal** modems are printed circuit boards that are connected inside the CPU, and the phone line goes into the back of the computer. An internal modem will usually also work as a fax.

Facsimile systems are usually called fax. To use a fax machine you must firstly dial the number of where you want to send the fax to, by pressing the buttons on the machine. You can then feed in pages carrying text, diagrams and photos, rather like putting them into a photocopier. The difference is that the copy is produced out of the other fax machine, which could be the other side of the world.

If the PC contains a **fax/modem card**, then the user can send a document prepared on the computer through the modem card to another fax machine, or to another PC containing a modem card. All you need is the phone number of where you want to send it.

Setting up communication systems

To set up systems like these, the user firstly has to arrange things as described above. This usually means plugging the modem into the back of the computer and into a telephone socket, and installing the communications software. The system then has to be **configured** before it will work properly. To work properly, the system has to be configured, which means doing the three following things: setting the communication modes, protocols and phone numbers.

Activity 4.8

Check back to Element 4.1 if you have forgotten what the following mean:
- simplex and duplex
- serial and parallel
- baud rate
- parity bits.

The communication modes are usually fixed by the kind of communication system being used. For example, fax is always half duplex. Long-distance communications are always serial rather than parallel. Protocols must be set to match what the receiver will expect – the baud rate should be the highest that the receiver can deal with and the number of data bits, parity and stop bits must be set correctly. The telephone number to be dialled must also be set. Communication software usually deals with these settings in one of two ways:
1 The phone number, parity and so on are entered, the number dialled and the communication takes place. The settings are not saved.
2 If the user is likely to communicate with the same service many times he or she can save the phone number, baud rate and other settings as a certain 'session'. Then he or she can simply select the session to use instead of inputting the settings each time.

Accuracy checks – echoing, parity checks

In the game 'Chinese whispers' people sit in a circle, and someone starts by whispering a message to the person on their left. The message is passed on and eventually returns to the person who started it – but usually the message has changed. Messages sometimes pick up errors as they move through a communications system. To deal some forms of accuracy check are needed. You will already have found out about parity checks in Element 4.1. Another way of checking the accuracy of data transmitted is to use **echoing**.

Echoing means that the receiver sends the message back to the sender, who can see if it was sent correctly. For example, when someone keys in their user ID when logging on what they type is displayed on the screen, or echoed back to them, so that they can check that they have hit the correct keys. By contrast, a password is *not* echoed back on the screen – it appears as asterisks, or nothing. This will prevent unauthorised people from seeing the password.

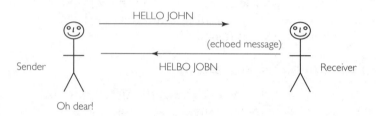

Figure 4.7 Error detection by echoing. The data received is echoed back to the sender. If the sender receives the same data as it sent out, the data has been transmitted correctly

Security issues

Because communication can take place over a long distance, you cannot be *sure* who you are 'talking' to or who might be eavesdropping on your conversation. This means that security can be a problem. One way of solving the problem is **encryption**. An encrypted message is 'scrambled' into a special code before it is sent. The receiver can only make sense of the message if they know how to decode (decrypt) it.

Suppose we want to encrypt the message HAVE A NICE DAY. By putting the letters into a 5 × 4 grid, working across then down, like this:

```
H   A   V   E
.   A   .   N
I   C   E   .
D   A   Y   .

.   .   .   .
```

and then taking the letters out, first going down, then across you will get the message

H.ID.AACA.V.EY.EN ...

This is the encrypted message you would send. To decrypt it, you would put it into a 5 × 4 grid working down then across, and read it back out going across then down.

Activity 4.9

Decode the message

W.IM.HANE.A.ES.TF.S.

using the method just described.

To add further security, many systems use **user IDs** and **passwords**. Users have to log onto a system, and the user ID tells the system who they are. The password is entered to prove the user's identity.

Activity 4.10

Your user ID is not secret, but your password is. List the bad things that could happen if other people knew your password.

Each user has a set of **privileges**, which means what they are allowed to access and do on the system. For example, they might be allowed to read some files, save to some files, delete some files, log on only at certain times.

Test questions

1 When you log on to a system, you type in your user ID, and this is displayed back to you on the screen as you type. This is called:
   a Parity
   b Carriage return
   c Rotation
   d Echoing

2 For security purposes you are allowed to change some files on a system but not others. This is known as:
   a A control command
   b A privilege setting
   c Encryption
   d A user password

3 What happens if your data is encrypted?
   a You can tell if there is a transmission error
   b It will take longer to send a message
   c It will be quicker to send a message
   d Hackers cannot intercept your message

4 When you log on, the system knows who you are because of:
   a Your user password
   b Data encryption
   c The access method
   d Your user ID

Element 4.3: Examine computer networks

Introduction

This element is about the different kinds of computer networks and how they are used.

Types of network

There are three kinds of network – local area networks (LANs), public wide area networks (WANs) and private WANs.

Local area networks

A LAN connects a group of computers that are fairly close together – usually in the same room or the same building. Less often, computers in buildings on the same site are connected on the same LAN. If the connection is so extensive that it crosses land not owned by the organisation, the network is not a LAN – it is a WAN. Colleges often have one or more 'computer rooms' where the computers are connected together – these are LANs. A small business might occupy a group of offices – finance, personnel, marketing, and customer orders. The computers in these rooms are connected by a LAN but if the business has another branch in a different city, the branches would be connected by a WAN.

Public WANs

Networks that go over long distances, such as between cities and beyond are WANs. A public WAN can be used by most people – it is available to the public. An example is the public telephone network that connects up most houses and businesses. Many of these phone lines are connected to computers through modems. Another example is the integrated services digital network (ISDN), which can carry digital computer signals at much higher speeds than phone lines.

Private WANs

A private WAN covers a large area, but can only be used by the organisation which owns it. The system is linked either by lines that organisation owns or by lines that the organisation leases, usually from British Telecom.

A bank would probably have a private WAN – for example, a customer can use a cash machine anywhere in the country, and the machine they use must obtain data (such as checking the PIN and account balance) from the branch holding that data. For security, the bank would use leased lines.

Components of a LAN

Workstations

The **workstations** are the computers that are connected together on the network. Some workstations are **dumb terminals** – they are only a keyboard and VDU. Dumb terminals cannot do any processing by themselves – any applications programs must be run in a processor somewhere else.

Most workstations are ordinary PCs that have been adapted to work on a network. They have a keyboard, VDU and CPU and can run programs in the same way as a 'stand-alone' computer. The PC might have its own printer connected in the usual way. Most workstations also have floppy and hard disk drives. Some sites use workstations with no floppy or hard drives, as a virus precaution and to prevent users installing unauthorised software.

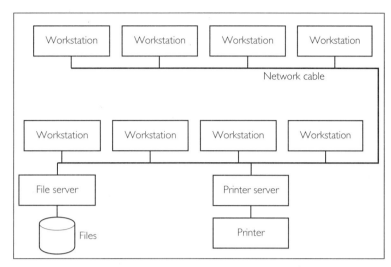

Figure 4.8 How a LAN might be put together

Network cabling

The computers on a LAN are usually connected by cables that carry the data between them. One type of cable is **coaxial** – this is made of one wire in the centre, surrounded by insulator, and then surrounded by a cylindrical mesh of fine wires connected to ground. This is the same as TV aerial cable. Other network cables are called **twisted pair** cables – each connection has two wires twisted around each other to cancel out any interference on the line. A third type of network cable is **fibreoptic**, which carries the data on pulses of light down transparent fibres.

A few workstations are linked to the network via wireless link, using radio or infra-red. They have no network cable. This is useful if the workstation is a hand-held computer which is moved around.

Network cards

All a PC needs to work as a network workstation is a network interface card. The card usually plugs into the **motherboard** – the main printed circuit board of the PC and the one that carries the microprocessor and memory. The network cable is plugged in to the connections on the card that appear at the back of the PC.

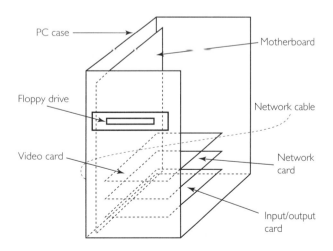

Figure 4.9

File servers

A **file server** is a computer on the network which has large hard disk drives and which is used to store users' files. When users want to save work, they can use a floppy disk or hard drive on their workstation, or a network drive. If the data is saved on a network drive it is sent down the network cable to the file server, where it is saved. Because the file server is dealing with many users, it needs to have a fast processor, lots of memory and high-capacity high-speed disk drives.

Network software

This is the software that is needed to make the network work and runs in two places – the file servers and the workstations. Most of the network software runs in the file servers. This deals with users, checking their ID against their password and allowing them access as they have been set up. It also lets users read and write files on the server as they request. A smaller amount of software runs on the workstations. This checks what the user wants, and routes requests for files on network drives to the file server.

Printer servers

A printer may be connected directly to a workstation, in which case it is used just as if it was attached to a stand-alone computer. However, printers are expensive and are not in constant use, so sharing a printer between several users over a network saves costs and means that the printer is used more efficiently. One way to do this is to connect the printer onto the network through a **printer server**. This is a device which routes data from the cable to the printer where needed. Some print servers are built into the printer, so the printer can be connected directly onto the network cable. Another way is to connect the printer to the file server. The file server runs the software needed. Either way, it means that a user at one workstation can print out their work on a printer somewhere else on the network.

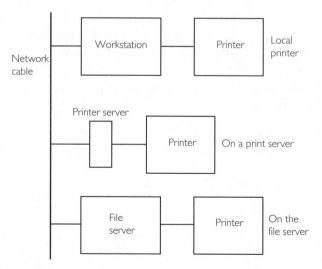

Figure 4.10 Printers on a LAN

Activity 4.11

Make notes on the network components described above.

Network topology

The 'shape' used to connect the components on a network is called the **network topology**. On a LAN, the three topologies used are **bus**, **ring** and **star**. These are shown in Figure 4.11. The things on the network are workstations, printer servers and file servers.

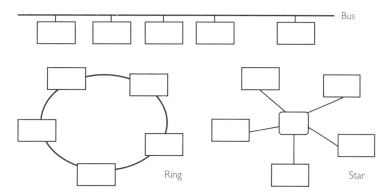

Figure 4.11 Bus, ring and star topologies

On a bus network, the components are connected to a single length of cable using 'T-piece' connectors. This is very simple, but if there is one break along the cable, the whole network stops working. On a ring, the cable goes into and out of each station, forming a circle. A single piece of data, called a token, is passed around the ring by the stations. A station can pass a message on only if it picks up this token and the network is otherwise free. On a star network, a central specialised device routes messages from one station to another.

The topology used in WANs is usually **mesh topology**, as shown in Figure 4.12. The nodes on the network are communications centres, such as telephone exchanges. Mesh networks are very reliable, since if there is a fault on one 'leg' a different route can be found around the faulty section. They are also efficient – a lot of traffic on one leg will slow down transmission, but other routes are found automatically to a faster path.

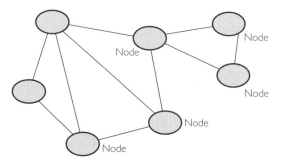

Figure 4.12 Mesh WAN

Activity 4.12

Draw a diagram showing bus, ring, star and mesh topologies.

Network services

People use LANs and WANs in different ways according to their needs. Many different facilities are offered and some of these are described in this section.

Bulletin boards

Bulletin boards are run by small businesses, clubs, special interest groups and some individuals. The bulletin board is run on one computer, connected to a modem, and other people connect to it using their own communications software and modem.

When you first access a bulletin board, it asks you to register and allocates you a user name and password. You will use these every time you access the board.

On a bulletin board you can:

- Read information put there by the 'sysop', the person who runs the service.
- Send questions and messages to the sysop. The sysop might deal with these him or herself, or may publish them so that other people can reply.
- Follow and take part in 'discussions'. People send messages in, and others respond.
- Download files to your own computer.

Electronic mail

Using electronic mail (or e-mail) you can send messages to people through the computer network instead of using the letter post, or 'snail mail'. E-mail is sometimes used on a LAN to send messages between people working in the same building but it can also be used over a WAN, to send messages to people thousands of miles away. When the e-mail message is sent, it is stored somewhere on another computer – on the file server of a LAN or possibly on a large computer over a WAN.

You write your e-mail message using a word processor or simple text editor. You must give the message a subject (which tells briefly what the message is about) and need to include the e-mail address of the person or people you are sending it to. When the person to whom the message is sent logs on to the network and checks their e-mail, they will see a list of the messages waiting for them, the subject of each message, who sent each one and the date it was sent.

The e-mail software will then give the user the choice to:

- read the message now or leave it till later
- delete the message
- reply to the message
- send new mail.

It is possible to 'attach' another file to an e-mail message, so you can send a spreadsheet or a graphics image, for example if you need to. It is also possible to 'broadcast' the same message to many people. This is often used for advertising, and results in 'junk e-mail'.

Conferencing

You cannot have a 'live' conversation with e-mail, but you can with **conferencing**. With conferencing two or more people on the system (a LAN or WAN) at the same time can send short messages immediately to each other. These messages will appear on their screens almost straight away, so that a conversation can take place. Conferencing can be used for idle chat or serious discussions. This is sometimes called **teleconferencing**. As an extension to this, if the users have computers with a video camera and microphone, they can see and hear each other. This is called **video conferencing**.

File transfer

A file you need might be stored on the hard disk of another computer, but if the computers are on the same network you can use file transfer to copy it to your computer. On the Internet this is called **ftp**, file transfer protocol.

The files you transfer could be anything, from word processed documents to graphics or program files. It is usual to talk about **downloading** files to your system, and **uploading** files from your system to a remote site. You must be very careful when downloading files from another system – the files you download could be carrying **viruses**. You should always check files using anti-virus software as soon as they are downloaded.

Database interaction

Databases can be stored on networks and accessed remotely. The database might be on a LAN or a WAN. The user can basically do two things with it:

- search the database for information
- change or add information into the database.

Imagine a company which uses a LAN. A member of staff might need to telephone a customer, but not know the phone number. They could use their computer to look up the customer's number held in a database on the file server. You could access the Internet from your home computer to plan your holiday by finding out the availability of aircraft flights to where you want to go.

Activity 4.13

Make notes on the different types of networks, and the services available.

Benefits of networks

Having a network causes some extra expenses, since special hardware and software are needed. Nevertheless, networks bring many benefits, which more than outweigh the costs.

Centralised security

It is easier to keep data secure on a network that stores the data centrally on one or a few file servers, because:

- User IDs and passwords make sure that only authorised people can use the system.
- Access rights can be controlled so that the access of certain individuals can be restricted to certain files and directories. This is described further below.
- More money can be spent on the disk drives on the file server to make them more reliable. For example, **disk mirroring**, in which an automatic copy of one disk is made on another, can be used.
- Backups can be taken reliably. It is easier to just back the files up on the file server than to get all the different users to back up their own disks.

Centralised support

Computer support means helping users to overcome problems, like dealing with faulty computer hardware or software and setting up systems. A network can help with support, since users can send descriptions of their problems over the network, and receive suggestions how they can fix things for themselves. The support team can also access the user's machine directly over the network, and fix any problems.

Shared data

A city council's offices would have several departments – for the repair and maintenance of council houses, for collecting Council Tax, for collecting rent, for example. It would not be a good idea for each department to keep their own separate data files on council houses because the data files must be kept up-to-date. Any change to one file must be repeated through all of the files, and it would be impossible to be sure which file is the most up to date at any one time. It is much better to have only one data file that all users share over a network.

Shared hardware

On a network expensive hardware can be shared, and accessed by many users, so the cost is reduced. Examples of hardware that can be shared are:
- disk drives on the file server
- printers and plotters on printer servers
- CD-ROM drives
- communication devices such as modems forming gateways to other networks

Shared software

Often on a network software is stored on the file server, and the users load it from there and run it on their own machines when required. This is better than installing the software onto the hard disks of all the network stations for several reasons.
- It is quicker to install software on one file server than on all the workstations.
- A licence is required for each user. The business will buy a licence for, say, 50 users for the software. It is easier to control the number of people using the software at the same time on a network than if the software was installed on many different machines.
- If users put software on their own machines, they might do it incorrectly, use unreliable software or introduce viruses onto the network.

Teamworking

A team of people might be working on a project such as a brochure advertising their company's services. They might have a meeting at the start to plan out the contents of the brochure. One person might write the text, another person draws some diagrams, while a third obtains some photographs. While they are doing this the team members might have more ideas and have to send notes to the other people. Then the text, diagrams and drawings have to be put together for the final brochure.

Teamwork can be enhanced by using a network:
- they can arrange meetings over the network
- messages can be sent quickly by e-mail
- meetings can be held by video conferencing
- the team members can work on the files separately, and when they are ready 'publish' copies on the network for other members of the team to work on or incorporate into another document.

Activity 4.14

Make notes on the benefits of network use as described here.

Security

There is a risk that data on a network could go to the wrong place, or be intercepted by the wrong person. Also, as files are stored together a file might be accessed by an unauthorised person. Extra security precautions are therefore needed on a network.

Users need to log on to the network before they can use it, which means they have to give their user ID – usually a shortened version of their name. The user ID lets the network software know which user is which, and this is important because of access rights. As they log on, the user also has to enter a password. The purpose of this is to 'prove' that the user ID they have entered is correct. The password is to confirm who they are. A person's password should be kept secret so that no one else can use it.

Access to files on the network is controlled using the idea of **access rights** or **permission settings**. Figure 4.13 shows how this might be set up. The network drive, from the root, is divided into user directories, where users store their files, and public directories, where shared files are kept. The public directories contain files that everyone would find useful, such as clip art. Applications software programs, such as a word processing program, are also kept on the public directory. In the user area each user has their own directory, and they can split this into sub-directories as they like.

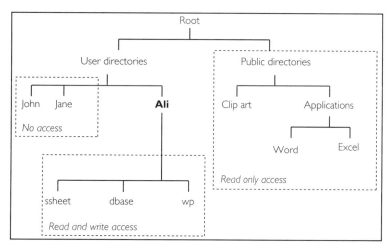

Figure 4.13 Access rights on a network

Figure 4.13 gives an example of how the user Ali can access the network. He has read-only access to the public directories – he can load applications and copy clip art, but he cannot change or delete files here. Ali has read and write access to his own directory – these are his own files, so he can read them, store new versions, and delete them as he wants. Ali has no access to other users' directories – he cannot even find out what files are stored there.

Legal issues

A number of laws relate to computer use, especially over a network.

The **Data Protection Act** is important, and covers three key points:

- It is about data about people.
- The data held on computer about people must be accurate and up to date. Backups must be kept, the information in the files must be updated

promptly, and must be protected from hackers who might falsely change the data.

- The data must be disclosed *only* to the people who need it for the purposes for which it was collected. In other words, the wrong people should not be able to get at the data. For example, the VDU of a computer at a reception area in a building should face away from the public, so that people cannot read what is on the screen.

Another important legal area is **copyright**. Users should not be able to copy software off the network for which they do not have a licence. People's work, such as their designs and drawings, are normally their own copyright, and no one should be allowed to copy this unless authorised by the copyright holder.

A common problem of **computer misuse** is 'hacking'. **Hackers** try to get access to areas they are not authorised to see by guessing or stealing passwords. Many hackers are malicious, and corrupt data stored in the areas they break in to. Hacking is a criminal offence.

Health and safety legislation to do with computer use is also relevant to people working on networks. Important points are:

- No drinks should be brought near computers – a mug of coffee spilt on a keyboard can give you an electric shock.
- All rooms containing computers should be equipped with electrical fire extinguishers.
- Good lighting is essential for avoiding distracting reflections from VDU screens.
- Good seating which will not tip over and which supports the back aids posture and so prevents neck and muscle strain.
- Users should take frequent breaks from the VDU and should not work on screen for prolonged periods because they could damage eyes, neck and wrists.
- Employers of workers who have to use a VDU as part of their job must pay for regular eye tests.

Activity 4.15

Make notes on the security requirements of networks.

Test questions

1. A company has four branches in different cities. The branches are linked, but cannot be accessed by members of the public. What type of network is the company using?
   a Public wide area network
   b Private wide area network
   c Local area network
   d Small area network

2. A team of scientists in a university use a network to take part in meetings, while staying in their own laboratories. What system are the scientists using?
   a Teleconferencing
   b Database interaction
   c Time management
   d Bulletin boards

3 A stockbroker uses a network system to find out the prices of shares before buying and selling them. What system is she using?

 a Electronic mail

 b Foreign access

 c File transfer

 d Database interaction

4 A small company that writes and sells software runs a computer, which users of the software can access and post queries about how to use the program. Which system allows users to exchange information about software use?

 a Database interaction

 b Telecommuting

 c Bulletin boards

 d Video conferencing

5 A company keeps information about its staff on computer. Why must the company ensure adequate security measures are undertaken?

 a To meet legal requirements

 b To avoid data being entered twice

 c To make information more accessible

 d To ensure information is correct

Element 4.4: Use a computer network

Introduction

This element is about the practical use of a computer network. You will learn some rules about the effective and legal use of network facilities, and demonstrate them in practice.

Log on procedures

Users must **log on** before they can use a network. You probably need a user ID and password before you can access your college network.

Activity 4.16

Find out the procedure for logging on to your college LAN. Make sure you know how to load applications (such as a word processor and a spreadsheet), save files and print them out.

File management

File management means keeping your computer files well organised and up to date. This includes grouping them in organised areas, deleting old files that you no longer need, protecting files from accidental deletion and moving files from place to place.

Sub-directories

A **directory** is a section of the disk on which files are stored. You probably have you own directory on the network drive. A directory can be split into smaller sections, called **sub-directories**. For example, if this course is taught by several lecturers who issue their own assignments, you could use a separate sub-directory for each lecturer's work. Using sub-directories makes it much easier to find your files.

Deleting files

Old files which are no longer needed should be deleted – they waste disk space, and distract you when you are looking for important files. Note that deletion is essentially a permanent process. You need to think carefully before you delete a file and should avoid deleting any useful files.

Copying files

It is often useful to be able to copy files. For example, if your lecturer places a file containing an assignment on the network, you will need to copy it and save it with your own filename.

Moving files

You might need to move files from one drive to another – for example from a floppy disk to a network drive. Or you might move files between directories, for instance when you create a new sub-directory and want to move some files into it.

File protection

The network manager will give users certain access rights, which will control the network areas they can access. You should also protect your own files, by making important files read-only. Usually files are set to be read–write – this means you can both read them and save alterations to them. If a file is read-only, you can load it but not make any permanent changes to it. This means you cannot inadvertently overwrite or delete an important file. If you really want to change the file, you must first make it read–write, and then save to it – something you could not do accidentally.

Backups

You have seen in previous elements the importance of backups. These are copies of important files, made so that if a problem occurs with a file you can go back to the last backup. Your files on the network may be backed up for you automatically. If not, you should arrange your own backup procedures, perhaps by copying files to floppy disks.

Activity 4.17

1 Talk to your college network manager, and find out how you can
   a create your own sub-directories
   b delete files
   c copy files
   d move files
   e make file to be read-only and read-write.
2 Find out if the network drive is backed up, and if it is not, back up your own files.

Copyright

People's work such as designs, drawings and text documents are normally their own copyright, and it is illegal to copy material without their permission. The same is true for most software – you can use it *only* if you have a licence to use it. Unauthorised copying of software is illegal.

Confidentiality

Confidential material should not be shown to anyone except those who have the right to see it. For example, the college may have details of any special medical conditions you may have. These are confidential, and only the people who need to see these details (such as first-aiders) should have access to them.

Much of the data held on computers about people is confidential. It must be protected by the methods described in Element 4.3, such as controlled access rights. The information is still confidential when it has been printed out, so hard copies should also be handled carefully. Hard copies of personal data which are no longer needed should be destroyed.

Activity 4.18

1 How does your college control software copyright? How do they make sure that software is not being used illegally?
2 How does your college ensure the confidentiality of personal data, such as students' addresses and staff salaries?

Test questions

A network manager insists on the following rules to ensure security on the network:

    a Printouts of personal data must be shredded after use
    b File backups must be stored at another site
    c No drinks are to be taken into the computer room
    d Anti-virus software must be run on all computers

1 Which of these is needed in case there is a fire?
2 Which protects confidential data?
3 Which rule ensures that files are not corrupted?
4 How can you organise your files so it is easier to find the correct one?
    a Use backup facilities
    b Use file protection facilities
    c Keep copies on floppy disk
    d Keep files in suitable sub-directories
5 You have accidentally deleted one of your own important files. How can you make sure you don't do this again?
    a Delete unwanted files
    b Do not drink near a computer
    c Make important files read-only
    d Use anti-virus software

Assignment A4.1

This assignment provides portfolio evidence for Element 4.1, and also the following key skill elements:

Communication 2.2:   Produce written material
Information Technology 2.3:   Present information

1 Find out about the broadcast communication systems of a local organisation. Here are some ideas:
   - local FM radio
   - local or national television station
   - mobile telephone network
   - CB radio
   - ham radio
   - air-traffic control at a nearby airport
   - police communication
   - cable TV.

Telephone the organisation to explain that you are doing a GNVQ assignment and would like some information on how their communication system works. You may have to try several before you find one that is prepared to supply you with what you need. They might send you some printed information, or you might be able to arrange a visit. Present a report on what you discover. Prepare a letter using a word processor thanking the organisation for their cooperation, and fax it to them.

2 Put your notes from Activity 4.4 in your portfolio.
3 Put your notes from Activity 4.6 in your portfolio.
4 Write a short report on either your college's LAN or the Internet.

Assignment A4.2

This assignment provides portfolio evidence for Element 4.2, and for the following key skill element:

Communication 2.2:   Produce written material

You work as an office junior in Old and Flaccid, a firm of solicitors. They do a lot of house conveyancing work looking after the legal details involved when people move house. Unfortunately they are getting a lot of complaints from clients, who say that the four or five months they take to complete the work is too slow. Old and Flaccid's excuse is that the post causes delays. In order to provide a faster service, Mr Old has asked you to look into better communication systems. This is what he wants you to do:

1 Write a report on what must be done to set up a communication system.
2 Fax the report to him (your lecturer will give you details of phone numbers).
3 Download and print out a file from a remote information service (this might be a Web page, something from Compuserve or America On Line – ask your lecturer for details).

Assignment A4.3

This assignment covers the portfolio evidence for Element 4.3, and also the following key skill elements:

Communication 2.2:   Produce written material
Information Technology 2.4:   Evaluate the use of IT

Write a report on networks from the notes you have made throughout this Element on the following areas:
- types of networks and services
- benefits of network use
- network components
- network topologies
- security requirements.

Assignment A4.4

This assignment provides portfolio evidence for Element 4.4.

Your lecturer will make a Record of Observation of you doing the following:
1 Logging on to the network with your password.
2 Creating a sub-directory.
3 Deleting old files.
4 Loading a word processor from the network, writing a document, saving it and printing it out.
5 Loading a spreadsheet from the network, entering some data, saving it and printing it out.

CHAPTER 5

Introduction to software development

Element 5.1: Explore software production
Element 5.2: Design a program from a given specification
Element 5.3: Produce a program from a given program design

What is covered in this chapter

- The stages in the software development life cycle
- Software testing
- Program development documentation
- The features of procedural programming languages
- Program design from a specification
- Program production from a design

You will need the following resources for your portfolio:
- The systems life cycle you will draw in Activity 5.2
- Notes of program development from Activity 5.6
- Notes on program development document from Activity 5.7
- The explanation of programming language features from Activity 5.8
- Assignment A5.2
- Assignment A5.3

Introduction

You saw in Chapter 1 that the **hardware** of a computer system, the electronic machinery, does nothing by itself. It is the **software**, the many coded instructions, that tells the computer what actions to carry out.

This unit studies how software programs are made. You will learn about programming languages, how to design a program from what a user wants, and how programs are actually written and tested. As part of this you will design and produce a software package for yourself. The unit has three elements. The first element looks at the principles behind writing software, programming languages and documentation. You will then put these ideas into practice – by designing a program in the second element, and producing it in the third.

Element 5.1: Explore software production

Introduction

This element covers the 'theory' of producing programs. It looks at the various stages in producing a program to meet a user's needs, the documentation involved, and the features of typical programming languages.

Hardware and software

Computer systems are made up of hardware (keyboards, VDUs, disk drives etc.) and software. Software is a series of instructions to the computer and stored on disk. The macro you produced in Unit 1 is a simple piece of software.

In Element 1.2 you saw that software is usually classified into two types – systems software and applications software. **Systems software** are the programs that make the computer work, controlling disk drives, keyboards, memory and so on. The operating system (MS-DOS, Windows, UNIX, MacOS etc.) is systems software. **Applications software** carries out tasks to meet the needs of the users in the real world, such as looking after stock control in a supermarket, keeping track of bank account balances, and storing medical records in a hospital.

Activity 5.1

Make up and complete a table of the software packages available for the computer systems you use.

Title of package	Purpose	Systems or applications software?

Life cycles

The **life cycle** of a piece of software describes the stages it goes through, from initial design to production to replacement by another version. Living things have life cycles – they are born, they grow up, and eventually they grow old and die. The same is true for software packages. A program is produced and put on sale. Users buy it and use it. After a while (usually a few years) a new version of the old package is brought out, or a completely new product is released. Users start to use this new program, and so the cycle continues.

Why do software packages have limited lives? Buying a new version costs money, and people do not usually spend money without good reason. There are a number of reasons why a program does not last forever:

- *Improved versions are produced.* A package may be used by millions of people, but after a while it will be clear that it contains **bugs** (faults) or lacks useful features. As a result the package will be partly or wholly rewritten, and released with a new version number.
- *Improved hardware is produced.* This is often a faster processor – for example a series of microprocessor chips has been developed for IBM-compatible PCs – the 286, 386, 486, Pentium. New versions of software are often needed to make full use of a faster processor.
- *Systems software improves.* For example, the systems software on IBM-compatible PCs has progressed from MS-DOS to Windows and then to Windows 95, and this development is likely to continue. The systems software becomes easier to use, runs faster or has fewer bugs. Usually applications programs have to be rewritten to run on a new operating system.
- *New user needs develop,* especially for bespoke software, where a package is written just for one customer. For example, software could be written for an

137

airline to use to schedule flights and book seats. That airline might then set up an alliance to cooperate with another company, and they might want to book passengers on the other company's flights if their planes were full. The software would have to be rewritten so that they could do this.

Activity 5.2

1 Find out the name of the operating system used by the college computers, and its version number (probably the easiest way would be to ask your lecturers).
2 By using reference books and software manuals, find out the date that Version 1.0 of this operating system was released, and try to identify some of the differences between it and the current version.

The development life cycle

Writing a program is only one step in the overall process of producing a new package. Usually a team of people have to work through several stages, and we will look at these in the following sections. These stages may themselves be split into steps. Table 5.1 summarises the process.

Table 5.1 The process of developing new software

Initial study	A study to gather background information and decide whether to progress further
Systems design	Finding out the data involved in the system, and how it needs to be processed
Program development	The programs needed are written
Implementation	The programs are installed on the hardware and the system started up
Maintenance	Any problems arising as the system is used are fixed. The way the system is working is reviewed continually, and eventually a decision is made to develop a new one

Activity 5.2

1 Look at the life cycle diagram in Figure 5.1 and decide which of the following stages should go into which box:

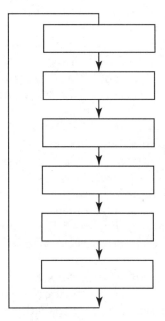

Figure 5.1

- program development
- maintenance
- initial study
- system design
- implementation
- review and start new version

2 Copy the diagram, titling it 'Systems Life Cycle', and complete it. Keep the completed version for your portfolio.

Initial study

This is the first step. The main idea at this point is to avoid wasting money, which will happen if the project is abandoned at a later stage. An outline of the users' needs is drawn up, an estimate is made of how long it will take to produce the final package, and the cost estimated. This gives an indication of whether it is a good idea to go ahead on the project, and an idea of what will be involved.

System design

At this stage an overall design for the system is produced. There are two important decisions to be made at this point.

- The data needed in the system – names and addresses of people involved, dates when things happened, amounts of money involved? Usually data will be included only if it is essential. One way to decide whether the data is essential is to try to foresee what might happen if something is not known – if it is likely to cause problems later on, then the information is essential.
- What kinds of data processing are likely to be needed? For example:
  - How is data going to be captured? Examples of data capture are reading a barcode, writing on a questionnaire and later entering it through a keyboard, or reading a magnetic strip as on a credit card.
  - How will the data be stored? Data is often stored in a file, and retrieved when it is needed. On PCs data is usually stored on a disk.
  - How is data to be moved around? Data often needs to be moved, sometimes very small distances, such as from one part of the computer's memory to another, sometimes from one machine to another.
  - What sort of output is required? Usually reports are needed, on a printer or screen.
  - Are any calculations to be carried out on the data?

Activity 5.4

A college library lends books to students. Students can borrow up to five books at a time, for up to three weeks each and can reserve books. Which of the following are essential data items for this system?

- The date a book is borrowed
- The librarian's home telephone number
- The number of pages in each book
- The titles and authors of the books in the library
- Whether a person is a student at the college
- A student's date of birth
- Today's date

- Whether the student has passed their driving test
- The date a book is returned
- How tall the librarians are
- The name of the student who borrows each book

Program development

Once the processing needed has been decided on, it is possible to go on to produce the software. This involves the following steps:
- program specification
- program design
- coding
- testing and debugging.

Program specification This sets out clearly *what* the program must do (rather than *how* it will do it). The specification will cover:
- the purpose of the program
- the data that needs to be input into the system and how it will be input – through the keyboard, a mouse, a barcode reader or other method
- the information the system will output – it does not matter at this stage how the data comes out, just what the output data is
- the processing needed – what must be done to the data entered
- any constraints (special requirements) on the system – it might have to run on a particular operating system, may be limited in the amount of memory it can take up or run at a particular speed, for example.

Activity 5.5

The program specification given below is for a program to convert yards, feet and inches into metres. However, it is incomplete. Complete the specification.

Purpose:	Convert yards, feet and inches into metric lengths
Input:	How many yards, … and … the length is
Output:	…
Processing:	Convert the length into metric
Constraints:	Must be a Windows program, and be very easy to use

Program design The program design follows on from the specification, and covers in more detail how the requirements will be met. The following aspects must be covered.
- The way the data will be input – whether to use a keyboard, a mouse, a scanner or other device.
- Decisions must also be taken about the way the user will input commands to the system – how the user interface will work. This could be in the form of a command line, a set of menus or a GUI. This might be part of the operating system (as in Windows) or the software may need to be written specially.
- The program specification spells out what data must be output, but the design must include the peripheral devices to be used and the format needed for output. For example, if a table is to be printed out, what order of rows and columns will be used?
- How the data will be stored – in RAM, for use while a program is running (in which case it will be lost after the program ends, since the memory will then be used to store other data) or on disk for use at a later date.
- The processing required – what the software needs to do with the data.

Examples are to look something up in a file (such as to find out if a borrower is really a member of the library), to compare data (to check a borrower has not borrowed more books than is allowed at one time) or to do some arithmetic (such as multiplying the fine per week by the number of weeks the book is overdue).

- The algorithms to use. An **algorithm** is a method of doing something. For example, it is often necessary to sort data into order – and the computer must be told in the program how to do it. There are many different sorting algorithms, and the program designer must know which method is most appropriate to use.

Activity 5.6

Figure 5.2 shows Media Player, Microsoft's Windows program for playing audio CDs on computers with a CD drive and a sound card. A number of other useful facilities could be added, such as to allow the user to go forward to the start of the next track, or back to the start of the previous track. Try to improve the design of this program as shown in the window.

Figure 5.2

Coding 'Coding' a program means actually writing it in the programming language chosen. The programmer uses a **text editor** to enter the program lines and stores the resulting program disk. Most programs contain many thousands of lines of code and wherever possible the coder uses parts of old programs that are already written. A large program may be written by a team of programmers working together rather than just one person.

Testing Testing the software means finding the mistakes in it. Designing and writing software is very difficult, and often the first design is wrong, or the coding is incorrect. This results in **bugs** in the software which cause it to go wrong. The bugs might simply be small, irritating problems that make the program difficult to use or they may be major flaws which make it unusable.

Activity 5.7

What bugs have you come across in the software you usually use?

Testing the design The program may have been designed badly. For example, Figure 5.3 shows the window of a program designed to convert temperatures from Fahrenheit to Celsius, and vice versa. A little thought shows that this program has two problems – there is no way for the user to choose whether they are changing from Fahrenheit to Celsius or the other way round, and there is no easy way of ending the program.

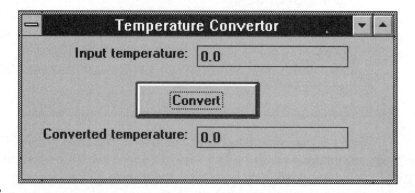

Figure 5.3

Activity 5.8

Re-design the program shown in Figure 5.3, removing these two problems.

Testing the coding Even in a well designed program bugs will appear because of errors in the program code. A **test plan** should be devised before the program is written, and then run on the program to find any bugs.

The test plan Before the program is written, a test plan should be compiled. This looks ahead to the finished program, and from the program design shows what 'should' happen in various circumstances. The test plan might take the form of a table with three columns. The first column in the table contains data the user might enter, or the input options they might choose. The second column shows what the program should do – perhaps worked out with a calculator. The third column is left blank until the program is tested, when what the program really does is entered.

For example, the user interface for a program to convert French Francs into Sterling might look like the one in Figure 5.4. If there are 7 Francs to the Pound,

Figure 5.4

the algorithm used by the program would be simply to divide the number of Francs by 7. A sample test plan for this program is shown in Table 5.2.

Table 5.2 Test plan for the program in Figure 5.4

User input	Expected output	Actual output
Francs = 7	£1	
Francs = 14	£2	
Francs = 17.5	£2.50	
Francs = Fred	'Invalid input'	
Francs = 0	£0	
Click 'close' button	Program ends	

The user input should be chosen to cover the following cases:
- Normal simple input (whole numbers such as 7 or 14 Francs giving £1 or £2).
- More complicated input (such as 17.5 Francs giving £2.50)
- The largest or smallest inputs allowed (e.g. 0 Francs).
- Input which is not allowed (such as a word rather than a number) should produce an error message (such as 'invalid input').
- All user actions (such as clicking the 'close' button).

Activity 5.9

The program used in the example above would not work if the exchange rate altered from 7 Francs to the Pound.
1 Alter the program design so that the user can change the exchange rate as necessary.
2 Draw up a test plan for the new program.

Debugging Once the program has been written, the test plan is carried out. If possible, small sections of program should be tested separately as they are completed – this will help to pick up errors and correct them as the program is developed. Data is inputted as planned, and the actual output compared with what is expected. If the output differs from the expected output there is a bug.

If a bug is found, the programmer must
- hunt down the bug in the program code
- find out why the code is wrong and
- correct the code.

The test plan must then be run again, to be sure that the fix has corrected the problem – and to check that the fix hasn't introduced any more problems.

Activity 5.10

Make your own notes on the stages of program development and keep them for your portfolio.

Implementation

Implementation means actually setting up the information system as planned. To do this
- any new hardware (computers, printers, phone lines and so on) must be bought and set up

- software must be written (or bought), tested, and installed
- data must be set up in the correct format
- any paper-based forms must be designed and copied
- users must be trained in the new procedures.

Maintenance

Once it has been implemented the system must be maintained in working order. Maintenance includes

- making small alterations to software as bugs are found
- contacting the suppliers of any bought-in software to sort out any problems caused by their product
- altering any data that has been corrupted in storage
- training new users
- fixing any problems with hardware – from little things like replacing the printer cartridge to big problems like a PC failing.

As the demands on the system increase, a point will be reached at which so many problems arise that the system is no longer workable. At this point a new system must be designed – and the systems life cycle begins again.

Program development documents

Documenting the development means writing down on paper the ideas, designs, plans, rules etc. The usual documents follow the steps in program development:

- Program specification – what the program needs to do, in terms of input, output, processing and constraints.
- Program design – how the program will meet the requirements in the specification.
- Listing of program code – a copy of the actual instructions in the program. It will usually include comments and variables – there are listings of small programs on pages 146 and 147.
- Test plan.
- Test results. These develop from the test plan.
- User instructions – the User Manual. This will have information on:
  - the sort of hardware needed
  - how to install the software
  - how data should be entered
  - the various processing options and how the user can use them
  - what the error messages mean and the actions that should be taken if one occurs.

Activity 5.11

Make your own notes on program development documents. Keep them for your portfolio.

Features of programming languages

A programming language is a special language in which computer programs are written. Many different programming languages are used – examples are Basic, FORTRAN, COBOL, Pascal, C and C++ (pronounced 'C plus plus').

In this element you will need to develop an understanding of the features of programming languages, and be able to give examples in one language. In

Element 5.3 you will develop your own piece of software, in the programming language in use at your college. This means you must become familiar with that language, and give examples in it. In this section, the language chosen is Pascal.

Exact syntax

Many programming languages use English words, like REPEAT, IF, INPUT. This does *not* mean that computers can understand English – in fact they cannot understand anything. A program is just a set of instructions telling the computer what to do. But you cannot write a program simply by writing down what to do in English – the computer is not intelligent enough to cope with this.

Programming languages have strict **syntax**. Syntax means the rules of grammar. English has strict rules of grammar in English – for example, it is incorrect to say 'The dogs is dangerous' (it should be 'The dogs *are* dangerous'). But if you break the rules of English, people can usually still understand what you are saying. It is different in programming – if you break the syntax rules of the language, the computer will not understand your program.

User interface

The user interface is the software the programmer uses when he or she is writing the program. In this situation, the programmer is the 'user'. The most obvious part of this is the **editor**, which is just like a word processor – in fact, a word processor can be used as a program editor. Through the user interface the programmer will access the **compiler**. A compiler is a piece of software which translates programs from one language into another. A computer can only carry out one particular language, called 'machine code.' The compiler must translate the program from the language it has been written in into machine code before it can be run. Short programs can be compiled very quickly on modern computers. Often the interface has the menu option 'Run', which appears to run the program straight away. In fact, it compiles the program first, but so quickly that it is not noticed.

The first version of a program nearly always has bugs in it. **Debugging software** is used to help the programmer find and remove these bugs. Sometimes the program will not even run, because the compiler cannot compile it. This produces an error message, telling the programmer what is wrong, and so fixing this is not too difficult. It is more difficult to fix problems when the program runs but goes wrong – when the output is different from the expected output. In this situation it may help to use the debugger to **single-step** through the program. In single-stepping the programmer controls the speed of the running program, making it carry out only one instruction at a time, and watching how things change.

Data storage in memory – variables

Almost all programs have to hold data in memory. Using a **variable** the programmer can reserve part of the computer's memory, store different values into it, and call those values back. As a simple example, suppose we want to write a program which will let the user type in two numbers, will add them together, and will show the result on the screen. This can be done using three variables. The two numbers entered by the user could be stored in two variables, which we could call x and y. The sum of the two is stored in a third variable, which we could call z. Finally the value of z is be output on the VDU. This process is shown in Figure 5.5.

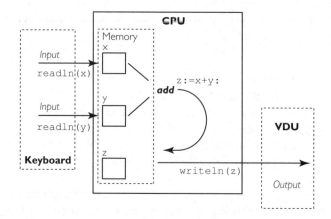

Figure 5.5

Here is a program in Pascal which will do this:

```
Program addprog;
var x,y,z: integer;
begin
readln(x);
readln(y);
z := x + y;
writeln(z);
end.
```

The line by line explanation of this is as follows:

Program line	Explanation
`Program addprog;`	The program title – it is called addprog
`var x,y,z: integer;`	This tells the computer that this program uses three variables called x, y and z, and that they will be whole numbers (integers). The computer would put aside enough memory to hold three integers.
`begin`	Marks the beginning of the program
`readln(x);`	Inputs a whole number (from the keyboard) and stores it in memory at the place called x
`readln(y);`	Reads in another number and stores it at y
`z := x + y;`	This tells the computer to add x and y, and to store the result in the memory `location z`
`writeln(z);`	This is an output instruction, telling the computer to output (on the screen) the number stored in location z
`end.`	Marks the end of the program

The next section will describe the ways various actions are dealt with in Pascal.

Input

Any kind of data may be read (input) into the computer, through any input peripheral – such as a mouse, a barcode reader or a light pen. Data is most commonly input through the keyboard. The instruction in Pascal

```
readln(v);
```

reads in a value from the keyboard and stores it in memory, in the variable called v.

Output

Output is the data the computer sends out, through a printer, screen or other output peripheral. This data could be in any form, such as a number, a word or a picture. In Pascal the output instruction

```
writeln(v);
```

displays the value of the variable *v* on the screen.

Mathematics

In Pascal, the computer is instructed to do arithmetic in a way very similar to normal mathematics, except that the asterisk (*) is used for multiplication, and the solidus (/) is used for division. Brackets might be needed to make the computer do one piece of arithmetic before another. The computer will carry out the instruction in brackets first. For example, suppose we want the computer to find the average of two numbers *a* and *b*. We must tell the computer to first add them up and then divide the result by two. In Pascal this instruction would be:

```
average := (a+b)/2;
```

String handling

String handling means inputting strings from the keyboard, outputting them on the screen or printer and processing them in various ways. A **string** is a series of characters, such as a word or a sentence. Characters are anything on the keyboard – letters of the alphabet, numbers, punctuation marks and spaces. Characters stored in a computer are coded into numbers – a common code is called ASCII. In Pascal, the function 'chr' gives the character with a certain code number. For example, the character 'A' has the ASCII code 65, 'B' is 66 and so on. A program in Pascal to read in a number from the keyboard then output the corresponding character, is

```
Program codes;
Var x: integer;
begin
readln(x)
writeln(chr(x));
end.
```

Data types

In a computer all data is stored as streams of ones and zeroes – integers (whole numbers), numbers with decimal places (sometimes called **floating point numbers** in computing), sounds and pictures (bitmaps).

Number In Pascal there are two types of numbers – integers and numbers with decimal fractions (these are called **real numbers**).

Character The character data type in Pascal is called char. For example,

```
Var
i: integer;
r: real;
c: char;
```

tells the computer there will be three variables in a program, called i, r and c, and that i will be an integer, r will be a number with decimals, and c will be a character.

Control structures

Control structures let the programmer control which program instructions the computer will carry out, and how many times. In this element you must study three control structures – **iteration**, **selection** and **subroutine calls**.

Iteration Iteration means repeating – doing something several times. In a program this is shown as a **loop**. In a loop some instructions are carried out, then the program goes back to the start and does them again a certain number of times. One kind of iteration in Pascal is called a *for* loop. For example, a program to display 'Hello' on the screen 50 times would look like this:

```
Program hellos;
Var counter: integer;
Begin
for counter:= 1 to 50 do
        writeln ('Hello');
End.
```

Selection Selection occurs when there are two alternative parts of the program, and the computer takes a logical decision to follow one route or the other depending on data input when the program runs. In Pascal this is controlled by the word *if*. For example, the program below reads in a number from the keyboard, and if it is less than 50 it displays 'small', otherwise it displays 'large'.

Program code	Explanation
`Program condition;`	The program title
`Var x:integer;`	It will use one variable, called x
`Begin`	Begin the program
`readln(x);`	Input a value for x
`if x<50 then`	If it is less than 50, then …
`writeln ('Small')`	Display the word Small
`else`	but if it is not …
`writeln ('Large');`	Display the word Large
`end.`	The end of the program

Subroutines A subroutine is a part of a program. Very large programs with many instructions are very difficult to program correctly. It is better to split up large program into smaller sections, which can be dealt with more easily. These small sections are called **subroutines**, or **procedures** in Pascal and many other languages. The computer will start at the beginning of the main program, and continue normally until a subroutine 'call' is reached. The computer then branches to the subroutine and follows the instructions in it. At the end of the subroutine, it returns to the main program and carries on. This is summarised in Figure 5.6.

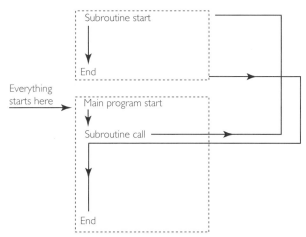

Figure 5.6 Using subroutines

Subroutines in Pascal In Pascal a subroutine is known as a procedure. The procedure is written as a small program, like this:

```
Procedure name;        The procedure title
begin                  The start
    ...                What to do in the procedure
end;                   The end
```

The procedures come before the main program. To call the procedure, which means to make it run, the programmer simply writes the name of the procedure. For example, if you have written a procedure called *getdata*, then to make it happen you simply write:

```
.....
getdata;
.....
```

in the main program at the place you want the subroutine to run.

As an example, here is a program with three procedures. The program inputs two numbers, puts them into order, and then outputs them. The first procedure is called *getdata*, and it inputs the two numbers. The second procedure is called *order*, and it puts them into order, smallest first, using an *if*. The third procedure is called *showresult*, and it outputs the numbers. Variables *x* and *y* are the two input numbers, and *small* and *big* are the numbers put into order. All you will write in the main program is:

```
begin
getdata;
order;
showresult;
end.
```

since it just calls the three procedures. Here is the whole program:

```
program procs;

var x,y,big,small: integer;

Procedure getdata;
begin
```

```
writeln('Enter two numbers');
readln(x);
readln(y);
end;

Procedure order;
begin
if x>y then
      begin
      big:=x;
      small:=y;
      end
else
      begin
      big:=y;
      small:=x;
      end;
end;

Procedure showresult;
begin
writeln('In increasing order the numbers are');
writeln(small);
writeln('and');
writeln(big);
end;

begin
getdata;
order;
showresult;
end.
```

User interface

Here the user means the programmer, not the person who will use the program. The user interface has several parts. The editor lets the programmer type in the lines of program, and save them to disk. The editor must have basic features – entering text, deleting mistakes and correcting them – and usually also allows block deletes, copy and move, search and replace. A **debugger** helps the programmer to find bugs in the program. It does this by allowing the programmer to carry out the program one line at a time, checking the flow of execution and seeing what happens after every step. Translating code usually means using a compiler. On a DOS-based machine the programmer saves his or her work in Pascal into a file with the extension .pas, such as procs.pas. The compiler translates this into a program in machine code, called procs.exe. When the program is run, the program procs.exe is actually the one that is executed. Most modern systems possess an **integrated development environment** (IDE). This has an editor, debugger and interface to a compiler on one screen.

Activity 5.12 ───

Make notes on the features of the programming language you will use – either Pascal or the language you use at your college. To cover the range, use the following headings:
• Control – iteration, selection, subroutines

- Data types – number, character
- Functions – mathematics, string, input, output
- User interface – editor, debugger, compiler

Element 5.2: Design a program from a given specification

Introduction

In this element you will put into practice the features of program design covered in Element 5.1 by producing a report. This report will include the design for a program, covering the purpose of the program, input and output designs, a data dictionary and a definition of how the data will be processed. The program specification will be given to you.

Design documentation

Design documentation needs to include the following items.

Program specification
This details what the program should do. The program specification will be given to you.

Input and output designs
The input design should show what data the user will need to input and what the user interface will look like. This will depend on the operating system you will be using – a GUI or a character-based interface. The output design will show how the results of the program will be output. In a GUI you might get input and output through the same window.

A data dictionary
A data dictionary shows the data that will be used in the program. It should be in the form of a table, with headings to indicate what the data means, the name of the variable in the program, what data type it is, and what the correct values of the data are. There is an example in the next section.

Processing definition
This should say how the input data will be processed. Some of the processing will be arithmetic, and you should show the formulas that will be used to calculate results. You must also show the **constructs** you are using – selections (usually these will be *if* statements) or iterations (loops and repeats, using *for ... next* or other loops). In a GUI like Windows, selection might be done by the user deciding which button to click, and iteration by allowing the user to do so several times before clicking the 'close' button. The processing definition could be in the form of diagrams, as in the example in the next section.

Sample report – a payroll system

This section includes a program specification as it might be given to you. It then shows how you could go on to produce the other parts of the report.

Program specification – payroll
Purpose: to calculate the details for a payslip, showing gross pay, deductions and net pay.
Input: The number of hours worked, and the rate of pay per hour.

Processing

Gross pay means the amount earned before any deductions (income tax, national insurance contributions, pension contributions, etc.) are taken into account. If the person does not earn very much (perhaps he or she has a part-time job) the deductions are small or even nothing. *Net* pay is the amount the person actually receives. The processing in this program is slightly simpler than how it is really done.

Gross pay = hours worked × rate of pay per hour.

If the gross pay is less than £30, the deductions are zero. If the gross is more than £30, income tax (22% of the gross pay) is deleted, and the national insurance contribution is 6%.

Net pay = gross pay – deductions.

Output

Gross pay, tax and national insurance deducted, and net pay.

Constraints

The program should do a payroll run for a batch of four employees. It should be able to do as many payroll runs as required. This specification would be given to you by your tutor. The next parts of the report are what you would have to produce.

Input and output design

The user interface in Windows could look like the one shown in Figure 5.7.

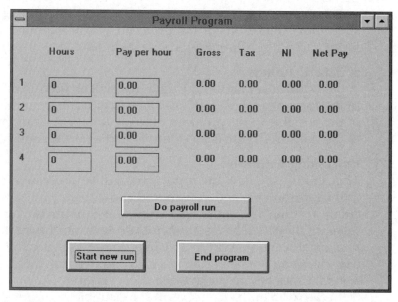

Figure 5.7 A sample user interface

The user would enter the hours and rates of pay for four employees, then click the 'Do payroll run' button. If they click the 'Start new run' button, the screen will return everything to zero. The user can continue until they click the 'End program' button.

If a character interface is used instead of Windows the following dialogue might be seen.

```
Employee 1 - enter hours worked ...
```

which the user would input, then

```
Enter rate of pay …
```

which the user would input. Then the computer would output

```
Employee 1 - gross pay = … tax = …
```

and so on. This would repeat for the other three employees, then the computer would output:

```
Another run? (y/n)
```

and this would repeat if the user entered 'y'.

Data dictionary

The data dictionary should be a four-column table, as shown in Table 5.3. The description should explain the purpose of the data, or what it represents. The name in the program should be the actual variable name which corresponds to this. The type means what type of data it is – 'real' means a number with a decimal fraction, needed to show amounts of money in pounds and pence like £34.80; an integer is a whole number. The constraints are any limits on the allowable values for the data.

Table 5.3 A sample data dictionary

Description	Name in program	Data type	Constraints
Hours worked	Hours	Real	
Rate of pay	Rate	Real	
Gross pay	gross	Real	
Income tax	tax	Real	
National insurance	ni	Real	
Net pay	net	Real	
Count of employees	n	Integer	Counts up to four
Users reply to 'another run'	reply	Character	y or n

Processing

Figure 5.8 shows the overall processing. The calculation is carried out for four employees, and so is an iteration. The payroll run may be repeated several times, so is another iteration.

One selection is made according to whether the user replies 'yes' when asked if they want another run. There is another selection in the calculation of the pay details, since the deductions depend on whether the gross pay is over £30. This is shown in Figure 5.9.

The rest of this section gives program specifications taken from business and science which you could use for more practice – or you could choose on as the basis of the report for your portfolio.

Currency conversion

Purpose

To change one currency (pounds sterling) into another (US dollars). This is what might be done at a bank or a Bureau de Change.

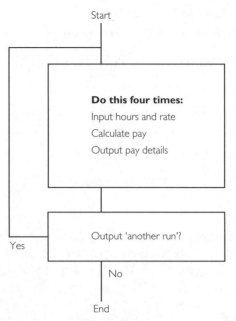

Figure 5.8 Overall processing for the payroll program

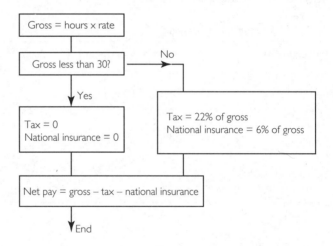

Figure 5.9

Input
Amount of money in pounds, and the current conversion rate (pounds to dollars).

Output
The amount of money in US dollars.

Processing
The amount in dollars is the amount in pounds × the conversion rate (at the time of writing £1 = $1.55, but check the current rate before you do the calculation). A commission is charged, either $5 or 1% of the total, whichever is greater. The amount given in dollars should be shown less this commission.

Constraints
The program should convert a batch of four amounts. The user should be able to do as many batches as needed.

Estimation

Purpose
This program is to be used by a small business (such as a plumber). Someone offers them a job to do, and they need to produce a quote of how much the job will cost. The program must calculate the total cost from the details.

Input
A description of each item needed for the job (such as 'double radiator'), its cost, and the amount of each item needed.

Output
The total amount to be charged for the job.

Processing
The cost of each item = number required × cost. These costs should be added up. To give a reasonable profit margin, £50 or 5% should be added to this total, whichever is the greater.

Constraints
The program should cope with five items per job. The user should be able to do as many jobs as needed in one program run.

Mortgage calculator

Purpose
To be used to find how many years would be needed to repay a mortgage on a house.

Input
The rate of interest, the annual repayment, and the amount borrowed.

Output
The amount left owing at the end of each year, and the number of years remaining before the mortgage is paid off.

Processing
For each year,

Interest = amount outstanding × rate of interest.
Amount outstanding at the end of the year = amount at start + interest − repayment.

This continues every year until the amount outstanding falls to zero.

Constraints
If the annual repayment is less than the annual interest, the mortgage would never be repaid – and the program should say this. The program should do as many mortgage calculations as are required.

Break-even analysis

Purpose
To work out how much business you have to do before you start to make a profit. If you do not sell very much, you will receive less in sales income than you spend in keeping the business running. If you sell a lot, your income should exceed your expenses.

There are two kinds of costs. *Fixed* costs do not depend on how much business you do – such as the rent. *Variable* costs are the cost of making each item.

Income is how much you get for selling each item. You start to make a profit when your income is bigger than your costs.

Input
The fixed cost, the variable cost per item, and the income per item.

Output
The number of items to be sold before you make a profit.

Processing
The idea of this is to work out the profit for selling 0, 10, 20 items and so on. We stop when the profit is more than zero.

Set number sold = 0
repeat
    increase number sold by 10
    calculate:
      income = sales per item × number sold
      costs = fixed cost + manufacture cost per item ×
        number sold
      profit = income − costs
until profit is greater than 0

Constraints
The program should do as many break-even analyses as needed.

Sales invoice

Purpose
The program will calculate an invoice for a customer who has bout something by mail order.

Input
A description of each item on the invoice (e.g. 'T shirt medium blue'), a unit price (price of each item) and the quantity sold.

Output
The total amount due.

Processing
For each item, cost = unit cost × quantity.
   The cost of all items should be added up. VAT should be added at 17.5%. Postage and packing is charged at £2 or 5%, whichever is greater.
   Overall cost = total cost of all items + VAT + postage and packing.

Constraints
The program should cope with five items on an invoice. It should do as many invoices as needed.

Temperature conversion

Purpose
The program should change temperatures measured in Fahrenheit to Celsius, and vice versa.

Input
The temperature in degrees on one scale.

Output
The same temperature on the other scale.

Processing
Fahrenheit = Celsius $\times$ (9/5) + 32
Celsius = (Fahrenheit $-$ 32) $\times$ (5/9)

Constraints
The user should be able to control which scale is being converted to which. The program should convert as many temperatures as required.

Ohm's law

Purpose
Ohm's law states that, in an electrical circuit

$$V = IR$$

where V = voltage, I = current and R = resistance
A program is needed to calculate V given values for I and R or to find R from values of V and I ($R = V/I$).

Input
Two quantities (I and R or V and I).

Output
The third quantity (V or R).

Processing
The calculation is $V = IR$ or $R = V/I$.

Constraints
The user should be able to choose to find either V or R. The program should do as many calculations as are needed.

Height of projectile

Purpose
If a projectile (such as a cannon ball) is fired vertically into the air, its maximum height in metres, h, is given by the formula

$$h = \frac{v^2}{2g}$$

where v is its initial speed in metres/second, and g is the acceleration due to gravity, 9.81 metres/second^2. The program should calculate h given v.

Input
The initial speed v.

Output
The height reached.

Processing
The calculation would be written in BASIC like this:

```
h = v*v/(2*g)
```

Constraints
The initial speed v must be greater than 0 – if the user enters a negative value,

the program should give a suitable error message. The program should deal with as many calculations as are required.

Element 5.3: Produce a program from a given design

Introduction

In this element you will write the program designed in the previous element. You need to produce the following documentation:
- program listing
- test plan
- results of testing
- user instructions.

Program documentation

Program code listing

The program listing is a printout the lines of program code written in a high-level language such as BASIC or Pascal. The main program and any subroutines used should all be listed, and it should be clear how the program is structured.

Test plan

The test plan should show what test data you intend to enter, and what output you expect as a result. You will probably have to use a calculator to work out the results the program should produce. There is an example of how the test plan is drawn up in Element 5.1.

Results of testing

This should show what the program actually does.

User instructions

These are what you would expect to find in a user manual if you bought a software package. The user instructions should be divided into three sections:
- how to start the program
- how to use the program, giving examples of the program in use
- error handling – what sort of errors might occur, and what the user should do in response to error messages.

The program on payroll designed in Element 5.2 will be produced here as an example. The language used will be Pascal and the program will be written for a character-based user interface.

Program example – payroll

Introduction

This program is intended to do payroll calculations for a batch of four employees, repeated as needed. The program was designed in Element 5.2

Program listing

Most languages let you put **comments** into the program. Comments are notes about how the program works, which part does what, explanations and so on. In Pascal comments are enclosed in curly brackets {like this}, and these are used in this listing.

```
program payroll;   {the program header}

{The next section declares the variables that will be used. This
is the same as in the data dictionary in the design}

var hours, rate, gross,tax,ni,net:real;
    n:integer;
    reply:char;

begin {start the program }
repeat  {start a loop for repeated runs }
    for n:=1 to 4 do    {count 4 employees in one batch }
      begin
      writeln('Employee number',n); {output which employee}
      writeln('Enter hours worked');
      readln(hours);     {input hours worked}
      writeln('Enter rate of pay per hour');
      readln(rate);      {input rate}

      gross:=hours*rate;{find gross pay}
      if gross<30.00 then      {if less than 30}
        begin
        tax:=0.00;         {tax and ni zero}
        ni:=0.00;
        end
      else
        begin
        tax:=0.22*gross;       {else tax is 22%}
        ni:=0.06*gross; {and ni 6% }
      end;

      net:=gross-tax-ni;{calculate net pay}
      writeln('Payslip. … '); {output results}
      writeln('Gross = ',gross:6:2);{use 2 decimal places}
      writeln('Tax = ',tax:6:2);
      writeln('NI = ',ni:6:2);
      writeln('Net pay = ',net:6:2);
      writeln('_____');
    end; {end this batch of 4}
    writeln('Another run of 4? (y/n)');
    readln(reply);{do another batch?}
until reply='n';   {stop if say no}
end.      {end the program}
```

Test plan
These outputs have been worked out with a calculator:

Inputs		Expected output			
Hours	Rate	Gross pay	NI	Tax	Net pay
0	0	0	0	0	0
2	5	10	0	0	10
10	10	100	6	22	76
20	2	40	2.40	8.80	28.80

Test results

Using the inputs in the test plan, the actual output from the program is given below (if possible you should put actual printouts in your portfolio).

```
Employee number 1
Enter hours worked
0
Enter rate of pay per hour
0
Payslip …
Gross = 0.00
Tax = 0.00
NI = 0.00
Net pay = 0.00

_____

Employee number 2
Enter hours worked
2
Enter rate of pay per hour
5
Payslip …
Gross = 10.00
Tax = 0.00
NI = 0.00
Net pay = 10.00

_____

Employee number 3
Enter hours worked
10
Enter rate of pay per hour
10
Payslip …
Gross = 100.00
Tax = 22.00
NI = 6.00
Net pay = 72.00

_____

Employee number 4
Enter hours worked
20
Enter rate of pay per hour
2
Payslip …
Gross = 40.00
Tax = 8.80
NI = 2.40
Net pay = 28.80

_____
```

The actual output agrees with the expected results.

User instructions

Congratulations on purchasing STP Payroll, the miracle breakthrough software package from STP! It will solve all your payroll problems, and is very easy to use, as this manual shows ...

Program loading This is a DOS program, stored on disk in a file called payroll.exe. To run the program, you need to be in DOS, in the directory containing the program. Simply type in the name of the program. For example, if the program is on drive c: you would type

```
c:\>payroll
```

Examples of use

The program will ask for the hours worked and rates of pay. These should be entered through the keyboard, finishing each with 'Enter'. The computer will then output the gross pay, tax, national insurance and net pay. After four employees, the computer will ask whether you wish to do another run. Entering anything other than 'n' will result in another batch of four payslips.

Here is an example of an actual program run:

```
Employee number 1
Enter hours worked
4.5
Enter rate of pay per hour
5
Payslip ...
Gross = 22.50
Tax = 0.00
NI = 0.00
Net pay = 22.50


Employee number 2
Enter hours worked
3
Enter rate of pay per hour
3.45
Payslip ...
Gross = 10.35
Tax = 0.00
NI = 0.00
Net pay = 10.35


Employee number 3
Enter hours worked
50
Enter rate of pay per hour
3
Payslip ...
Gross = 150.00
Tax = 33.00
NI = 9.00
Net pay = 108.00
```

```
Employee number 4
Enter hours worked
3
Enter rate of pay per hour
50
Payslip …
Gross = 150.00
Tax = 33.00
NI = 9.00
Net pay = 108.00

Another run of 4? (y/n)
n
Press any key to return to Turbo Pascal
```

Error handling The only problem you are likely to come across is if you key in words rather than digits – for example:

```
Employee number 1
Enter hours worked
one
Runtime error 106 at 0000:0133.
```

Run the program again, using digits only.

Now, you can go ahead and use STP Payroll without a care in the world!

Assignment A5.1

This assignment provides evidence for Element 5.1 and for the following key skills:
Communication Element 2.2:   Produce written material

Put into your portfolio the following:
- The systems life cycle you drew in Activity 5.2.
- Your notes on program development from Activity 5.10.
- The notes on program development document you prepared for Activity 5.11.
- Explanation of programming language features (from Activity 5.12).

Assignment A5.2

This assignment provides the evidence for Element 5.2, and the following key skills:
Application of Number 2.2:   Tackle problems
Communication 2.2:   Produce written material
Communication 2.3:   Use images

Choose one of the program specifications given in Element 5.2 (or one given to you by your lecturer) and produce a design for the program. Your design should contain the following sections:

1 The specification as given to you.
2 Input and output designs – the user interface.
3 A data dictionary – a table as shown in Element 5.2.
4 Processing definition – using diagrams as in the examples shown.

Bear in mind that you will have to implement this design (that is, write the program) in Assignment A5.3.

Assignment A5.3

This assignment covers evidence for Element 5.3, and also for the following key skills:

Application of number Element 2.2: Tackle problems
Communication Element 2.2: Produce written material

Following the design you worked out in Assignment A5.2, write the program. You must hand in documentation with the following sections:

- Program listing
- Test plan
- Results of testing
- User instructions

CHAPTER 6

Technical support (intermediate)

Element 6.1: Install a microcomputer system
Element 6.2: Undertake housekeeping duties
Element 6.3: Provide user support

What is covered in this chapter

- Stages in installing a microcomputer system
- Procedures for reporting errors
- Computer technician housekeeping duties
- Computer user support activities
- Planning and installing a microcomputer system
- Devising, carrying out and logging computer technician housekeeping duties
- Providing and logging user support activities

Resources you will need for your Technical Support file:
- Written answers to the activities in this chapter
- Written answers to the questions at the end of the chapter
- Completed Assignments A6.1, A6.2 and A6.3

Introduction

Most users of IT are not interested in the technicalities of computer hardware and software – they just want to use it as a tool. Users want a system that's easy to use. This means that

- it should start up in the program that they usually use when first switched on
- it should be easy to get to other programs that they want to use
- backing up should be automatic
- data is safe from loss or corruption
- data is safe from interference by other people.
  Users want hardware and software that works correctly. They require
- hardware that is clean and works properly
- paper and disks to be available when needed
- faults to be repaired immediately.
Users want help with hardware and software at the point of need. This includes
- help with new tasks
- help when things go wrong
- manuals are available.
The job of an IT technician is to make life easy for the user. This chapter looks at the chief tasks of a computer technician, which are

- to install new hardware and software to give the user an easy-to-use system
- to look after computer hardware, software, consumables and accessories
- support activities by helping users with hardware and software.

Element 6.1: Install a microcomputer system

Installing a microcomputer system involves
- checking the equipment
- connecting the hardware
- testing the hardware
- loading and customising the software
- testing that the software works
- testing the software with all the peripheral hardware
- handing the system over to the user.

Checking the equipment

When new equipment is delivered the first thing to do is unpack it, being careful to keep all the packing material and boxes, as they have been designed especially for the equipment, and you might need them to send back anything that's faulty.

The computer may come in one box, or may be packed as several units. The monitor, keyboard and mouse may each be separately packed. If so, each separate box will contain its own packing, manuals, guarantee and registration card. With the computer should be disks containing copies of the software needed to operate the computer (the operating system). This has probably already been installed. A new peripheral device (printer, scanner, modem, etc.) will also be provided with manuals, guarantees and any software needed to run it. However, it will probably *not* come with cables for connecting it to the hardware.

Checklist for unpacking computer hardware
1 Find the packing list.
2 Check all equipment against the packing list. If anything is missing chase it up immediately.
3 Collect manuals together.
4 Collect guarantee forms together.
5 Put all packing materials back in the boxes. These should be stored in case anything goes wrong and the equipment must be returned.
6 Read the chapter in the manual about installing the equipment.

Connecting hardware

The hardware will need connections to a power supply and other parts of the installation.

Many CPUs have both inward and outward connections for electric power, so even if the monitor is separate from the CPU, it can obtain power from the CPU.

The electric cable you will need to connect the CPU to the mains has a normal 13-amp plug at one end (Figure 6.1) and a female socket (Figure 6.2) at the other end. This type of cable is called a kettle lead and is available from any electrical or computer store. The mains lead should be supplied in the box with your CPU, or attached to the CPU. A separate VDU is often supplied with a cable with a socket at one end and a plug at the other and it can then take its power from the CPU so that both can be switched on and off together. If it is not supplied, and the VDU is separate from the CPU, you will need another kettle lead. In this case you will also need two wall sockets.

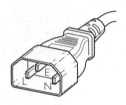

Figure 6.1 Male power plug

Figure 6.2 Female power socket

Computers work on voltages other than that supplied by the electricity board so need their own power supplies. The power supply is often built into the main processing unit so no outside connections are required. Where it comes as a separate unit – this is usual with laptop computers to keep them portable – the proper connection is required. There seems to be no standard between computer companies either as to power supply voltage or plug – so make sure that you have the correct ones with any computer that you buy.

There are several standards for connecting peripheral devices to a CPU. You can see a few plug configurations in Figure 6.3. All of these can be either male or female – and there is always the possibility of non-standard configurations, so always check the back of any CPU or peripheral device before making up or buying a lead. Most printer cables are standard for serial printers but beware if someone gives you an old printer.

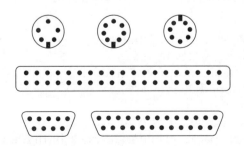

Figure 6.3 A selection of plug configurations for peripherals

Activity 6.1

1 Check out one or two of the installations in your educational establishment. List the peripherals (this should include the monitor and floppy disk drives) and draw or describe:

   a the connections between the peripheral and the computer

   b how the device receives power

   c media required for the peripheral.

2 Make a collection of catalogues and brochures describing computer peripheral devices and cables.

Checklist for installing hardware

1 Connect the computer according to the instructions in the manual using the proper cables.

2 Check that the plugs have the correct fuses.

3 Switch on the computer and monitor first.

  • A light should come on to indicate that the CPU is on, if not check the connection between the CPU and the electricity socket. If there is an external power supply, check that its light is on. A light should also come on to indicate that the monitor is on; if not check the power supply.

  • The bootstrap program should start up. This is a program which is hard wired (i.e. it is built into the computer). It is usually a self-checking program to test the computer's internal memory. Something should show on the monitor.

  • The bootstrap program probably then checks the floppy drive for an operating system: the indicator light should come show on the floppy disk drive and it will make a noise.

  • The bootstrap program then looks at the hard disk drive: the indicator light should go on and the operating system should load up. This should all show on the monitor.

Computers do differ from each other, so

IF ALL ELSE FAILS – READ THE INSTRUCTIONS!

A brand new computer that doesn't work

A new stand-alone computer which no one has ever used before will be supplied with a hard disk drive and a Windows-type operating system. If electricity is obviously coming through to the computer but it doesn't boot the internal connections might have vibrated loose in transit.

Providing this does not invalidate the guarantee, disconnect the electricity supply and take the back off the computer. Keep all the screws carefully, making a note of where they all go. Be gentle so as not to break off any small pieces of plastic. Check all the connections between internal cables and their sockets and press them together firmly. There may well be some spare ribbon cables with plugs or sockets hanging loose – don't worry about them, they are for extra drives. Do the same for chips which are not soldered in. Put the computer back together. Reconnect the electricity. Try to boot again.

If it still doesn't work ring the help line.

Ringing a help line

1 Make a note of the problem – in detail – before you pick up the telephone. Reproduce the problem and keep your notes with you. Have the telephone by your computer and keep your registration number with you.

2 Ring the number given. You may have to ring several times before getting through, and you may be on hold for some time once you are through, so be patient.

3 The operator can often talk you through a solution to your problem. If you have the computer in front of you, you can follow the instructions as given and can ask further questions if you need to without ringing up and waiting again.

Second-hand computers

Technology changes very rapidly and many organisations and individuals change computers fairly frequently. A second-hand machine can be a very good buy. Some commercial companies are prepared to give second-hand machines to charities and educational establishments.

If the second-hand microcomputer comes with an internal hard drive and a fairly modern operating system which uses standard floppy disk formats it can still be used for work. If there is no hard drive, or non-standard floppy disk drives then the machine may be fun to play with but will not be suitable for serious work. Second-hand computers which do not run Windows will need old software to run on it – and software, like hardware, goes out of date quickly. You will find it difficult to obtain support from the manufacturers for out-of-date software and hardware.

Installing a printer

If you are installing a stand-alone microcomputer, you will probably also be installing a printer.

1 Unpack the printer and put it together according to instructions in the manual.

2 Load ink, toner, printer ribbons etc. according to instructions in the manual.

3 Load paper according to instructions in the manual.

4 Plug the printer in to the mains.

5 Switch the printer on and check that the correct indicator lights are on.

6 Run the printer self-test. This should be described in the manual.

7 Connect the printer to a suitable printer port on the CPU using an appropriate printer cable.

Installing the printer driver Switching the computer on when the printer is plugged in should **initialise** the printer and it should make some sort of noise to show that the computer and printer are communicating. The printer will only work properly if the correct **printer driver** (a program which may be part of the operating system, part of a word-processing package, or may come with the printer) is installed. The printer driver allows the computer to send instructions to the printer. If a printer driver comes on disk with the printer, follow the instructions for installing it. If you have a Windows operating system and an old printer which comes without its own printer driver, find the part of Windows that lets you install new printers. How to do this is shown in Figure 6.4.

If you are using Windows 95 choose:

Start up

Settings

Printers.

In both Windows 3.1 and Windows 95 a list of printers will appear. Choose your named printer from the list. You may need the original installation disks or CD-ROM for the operating system.

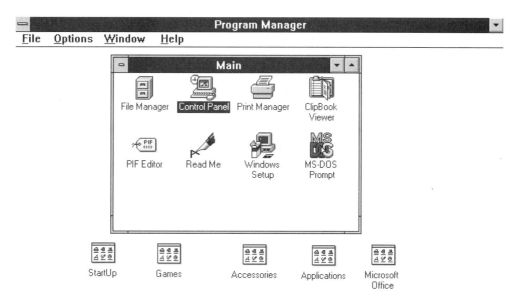

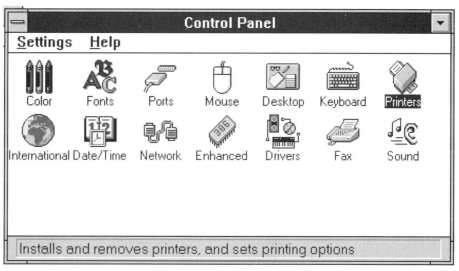

Figure 6.4 To install a printer in Windows, choose Main, Control Panel, Printers

If your operating system is MS-DOS, and you have an old printer then make a text file by typing:

```
COPY CON MARY
Mary had a little lamb
Its fleece was white as snow
^Z
```

(^z means hold the CTRL key down at the same time as pressing the key z.) This will make a text file called MARY containing the two lines of poetry that you typed in. Then type

```
PRINT MARY
```

The file should print out.

To use the printer with applications software in MS-DOS, you will have to use the printer driver that comes with your software package. You will install it either by using menus within the program or by following instructions in the manual for the program.

Activity 6.2

I Check out one or two items of application software in your educational establishment.

   a Write down the name of the software and the manufacturer.

   b Who is it licensed to, and what is the licence agreement?

   c Find the directory (or directories) on which the software is installed and list the main files.

   d Copy out the instructions for installing the software.

2 Collect copies of different software licence agreements.

Installing software

1 Unpack the software. You should be supplied with a disk or disks containing the programs, a manual and a registration card.

2 If the software is not new, check that you are legally entitled to use it. Has it been taken off the computer it was bought for or have you got a site licence?

3 Follow the instructions in the manual about installing the software. The newer the software the easier it will be to install.

4 While the software is installing, follow any instructions you are given on the screen. If it asks any questions that you can't answer choose the default (the answer they expect you to give). Be careful with this as it sometimes tells you something important – like you don't have enough disk space for the software. If this happens you will need help.

5 Try the software and make sure that you can:
   - get into the program from the operating system
   - get back to the operating system
   - save from the program
   - print from the program – if you haven't already done it you will have to install a printer driver at this point.

Customising software

By customising software you set it up for the user's convenience. How this is done will depend on the software used, your operating system, your applications software and sometimes even your hardware. You will need to use on-line help, explore menus and read the manuals for your software. Some examples of the sort of customising which can be done are shown below.

Customise the operating system

- Use an English keyboard – test that the ' and @ work correctly and that the £ sign appears rather than the $ sign.
- Use British dates – i.e. day/month/year in that order.
- Show the correct day and time – don't forget to get a.m. and p.m. correct.
- Make it easy to get into the applications software from the operating system – you may need to add an icon, or add the applications software to a menu.
- Make sure that the mouse (if you have one) works properly.

Customise the applications software

- Set up a working directory for the program.
- Set up the program to use this directory as a default.
- Set up the page size to suit your printer.
- Make sure that the default dictionary is UK English, or International English rather than US English.
- If there is a choice 'Options' on the menu, work through the options.

Customise the installation

- Virus checks will be done at start-up.
- Make it easy for the user to back up data at regular intervals. You might need a **batch file** to do this. A batch file is a file using operating system commands. You will need to demonstrate this and suggest a practice while you watch.
- Ensure that programs are closed and disk heads are parked before the user switches off. This is standard in Windows 95, but in other operating systems you might need to set up your own icon or create a batch file to do this.

Testing the software with the hardware

If you are familiar with the software, then devise a test plan to run through a few typical applications. At the least you should:
- test it with the printer
- test that the backup works properly
- test that you can retrieve work done previously.

Try the 'buttons' in WIMP software, try any menus in the software, try the commands in non-WIMP software. (WIMP stands for windows, icons, menus, pointers.) If you are unfamiliar with the package, then run through the on-line tutorial or work through the tutorial in the manual. The user is likely to be less familiar with the software than you are, and will expect you to be the expert.

Consumables

Make sure that you have a supply of the media that the installation uses – floppies, paper, printer ink etc. Tell the user where they can obtain what they need.

Accessories

Will the user need any accessories – mouse mat, document holder, wrist support, footstool? Make sure that he or she has what is needed or knows where to get them.

The ergonomics of working are extremely important, and it is particularly important that these are explained to a new or inexperienced user. Ergonomics is the study of how the environment affects the worker's efficiency. It is discussed in more detail in Element 6.3.

Does the organisation you are working for have any security requirements? You should follow the procedure for your company – such as engraving the kit with identification numbers, screwing it to the desk, registering it on the company inventory.

Activity 6.3

1 Look at one or two installations in your educational establishment and list
   a any consumables used
   b any related accessories
   c security measures used to protect the hardware.
2 Collect some brochures and catalogues for
   a computer consumables
   b computer accessories
   c computer security devices for hardware
   d software security.

Handing over to the user

1 Collect the manuals, disks and registration forms.
2 Write a help sheet, not more than two sides of A4, with simple instructions for beginners.
3 Arrange a suitable handover time.
4 Demonstrate the system to the user and answer any questions.
5 Give the user the help sheet.
6 Ask the user to demonstrate that he or she has understood your demonstration.
7 Put away the manuals and disks in a safe place.
8 Help the user fill in the registration forms and send them off.
9 Tell the user where to find any media they need.
10 Offer the user a catalogue of accessories so they can order any they need.

Dealing with problems

Whenever you are working with computers, you will hit problems:
• the hardware may be incorrect, damaged or parts may be missing
• the software may be incorrect for the hardware, files may be missing or damaged, may be on incorrect media for the hardware
• the instructions may be unintelligible or incorrect.

You will probably be able to sort out some problems for yourself, and with experience the number and types of problems that you can deal with will go up. At other times you will need to ask a more senior technician or the manufacturer for help. Most hardware and software companies have help lines.

Most companies employing more than one technician will have procedures for reporting problems, and as a technician you will need to keep a record of the problems you have been asked to sort out – both the ones that have been notified in writing, and those you have only been told about. You will need to record at least:

- the time and date you were notified of the problem
- who brought the problem to your notice
- what the person who told you about the problem said was wrong
- what you actually found to be wrong
- how you fixed the problem
- when you fixed it.

Activity 6.4

1 Find out the procedures for reporting errors in your educational establishment or any other organisation that you are in contact with.
2 Find out how well these procedures work from both a user and a technician.
3 Collect copies of any error report forms that are used.

Keeping records

You will need to duplicate the problem reported before you can fix it. Sometimes problems can be very hard to pinpoint or to fix. Problems can recur, and if you don't keep notes you won't remember what you did last time. Or you may be totally stuck and have to ring the help line, and then have forgotten how you duplicated the problem. So – *keep a diary* as you go along. Be very specific about what you did, and copy error messages off the screen – you probably won't remember that it said 'Error 57 at line AF8' unless you make a note.

When you start a new job, whether it's fixing a bug, or installing a new system, write down
- the date
- the time
- the location of the machine causing problems
- the name of the person who asked you to do the job
- the reported problem/requested task
- the steps you used to solve the problem – these should include:
  - the number of the step (starting from 1)
  - the time
  - what you are going to do next
  - a tick if you did what you wrote down with no problems
  - otherwise a note of what went wrong.
- your conclusions.

The numbered steps will help you next time you do a similar job. You write the time before starting the next step, and you write what you are going to do next. For instance:

3.   9.52   Unpack printer   done – but dropped the lid (not fixed on) cracked.
4.   10.03   Load ink and paper   ✓
5.   10.12   Self-test   ✓

Next time you have to unpack this make of printer, you will be more careful with the lid, and you'll also realise that it takes about 10 minutes to unpack it.

Where you are solving a tricky software problem, for example, you will need to be very specific about what you are doing – for instance if you have insufficient space to load a full version of Microsoft Word, then you need to say that you chose to customise the installation. The installation program offers a large number of files and you should choose the ones you want – and list what you chose. If the program eventually does not do what you want it to do, you can go back and change your choice, but you have written down what your first choice was.

In your conclusions you will have to report the cracked lid and get it replaced among other things that you want to say about the task. You will also need to make out a problem report form for it.

Activity 6.5

Design and produce the following.
1 A diary page that you could use.
2 An error or problem report form that you could fill in as you come across problems.

Planning a task

When attempting new jobs you should always **schedule** the job – that is, plan the tasks and the order of the tasks making up the complete job in as much detail as possible.

1 Name each task
2 Estimate the time that each task will take. You will get better at this as you gain experience. The more that you get into the habit of estimating time before a task and checking it afterwards, the quicker your estimations will improve.
3 Estimate the resources needed (human and material).
   • Will you need help with carrying equipment?
   • Can some tasks be done by other people at the same time as you are doing something else?
   • Will you need tools, cables, paper … ?
4 Plan where you are going to carry out the task. Will you work at your workplace or the user's?
5 Decide the most comfortable way to carry out the task. Get the ergonomics right.
   • Make sure that you have room to work by moving obstructions out of the way before starting.
   • You will need enough desk space for the equipment, your tools, manuals.
   • You will want to be able to reach switches without crawling under a table every time.
   • You will want to be able to reach the back of the machine without performing contortions.
   • If you are working at the user's place, what will they be doing while you work?

Always make a report on what you are doing. Leave room in your schedule to report in detail – right down to which keys you have pressed – what you actually do, and what appears on the screen. If you do this you will be able to report the problem fully if you need advice.

Test questions

1 List the stages required in installing a microcomputer system.
2 List the procedures for reporting errors.
3 List considerations for an **installation schedule.**

Element 6.2: Undertake housekeeping duties

Computer housekeeping

An organisation employing computer technicians will have certain standards for using information technology equipment, on:
- storage and safety of software and data
- storage and availability of consumable items
- storage and availability of manuals
- cleaning and management of hard disks, computers and printers.

Backing up files

Files should be backed up so that they can be restored if the original files are corrupted or lost. You will need backup copies of all programs running, and of all data on the system. Backing up files copies them onto another disk or tape – either as a straight copy, or compressed to save space on the backup disk or tape. Two well known compression programs are ZIP and ARC (short for archive). To get .ZIP files back a program called UNZIP is used. The program ARC can be used for compressing and decompressing.

Backups of programs

If you buy a program today it will come either on a CD-ROM or on floppy disks (until fairly recently, programs *only* came on floppy disks). A CD-ROM is laser printed and can only be damaged physically, so if you have bought a program on CD-ROM keep the disc safe and you will be able to reinstall the program if it becomes corrupted. Floppy disks are magnetic media and can be corrupted if they are near magnets or electric charges or get too hot, cold or dusty. They can also be damaged by faulty read/write disk heads and by computer viruses. It is therefore advisable to backup all floppy disks before using them.

Backups are there to back you up in an emergency – if all is well they are never used. This does not mean that they are not necessary. You can guarantee that the one program you have not backed up will be the one that gets corrupted!

Any organisation which hires computer operators will have some policy about backing up software. They may, for instance, buy multiple copies of software and not back it up because there are many copies. Or they may require the user to store his or her own original copies and have a central backup. You should stick to your company's policy.

In installations that carry out a lot of batch processing, programs are often removed from on-line disks until they are needed. As on-line storage becomes cheaper, and more processing is done on line this happens less often. When new programs are bought or existing programs are updated, the old program should be removed from on-line disks to make sure that all users convert to the new programs. Again, a large organisation should have a policy about what to do with data that has been generated by old programs, and whether copies of the old programs should be kept. It is usually best to convert old data if it is to be used again, as hardware is also updated and old software is unlikely to run on new hardware.

Laws about how long data must be kept still refer to data which can be seen unaided. Banks and other financial organisations store vast amounts of written material in warehouses to comply with the law, which has not yet been changed to allow data to be stored only on magnetic media.

Backing up data

Data stored on-line on hard disks runs the risk of corruption:

- Hard disks can crash. When this happens the read/write head hits the disk and physically damages it – and the data held on it. This can happen if a hard disk is carried or jogged in some way when the heads are not parked. Parking the heads moves them away from parts of the disk where data is stored, and reduces the risks to data.
- Bad sectors can corrupt the data. This happens particularly on disks which are very full or quite old.
- Users can delete files by accident. Various programs are now available to 'undelete' files that have accidentally been deleted but these only work if the deleted data has not been **overwritten**. Encourage the users you are looking after to call you as soon as they have lost data and to not use the machine until you have restored the missing data.
- **Viruses** can wreck data.

How often data is stored depends on its importance, and whether it is reusable.

- Data used in the day-to-day running of an organisation needs to be backed up frequently. Some businesses have dual systems running so all data is stored twice. If the organisation closes down every night, the data should be backed before switching off the machines. It may be possible to do incremental backups – to only back up data that is new since the last backup. It is faster to use tape for backing up than floppy disks.
- Batch processes back up data automatically as they run.
- Many transaction processes store data to a log file which can be backed up between backups of the main database files.
- Secretaries back up computer files as they would copies of letters or memos – if it is important to file a document, then it needs to be backed up.
- If all data is stored centrally on a network then the network manager must have a policy and a system for backing up data.

Storing backups

Backup disks and tapes must be kept dry, at the correct temperature, away from dust, magnetic and electrical fields and floppy disks should not be bent or stabbed. They must be kept handy for use when required. A second set of backups of important data should be stored on separate premises. Backups must be clearly labelled with

- filenames and file versions
- an indication of where one backup disk or tape fits into a sequence of several
- date (and possibly time) of backup
- date when the disk or tape can be recycled – they should be recycled when the data becomes obsolete but if the data they contain is confidential they should be wiped before recycling.

Homestart Database vers 3
Disk 2 of 6
29/11/96

Re-use after 31/1/97

Backups should be clearly labelled

Activity 6.6

Find out the procedures for backing up in your educational establishment or any other organisation that you are in contact with.

IT consumables
Information technology needs many **consumables**:
- Floppy disks are used for backups and for transferring data between one stand-alone computer and another. Floppies come in different physical sizes (generally 3.5″ or 5″) and hold different amounts of data. A 3.5″ disk may hold 720 kilobytes or 1.4 megabytes of data.
- Disk labels are not always supplied with the disks, and if disks are recycled they may well need new labels. Labels should fit the disk and be stuck on so they don't come off in the disk drive.
- Printers need paper. Some printers use ordinary paper, others use special paper. In Britain, sheets of paper are measured in A sizes. In the USA they are measured in inches. Most software is American and new software often defaults to American sizes.
- Printer ink, toner, ribbons etc. are needed by the printers for marking the paper. Almost every printer uses a different type of ink or ribbon cartridge. Most ribbon and ink cartridges can be reinked more or less successfully.
- Cleaning fluids and cleaning cloths are needed for cleaning screens, keyboards, mouse balls, etc.

It is often part of a technician's duties to look after the consumables and ensure they are available for use by information technology users. This usually includes budgeting for buying consumables, storing them, keeping stock and ordering more before the supply runs out.

Manuals
Manuals must be available when needed. To ensure they don't get lost manuals should be stored safely and logged out to users when required. If enough manuals are available each user may be allowed their own copy.

Activity 6.7

May produce evidence for application of number element 2.1.
1 Find out the procedures for ordering, storage and logging out of consumables and manuals in your educational establishment or any other organisation that you are in contact with.
2 Estimate how many consumables you personally use in a year, and what their value is. Show how you reached this estimate.

Management of hard disks

The hard disk must be kept free from **viruses**. Viruses are programs which have been deliberately written to damage data and programs. Successful viruses can reproduce themselves and copy themselves to other disks. A computer can catch a virus from a diseased disk or off the Internet, and will pass it on to floppy disks put into the computer. Programs are available that will check for known viruses, and remove them. Part of a technician's job is to check the hard disks for viruses and remove any they found. New viruses are always being invented so virus checking software must be updated frequently. Most organisations try to prevent viruses from getting on to the disks in the first place by not allowing users to bring in disks from elsewhere, but viruses have been found on the most respectable disks from well known software companies, and they can be imported over networks. Some computer users run virus checking programs every time they start up their machine. Keep your anti-virus programs up to date. Keep checking. Keep virus-free backups.

Keep hard disks tidy. Make sure that users use directories and sub-directories to manage their data. Make sure that when backing up, old files are removed. Users of a network will be sharing hard disk space. The technician will be responsible for setting up directories, passwords and access rights and looking after the shared disk space.

Cleaning computer equipment
- Keyboards should be clean and free from stickiness.
- Screens should be clean and free from glare.
- Floppy disk heads should be clean and free from dust.
- Mice should be clean, the ball should roll freely and a mouse mat should be used.

Activity 6.8

1 Find out from the technicians in your educational establishment what cleaning materials they use for keyboards, screens, disk drives and mice.
2 Write a schedule for cleaning one computer.
3 Using the diary you designed in Activity 6.5 clean one computer using the correct materials.

Looking after printers

The technician will need to make sure that shared papers always have paper and ink, and that they are working properly. In some organisations high-quality printers are kept in a separate print room, and can only be accessed by the technicians. There must be some **spooling** arrangement for use of shared printers so everyone can use them in turn without having to check if the printer is in use. A spooler is a program which puts files into a queue for processing. The main use of a spooler is to queue files to a printer, but it can also be used for other processes like backing up.

Activity 6.9

May be used to provide evidence for application of number element 2.2.
1 Find out the cost of paper and ink or ribbon cartridges for three different printers. Use this information to compare the costs of running the three printers.

2 Demonstrate how to:

   a re-ink a cartridge or ribbon

   b change the paper in a printer

   c change an ink cartridge or ribbon in a printer.

Housekeeping schedule

If you are going to perform **housekeeping** tasks, you must agree a schedule with the users. This schedule should include:

- the activity to be performed
- which machine or machines it is to be performed on
- an estimate of the time the activity will take.

If you are looking after several users it is worth making your schedules known to all of them so that they know where you are and when you will need access to their machines.

Housekeeping log

Always keep a **log** of all your activities, including your housekeeping activities. Your line manager will ask you to do this in any case, but it acts as a protection to you if one of your users complains that you have not cleaned their machine or repaired a fault. You are likely to be involved in several such disputes, particularly with people who are unhappy about using IT.

Case study

A day in the life of a computer technician

Datafit is a firm writing software for retail systems and banking. Every employee of the company has a computer on their desk, in some cases more than one. The main computers are networked and employees keep data both on the network disk and on their own hard disks. Everyone in the company (50–60 employees on two sites) is computer literate and there is one computer technician.

   The network is backed up every night at 2.00 a.m. and the backing up program runs on a timer. Sometimes people work late, or come in early, but there is never anyone around at that time. All new files or updated files on the network disk for each day are backed up. The five tapes are kept in a fireproof safe for two weeks, then they are reused. At the weekend all data is saved to a 4 gigabyte tape. It takes about half an hour. The company uses datatape, which is much smaller than normal audiotape and backs up much faster. If people store data on their own hard disks they back up their own – it is not the responsibility of the technician. A tape backup machine which plugs into the computer parallel port is available for people to make their own backups. It uses ordinary tape cassettes like the ones you have in an ordinary cassette recorder.

   As new software comes in, and it comes in almost daily, the technician numbers the disks and manuals, and indexes it. He then checks the disks for viruses – Datafit have had viruses on brand new disks from well known manufacturers, so they are very careful. Luckily they have not had any viruses on CD-ROMs. Any viruses the technician finds on floppy disks he removes. The company uses Dr Solomon's virus checker and receive updates several times a year. The technician then copies the disks and puts the originals and the manuals in the software cupboard open to everyone – he keeps the copies in his own cupboard. If people borrow the disks or manuals they are supposed to ask the technician, or sign them out. The company has not had enough trouble with disks or manuals vanishing to make it worth putting in a more complicated system. If the software is to go onto the network, the technician puts it on – it is then available for everyone. He does not put everything on the network because the network would soon run out of disk space.

The administration people deal with ordering of all consumables. They also copy the disks that are sent to customers, and recirculate used floppy disks.

When the network disk is full the technician removes anything older than today's date from the DUMP directory, which is used by people to send data to each other, or to store data temporarily. All the staff know that he does this. Then he looks at any software that has not been used lately and checks whether it can be removed from the system.

The technician sets up new passwords, individual e-mail accounts and passwords within the company's CompuServe account. Individuals can change their passwords, but so can the technician – this means that if they forget their password they're not stuck.

If someone does something stupid like pouring coffee over a keyboard, they will unplug it and bring it to the technician for a new one, but normally they clean their own machines (the company keeps a supply of methylated spirits for the purpose). They might take a mouse back and swap it for a working one. The technician will sort out anything which is easy to deal with, like cleaning a mouse or a coffee covered keyboard, but the company leases all its machines, so he will arrange for the leasing company to deal with any more serious problems.

The machines are sent back after three years' use. The technician wipes all the hard disks first by running a program which puts random ones and zeroes on the disk – deleting the data only deletes the disk index, not the data, and even reformatting a disk leaves data on the disk. This program is run three times to make sure all the data is removed.

The technician has little to do with printers. If any go wrong he calls the leasing company to deal with the problem, and administration orders consumables. He does keep up with the latest printers, so he can advise on new ones.

The technician doesn't keep a time log of his activities, but there are some things he does every day. Most of his time is taken up with 'firefighting', and all of those activities are logged on the firefighting file on disk. Every morning when he comes in to work he checks that the network is running and that the backup worked correctly during the night. He then puts the backup tapes in the safe and checks his e-mail. This will contain customer care jobs that have come in over night. He also uses the Internet to monitor development forums of hardware and software that Datafit use, such as Windows 95, Novel and US Robotics.

The 'firefighting' comes directly to the technician by e-mail or by phone from the company's second site. In one day he may have to deal with problems such as
- sorting out a problem with the network losing contact with the main printer
- restoring a corrupted file from the previous night's backup
- decoding some e-mail for someone – it had been compressed before sending and the recipient did not have the correct decompressing program
- recovering data from a 'dead' machine, and arranging for maintenance to replace it
- sending data to a customer using a modem – they did not have an e-mail address

- getting a room upstairs ready for a sales meeting with a customer this afternoon
- sorting out a machine from the second site which is not connecting properly to their network. To do this he may have to go over to the other site because the two sites use different networks, but he will check out the network card in his workspace first to try to save a journey.

Review questions

You have applied for a job as computer technician for a medical centre that uses seven networked computers and two printers, one dedicated to writing prescriptions and another general-purpose printer. Eight people have been short listed for the job, and when you get to the job interview you are asked the following questions. Answer them.

1 Why are file backups important?
2 How should you store floppy disks?
3 You will be in charge of computer consumables:
   a How would you make sure that you did not run out?
   b What data would you record when giving a packet of disks to one of the doctors?
4 How would you look after the hard disk drive on the system?
5 How would you clean a computer?
6 How can you be certain of removing data from a disk before recycling the disk?
7 For a named printer
   a write instructions for adding paper
   b write instructions for adding new ink or whatever it needs.
8 How could you stop manuals from going astray?
9 How would you draw up a housekeeping timetable for the centre?
10 What log will you keep of your activities?

Element 6.3: Provide user support

User support activities

It is difficult to draw an exact dividing line between housekeeping duties and **user support**. Some activities, such as keeping communal printers loaded and backing up communal data are clearly housekeeping, others like staffing a telephone help desk are clearly user support. When you are face to face with users the distinctions become more blurred. User support activities involve:
- identifying faults in the information technology system
- taking action to remedy the fault.

Fault identification
Faults may found in hardware, software, or both – or may be nothing to do with the hardware or software.

Table 6.1 Common hardware faults and possible solutions

Problem	Possible solution
No electricity to the computer system, or part of the computer system. Wall plugs must be switched on as well as switches on the information technology kit. It is quite common for new or nervous users, or even experienced users with other things on their mind, to forget to switch on a wall plug. If the lead goes from the plug to the monitor you may get the desperate call 'The computer is not working at all' because the monitor is blank.	Solve by plugging in and/or switching on.
Connections between parts of the IT system have come undone, are loose or are plugged into the wrong ports.	Solve by connecting correctly.
A peripheral device may appear faulty because it is not being used correctly, for instance the printer paper is incorrectly loaded or the user puts a CD-ROM into the drive upside down.	Demonstrate the correct use of the peripheral device and check the user doing it.
Coffee or other liquid has been spilt over the system. This is not normally a disaster, although sweet drinks will make mechanical contacts sticky and may stop electrical contact.	Most modern electronic component are not damaged by fresh water so the offending liquid can be washed away with fresh water and the component left to dry.
Dirty contacts on keyboard, mouse or other devices.	Clean with methylated spirits or proprietary cleaning fluid.
Faulty power supplies stop electricity getting at the hardware.	Replace the power supply.
Broken fuse.	Replace the fuse after finding the fault which caused it.
Faulty components.	Repair the components, replace them or have them mended.

A mixture of hardware and software faults This may be solved simply by changing a faulty peripheral and recustomising the software for it, or it might involve using the help line for both the hardware and software manufacturers, both of whom will blame the other. You will have to persevere.

External problems These are unconnected with the hardware and software of the information technology system and can be
- physical problems caused by the immediate environment
  - if they are related to the information technology system (see below under ergonomics) they may be sorted out by altering the physical layout of the system
  - if the problems are unrelated to the IT system you need to be sympathetic so as not to make them into psychological problems – but it is not part of a technician's job to cure them
- psychological problems due to stress; either
  - stress caused through using information technology (see below under technostress) or
  - outside stress – you can do nothing about this, but try not to add to the problem by showing scorn at what you perceive as the user's stupidity where IT is concerned.

Table 6.2   Common software faults

Problem	Possible solution
Network faults	
User comes up against built-in security, for instance the user forgets a password or tries to log into someone else's workstation.	Make sure he or she should be using that machine, and ask the network manager for a new password with the correct accesses.
Network is overloaded.	People will have to log off temporarily. In the long run the network must be upgraded.
Network is down.	Find out why. The network manager will need to restart it.
Application software 'faults' (a very large number of reported software faults are not in fact faults in the software, but are due to users not knowing the software very well)	
User has new (or a new version of) software and tries to use it like the last software or software version.	Explain the new software to the user, offer a manual. Be gentle – do not laugh.
User wants to do something that they have never done before and would like to know how.	Do not show them. Talk them through it – that way they will remember.
User has lost files – this may be because they do not remember the name of the file or the directory, do not understand directory structures, have not saved it or have deleted it.	With modern software, all these problems can usually be overcome Explain directory structures if the user does not understand them. Suggest the use of meaningful directory and file names. Show them how to look for files by type, date and time. Show them how to use file search software if it is available.
User has pressed the wrong button and does not know what has happened to their work.	If you know the software package, explain to them what they should do. Talk them through rather than showing them – they will remember it better. Above all, don't 'magically' sort out the problem with fast key strokes or they will keep repeating the mistake and you will have a job for life. If you do not know the software, talk them through using the menus, using the help facilities or even reading the manual.
Software has been incorrectly installed.	Reinstall it correctly.
Software files have been corrupted.	Replace the corrupt files or reinstall the software.
Faults in user-developed software.	This may involve you in helping debug their software and should only be attempted if you understand the software reasonably well. However, you could usefully provide a manual if they do not have one, or the telephone number of the manufacturer's help line.

Ergonomics

Ergonomics is the study of work and its environment, and it examines the conditions of work which are likely to lead to maximum efficiency. Ergonomic studies have led to health and safety legislation and work practices which lead to good working conditions for an office worker, and in particular for work with IT equipment.

Figure 6.5 shows a number of important features of working with IT equipment:

1   Eye height above ground is comfortable between 1 m and 1.25 m for 95% of seated people. The comfortable viewing distance is between 0.6 and 0.7 m.

Figure 6.5 Ergonomics of working at a computer

2 Keyboard top is comfortable approximately 0.7 m above the ground. It is important that the keyboard can be moved separately from the rest of the equipment, and that its angle is adjustable.

3 A wrist rest should be available.

4 The working chair should have an adjustable backrest to support the lower back. The chair should have no arm rests to allow maximum arm movement.

5 The seat height should be adjustable – comfortable height is approximately 0.4 m above ground.

6 The chair should be able to swivel so the whole body can be moved easily when changing between keyboard use and other activity.

7 Chair should be movable to make getting up and sitting down easier, and allow easy access other parts of the workspace.

8 Footrest should be available, especially for short people.

9 A minimum distance between seat and table of 0.2 m is needed for knee clearance. Since tables are usually of a fixed height (maximum height allowed is 0.7 m) it is important for everything else to be adjustable.

10 The screen should be free from reflected light. Ideally this should be accomplished by careful positioning of the screen relative to light sources, but accessories are available to deal with the problem of glare. Screen should be roughly at a right angle to the line of sight.

11 If data is going to be input from documents, manuscript holders should be attached to the screen. This makes sure that there are minimum head movements between document and screen.

In addition, the employers of people whose main duties involve working with VDUs are required to pay for regular eye tests. Staff should take frequent breaks from working with a VDU and keyboard, should be aware of the risks of repetitive strain injury and not ignore muscular stress symptoms.

Activity 6.10

May produce evidence for application of number element 2.2.

By measuring and by observation, check whether your educational establishment complies with the requirements listed above for

1 students
2 staff.

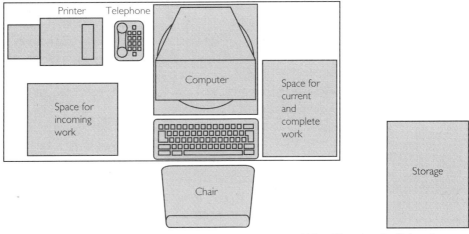

Figure 6.6 Planning a work station. Anyone sitting at this desk should be able to reach all that they need for their work, the largest 'stretches' being for equipment that they use least

Activity 6.11

May produce evidence for application of number element 2.2.

Design a work station for your own use. You will need it for running a users' help desk.

1 Choose a small room for it at home, or part of a room at school or college. Make a plan of the room.
2 Decide where to place the work station in relation to the window and door.
3 Decide what equipment you will need, and how you will arrange it.

Technostress Many people feel threatened by IT, and worry about using a new software package or piece of equipment. If something goes wrong, they feel put upon. When sorting out 'faults' for these people, you must be careful not to make them feel stupid. They are making perfectly understandable mistakes, and will make more if they feel harassed by you. 'People' skills can be very important in user support work.

Fault logging system

As with housekeeping, you will be required to keep:
- an **event log** to log your problem solving, which should include date, time, user, fault category, action taken
- records of work done so that you can report, either verbally or in writing, to your supervisor or senior technician as required.

Case study

Running a help desk

The help desk is run for customers of Datafit (described in the case study in Element 6.2). A list of questions was sent to the company and the customer care administrator gave written replies. These are summarised here.

What are your chief user support activities?

1 Take Incoming telephone calls from customers who have queries ensuring that name, address, telephone number, and 'full details' of query are taken.
2 Record any telephone queries together with any immediate response.
3 Acknowledge, on day of receipt, any customer queries received by letter post, fax or e-mail recording receipt and 'saving' master copy of communication.
4 Answer simple queries, if I know the answer.
5 Arrange transfer of more complex queries to the relevant person.
6 If the query is not straightforward and needs time to investigate, then I monitor the development of the answer at agreed intervals and inform the customer of development or anticipated delay.
7 Contact customer for any further information needed for any investigation.
8 Ensure the answer is transmitted to the person making enquiry. It may involve sending a software solution, not just a spoken answer.
9 Close query records and ensure records/filing are completed.

Describe your fault logging system

We have a form to fill in. I call it the 'blue form' – I print it on blue paper so that technicians notice it and give it priority. It is obviously important to look after our customers. At the same time I enter the problem on a fault report system on computer. I start with a reference number which is generated by the computer. I then ask for various details and carry out the following procedure:

1 I take down customer details – postal address, telephone number, fax number, mobile phone number, e-mail address etc. We may have some of these already on computer – if so, we check them with the customer.
2 What are the fault details – date, query reference number, operating system used, which program they are using, version number, what error messages are appearing.
3 The customer is asked to describe the symptoms of the error – what he or she is attempting to do, or what is happening in our software at the time that the error occurs.
4 We check back over any event already logged for this specific query in our computerised fault event log.
5 We find out the priority of the fault to the customer.
6 We also put on computer the name of the technician allocated the task of 'solving/answering' the problem.
7 Customer contact for this query.
8 Customer reference.
9 When it is finished I add total time taken to 'solve' query and the date that I can 'close' the query. We keep all the information on computer as we need to be able to access this log by customer name, query reference number, our program name, application name or error number. We need to be able to provide reports on what we are doing by all these access ways.

Can you explain the priorities, please and give examples?

1 If a customer has to close down their system because the error is not remedied then they obviously have first priority. This may occur in a supermarket if the back office system went down. Any large supermarket customer of ours will have a second system running in parallel, but this sort of problem must be attended to at once. If necessary we send someone out to them.

2 Second priority is if the customer will have difficulty running if the fault is not remedied. An example is a problem with backing up. Obviously the business is not in immediate danger, but it still needs a fairly fast turnaround.

3 A third priority would be a customer who would like, say, an enhancement made to their software.

What do you put in your event log?

We need an entry for each and every separate activity. We store the entries in chronological order and can access them by the specific fault (we may have met the fault before and not yet sent out a repair for the bug) or by query reference number. The log contains the following details:

- activity date
- activity number
- description of event (i.e. what occurred)
- reference to any communication we have had with them
- information about items and/or data which we have transferred to them, and how we made the transfer (by modem, e-mail, post)
- an ID of event recorder so we know who to query if the problem arises again.

How do you categorise your faults?

1 By type:
   - A *query* is one we can deal with immediately over the phone. I deal with very simple queries and I transfer the more complex queries to one of the technical staff.
   - A *support* problem, where the customer is using the software wrongly or wants to do something not catered for in the manual. These are dealt with by our technical staff.
   - A *fault* indicates something wrong with our software.
2 By urgency:
   - The problem must be dealt with immediately if the business is to survive.
   - The fault affects the customer's business, but they can survive a few days.
   - The fault is detrimental to the business, but they can still function.
   - The fault causes inconvenience but does not affect the running of the business.
3 By the number of our systems it affects:
   - A general problem affects all our software (e.g. we need to make it work efficiently on a new operating system).
   - A specific range problem affects only some of our software, perhaps only software to do with banking.
   - A specific product problem affects only one of our programs, perhaps the report writer.
   - A version problem affects only one version of the software. Not all our customers want to upgrade whenever we put out a new version.

General comments on fault logging system

Datafit has a partly computerised, partly manual system. Below is a list of 'daily activities'. The duties are split between administration staff, customer care administrator and the technical staff.

1 Hand out/remind duty support person with two copies of the paper Tele-logs (the 'blue forms' mentioned earlier).

2 Collect filled-in 'blue forms' and enter details into the Customer Care Reporting (CCR) system.

3 Issue 'blue forms' of any problems we have received by fax overnight and put a copy of any problems received overnight by e-mail in the fax in-tray to keep all the problems together for filing. 'Blue forms' are issued to the member of technical staff responsible for the development of the software covered by the problem (I have a list on computer) together with any files received from the customer. I enter the assigned person's ID (initials) in the box on the CCR system. A sample 'blue form' is shown in Figure 6.7.

Telephone Support Log		CC Ref. no.
Initials:	Date:	Time:
Name:	Company:	
Tel. number	Fax number:	
Operating system:	Program:	DP4 version:
Subject/description		
Response:		
Action needed:		
Approximate **time spent** dealing with this support call . . . . hours		

Fig 6.7 Example 'blue form'

4 Check the e-mail every hour or so, for messages and files relating to customer care and check that customer care messages have not gone to individuals without my knowing.

5 Enter activity (brief summary of outgoing faxes, files despatched, telemessages sent against relevant record in the CCR system.

6 Ensure a copy is kept of files sent out (to repair software bugs) or files received in (so we can reproduce the fault). We keep them as Zipfiles, which is a way of compressing them so they do not take up so much space. They are stored on the network.

7 Use Crystal Reports (a report writing program) to print reports as necessary:
   • summary of the activities of the last week or so
   • detailed activity on all CCRs raised since a given date
   • detailed activity on open CCRs since a given date
   • detailed activity for all CCRs for a given organisation
   • summary of all outstanding CCRs
   • any other reports requested from time to time by personnel for specific companies etc.

8 I use a manual filing system for the CCRs:
   • the top tray holds current/immediate/non-allocated CCRs requiring action within 24 hours
   • the middle tray is for CCRs that are being worked on/outstanding
   • the wall tray holds last month's closed CCRs
   • boxes are for last year's closed CCRs
   • main files hold a master copy of all communications to customers about faults.

9 I check once a day for fixed CCRs and outstanding CCRs and take action if necessary (e.g. remind the relevant technician that a customer is waiting for a reply).

Test questions

A user tells you that the computer won't come on when switched on.
1 How would you attack this problem?
2 How would you log the problem?

Assignment A6.1
Install a microcomputer system

This assignment provides portfolio evidence for Element 6.1 and also the following key skills elements:

Communication 2.1:   Take part in discussions
Communication 2.2:   Produce written material
Communication 2.3:   Use images

A local charity has been given a computer, associated hardware and some applications software by a generous donor. Your tutor will give you details of the hardware and software to install. You have been 'volunteered' to install the system.

1 Write a report to the charity describing the stages involved in installing the system.
2 Write out an installation schedule suggesting
   a timings
   b resources needed (human and material)
   c location and ergonomics.
3 Install the system
4 Demonstrate the system to the charity organisers
5 Write a report on the procedures they should use for reporting errors and requesting further help from you.

Assignment A6.2
Undertake housekeeping duties

This assignment provides portfolio coverage for Element 6.2.

Undertake housekeeping duties on equipment and for users as specified by your tutor and for a specified length of time. Having been given the specifications you should:

1 Describe the duties that you will carry out.
2 Agree a schedule of duties over the period.
3 Complete the duties, keeping a log.

Assignment A6.3
Provide user support

This assignment provides portfolio coverage for Element 6.3.

Undertake user support activities as specified by your tutor. Record your support activities:

1 Identify user support activities, giving three examples of activities you may be called upon to carry out.
2 Describe a fault logging system.
3 Design an event logging system.
4 Identify fault categories, giving three examples.
5 Carry out the required support activities.
6 Document the activities using your event log.

CHAPTER 7

Using software packages to satisfy user requirements through teamwork (intermediate)

Element 7.1: Design a solution to satisfy user requirements using teamwork
Element 7.2: Implement a prototype of the system design individually
Element 7.3: Evaluate the prototype implementations as a team

What is covered in this chapter

- Teamwork
- User requirements
- Presentations
- Facilities of software packages
- Application system testing
- User documentation
- Evaluation of software packages for a purpose
- Evaluation of applications
- Active participation in a team
- Performing a task fitting in with other tasks to create a team project
- Active participation in a presentation
- Examining advanced facilities of software packages
- Creating a prototype computer system
- Choosing the best option

Resources you will need for your Organisations and Information Technology file:

- Your written answers to the activities in this chapter.
- Your written answers to the test questions at the end of the chapter.
- Completed Assignments A7.1, A7.2 and A7.3.

Introduction

There are two main aims for this unit:

1 To set up a prototype application system using a software package. The stages of setting up an application system from the user requirement to the delivery of the final system are shown in Figure 7.9. This unit covers stages 1 to 5. You will have to design the system fairly fully, as you will need to demonstrate the design to the 'user' (your tutor). To do this you will need to design the **interfaces** between the user and the computer in detail – what the input and output screens look like, what will be printed or otherwise output. You will also need to decide what data must be stored, and how, to achieve the outputs, and how that data will be input. After you have agreed the design with the user, you will study an application package for suitability for

use, and build an **implementation** as close to the design as possible. You will then evaluate your program against the design.

2 To learn to work as part of a team in planning, presentation and evaluation. You will need to work together at the design stage, and in presenting the design to the user. You will need to plan a **presentation**, allot individual tasks and carry them out, and come together with a presentation. You then individually build a **prototype** system to the agreed design. Finally, you must demonstrate the prototypes to each other, evaluate all the prototypes fairly and choose the system that will be offered to the user.

Element 7.1: Design a solution to satisfy user requirements using teamwork

Working in a team

You will often be expected to work with other people, and you will not always be able to choose who they are. A job is often measured in working hours. If a job takes 40 working hours, then:
- it will take one person 40 hours to complete the job, or
- it will take two people 20 hours to complete the job, or
- it will take four people 10 hours to complete the job

but *only* if they work together as a team. If they don't it will take four people 50 hours (40 hours in which they each do their own thing plus 10 hours of argument). To work as a team they will have to:
- agree on a plan of work – they must split the job into separate **tasks** which can be done at the same time
- agree on who will do what tasks, and by when
- do the tasks, finishing at the agreed time.

Good teamwork is difficult. To make a team work at its best, and for you to play a useful part in the team, you need to think about a number of points:
- the formal organisation of a team
- team dynamics, or the informal organisation of a team
- relationships between team members
- your feelings about working as part of a team
- your relationships with other team members.

Formal organisation of a team

A team can be made up from people of equal status, with no official leader, or people of different status, in which case there is probably an official leader, and possibly other people with official roles within the team. An important role is that of secretary to the team, who may be a member of the team, or only employed by the team to record decisions, actions and meetings of team members.

A formal team organisation *must* be recognised by the team members. You might not like your boss, and you might think that you could do the job better – but if you do not treat your boss *as* your boss work can become very unpleasant (that is, if you keep your job).

In any sporting team you need a captain, and this is no different for a work team – you need a leader. The leader must perform several duties:
- chair team meetings – this means being in charge at team meetings
- make sure team members all have a chance to speak

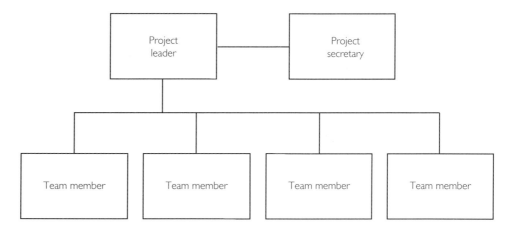

Figure 7.1 Organisation of a typical project team

- make sure that the team members agree on what to do
- check that team members are working between meetings, and arrange help if they need it
- report to the manager about how the team is doing.

Usually at work, the manager will choose the leader. If there is no team leader, these tasks become the responsibility of the whole team.

Recording team activities

It is important to keep a record of what the team is doing. Someone needs to write down what happens at a meeting (this is called 'taking minutes'), who is expected to do what task, and by when. The person who does the recording is called the secretary. If someone forgets what they should do they can refer to the written reminder. Everyone in the team knows what they, and the other team members, are responsible for. The manager who set up the team should also read the minutes to know how things are going. As soon as possible after each meeting, the secretary should write up the minutes to a standard format (see, for example, Figure 7.2).

```
Time, date and place of meeting:
People present:
Apologies from: (this is a list of the people who should have been at
the meeting but who were not but sent in an excuse)
1. Minutes of last meeting and matters arising (Read through the
   minutes of the last meeting and check that people have done what
   they should have done)
   Action by
2. Topic one (description of topic one, action(s) to take)
3. Topic two (description of topic two, action(s) to take)
4 …etc.
Penultimate   Any other business (this is where anyone can add a topic
to the agenda)
Last   Time, date, place for next meeting. Note of time meeting
finishes
```

Figure 7.2 A sample format for minutes of a meeting

For a team to work well, all members should agree on:

- aims and objectives
- decisions made by the team and by individual team members
- what actions each member is responsible for, and deadlines set for the actions
- what is likely to go wrong, and what should be done if it does.

These points should all be discussed in team meetings and minutes taken. Minutes should be circulated to all team members as soon as possible after meetings, preferably with each member's responsibilities highlighted in some way. The secretary also works with the team leader to set the agenda (list of topics to be discussed) for future meetings. If enough team meetings are held, the minutes will record everything that is going on.

Any decisions taken outside team meetings should be recorded in some central place – perhaps a notice board. A copy of all work in progress should also be kept in a central place – on a shared disk directory or in a drawer somewhere – so that if members are ill or absent for some other reason it should still be possible to use their work.

Activity 7.1

May produce evidence for communications element 2.1.

Your tutor will put you in a group of four to seven people, will choose one person as team leader, one person as secretary and one person to observe. The *team* consists of everyone *except* the observer. Your job as a team is to fill in the shaded boxes on the grid shown in Figure 7.3. To do this you should:

1 Think of at least two, and not more than four, reasons why
   a a team would work better with a leader
   b a team would work better if all members are of equal status.
2 Think of at least two, and not more than four, problems which might arise because
   a a team's leader has been chosen for them

	Team has a leader	Team members are of equal status
Advantages	1 2 3 4	1 2 3 4
Problems that might arise	1 2 3 4	1 2 3 4
Type of organisation chosen (tick one box)		
How to overcome problem listed above	1 2 3 4	1 2 3 4

Figure 7.3 Grid for team meeting for Activity 7.1

b all the members of the team are of equal status.

3 Decide whether your team will work best with a formal leader, or with all members having equal status. Tick the appropriate box on the grid.

4 How would you overcome the problems that you listed for this type of organisation?

During these activities
- the team leader must run the meeting
- the team secretary must record the meeting and produce minutes
- the observer, who should not take any part in the meeting, will make notes of the meeting using the observation sheet shown in Figure 7.4.

After the meeting each member of the group, team members and observer alike (no conferring), should fill in the summary sheet given in Figure 7.5.

OBSERVATION SHEET						
INDIVIDUAL BEHAVIOUR						
Place a tick in the box for a member every time their behaviour is described in the column on the left.						
GROUP MEMBERS	1	2	3	4	5	6
1 The team member made a new suggestion						
2 The team member took part in making a decision						
3 The team member agreed to a compromise						
4 The team member became angry						
5 The team member stopped listening						
6 The team member acted as peacemaker						
7 The team member interrupted						

Figure 7.4 Form for observer to complete (Activity 7.1)

SUMMARY OF GROUP BEHAVIOUR	
1 How did the team begin their task?	
2 Did the appointed leader control the team, or did anyone else seem to control it?	
3 How were decisions reached?	
4 Was there confrontation? If so, how was it resolved?	
5 Who spoke the most?	
6 Who spoke the least?	
7 Did anyone not take part at all?	

Figure 7.5 Summary form to be completed by all at the end of Activity 7.1

Group dynamics

The observer in Activity 7.1 studied the informal organisation of the group. This is sometimes called the group dynamics. He or she was observing how the group *actually* worked, rather than how it *should* have worked.

Your job as a team member is to make sure that the team achieves its aim. All members of a football team, for instance, should aim at their team winning the match. In a work team, all members should aim at the team finishing the work well, on time. Your job at the planning stage is to help make a good plan. The plan must work for the whole team, not just you. In the doing stage (while you are carrying out a task agreed by the team) your job is to do the task and to keep the rest of the team informed about your progress.

- Start the task in good time because things may go wrong. Tell the secretary that you have started.
- Ask for help if you are having problems with the task. Tell the team leader, and anyone who may be able to help, if you are having problems.
- If you are having problems that are unrelated to the task, but which may make you unable to finish on time, tell the team leader in good time so that someone else can finish the task.
- Help your team mates if they are having problems.
- Do not leave work at home. If you take work home, leave a copy of what you have done so far at your educational establishment. You should discuss ways of doing this with your tutor.
- Finish on time.
- At the evaluation stage, support your team mates.

Behaviour helpful for completing a team task
- Suggest an action which will help the team to complete the task.
- Ask for information if you do not understand either the task or what some-one has said.
- Explain the task, what you have said, or what you understand someone else to have said.
- Say something which is relevant to the task, even if it is not a suggestion, a question or an explanation.
- Summarise what you think people have been saying, if it makes things clearer.
- Take part group decisions.

Behaviour helpful in keeping the team working together
- Listen to, and think about, what everyone is saying.
- Make *positive* comments about team mates' suggestions. This is especially important if you disagree with the other person. If you want to disagree with a team mate, start by saying where you agree.
- Encourage your team mates. Say when you like a suggestion. Always think positively about a suggestion.
- Be prepared to change your suggestions to fit in with other people.

Unhelpful behaviour
- Trying to boss the rest of the team.
- Aggressive or stubborn behaviour.
- Saying or doing something just because no one is looking at you.
- Sulking, going to sleep or otherwise 'turning off'.

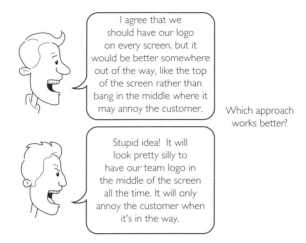

Figure 7.6 Disagree with a positive statement

Activity 7.2

May produce evidence for communications element 2.1.

Your tutor will put you in a group of four to seven people and will choose one person as an observer – this observer should not previously have acted as observer. The team consists of everyone except the observer. The observer will fill in the observation sheet shown in Figure 7.7 while the team is working. The team's task is to:

1 Read scenario 1
2 Hold a meeting to organise your team, decide how the input screen should look and how the profile printout should look.
3 Produce the minutes of the meeting.

Scenario 1

The company you work for, GNVQ Projects, does a lot of project work. They are doing some research into the efficiency of their project teams. To this end their researcher will be sitting in on team meetings observing team members, using a form like the one your observer is using.

At the end of a meeting the observer wishes this information to be fed into a computer. They want to print out a profile of each team member after a meeting, showing graphically how each person behaved at the meeting, so that the line manager can discuss group behaviour. They would also like to see if people's behaviour changes over the course of several meetings.

Your project team has been asked to design an input screen for the researchers, and to design the printout showing the team members behaviour profile graphically.

Relationships between team members

We do not need to like people in order to be able to work with them. However, we *do* need to feel comfortable working with them. We need to feel that they respect us and are confident in our abilities to produce our share of the work. In turn we need to respect our colleagues and be confident that they will not let

OBSERVATION SHEET							
	BEHAVIOUR	GROUP MEMBER					
		1	2	3	4	5	6
TASK WORK	Making a suggestion						
	Asking for information						
	Explaining something						
	Saying something to the point						
	Summarising the discussion						
	Taking a decision						
GROUP WORK	Active listening						
	Agreeing with others						
	Encouraging others						
	Making compromises						
SELF	Trying to dominate the group						
	Being aggressive or stubborn						
	Seeking attention						
	Withdrawing from involvement						

Figure 7.7 Observation sheet for Activity 7.2

us down. We respect someone if we admire some qualities in them. We do not need to agree with this person about how we work or how we might like to play. We do not need to want these qualities in ourselves. But we do need to think that in the other person these qualities can be seen as strengths. It is, in fact, very useful to a team for everyone to have different strengths. It can be useful when dealing with people outside the team if the team contains a wide variety of types.

Activity 7.3

List your own strengths and weaknesses as far as working in a team on an IT assignment are concerned. Think about how you rate yourself in the use of IT, in getting on with people, in working with others rather than by yourself, in working to a deadline and in responsibility. Write down four strengths and two weaknesses.

Can you think of any circumstances in which one of your weaknesses could be thought of as a strength?

We are confident that other people will not let us down if:
• they are realistic about their abilities, and will agree to perform a task only if they know that they can do it
• they are serious about their responsibilities
• we know that they will tell us if they are having problems
• they have not let us down before.
If we are working with people who we feel will not produce their share of the work, we will need to make sure that they tell us in time for us to do something about it.

Activity 7.4

Your tutor will put you in a group of four to seven people and will choose one person (who has not already been one) as an observer. The team consists of everyone except the observer. The observer must complete an observation sheet, as shown in Activity 7.2. The team should produce:

1 A list for each team member containing:
   a three reasons to respect them
   b two tasks in using a computer or giving a presentation that they will be good at
   c a mark on a scale from 1 (totally confident) to 5 (no way) on whether the team in general is confident that the team member can produce a chart for use in presenting the outcome of the meeting if asked to do so
      • before they go home today
      • tomorrow morning
      • this time next week.

2 Minutes of the meeting.
3 The observer should produce the behaviour sheet.

Fitting into a team

There are many advantages to working in a good team:
• you share the work
• you help each other
• between you, you will have many different strengths and talents
• the team will have more ideas than one person on their own
• if one person is ill, the work can still be done.

Equally teamwork can have its disadvantages:
• the outcome will not be your personal achievement
• you might come into conflict with others about the best way to work
• if another team member is especially good at something, you might not get the chance to do it
• you may have to do the work of other people if they are unable to do so.

Activity 7.5

Think about how you feel about teamwork. Read scenario 2, then answer the questions below.

1 If you were asked to work on the project described in scenario 2 as part of a team:
   a Which task would you most like to do yourself?
   b Which task would you least like to do yourself?
   c Which task would you find most difficult?
   d Which task would you find easiest?
   e Which task would you find easiest to discuss with a friend?
   f Which would you find most difficult to discuss with a friend?

2 Which of the following sentences most nearly describes your feeling about working as part of a team?
   a I like to work as part of a team.
   b I like to work with my best friends, but do not like team work otherwise.
   c I would prefer to work on my own, rather than with anyone else.
   d I hate working with others.

3 Give at least two reasons for your answer to Question 2.

Scenario 2

GNVQ Projects needs to know how much time is spent on each project so as to bill customers accordingly. Employees are asked to fill in a time sheet to help with this. The accounts department suggests that, at the end of every hour, each employee writes down the name of the project that they have been working on for most of that hour. This could be done on paper, for entry into a computer later on, or directly into a computer program. The company's accountants can then obtain a printout listing all staff hours spent on the project by date and time. The information should give totals per person and overall total.

You have been asked to:
- devise data entry screens and/or forms
- design a suitable printout form
- describe data to be stored, and data processes to be used.

To make sure that you understand the system you will need to perform two more tasks at the design stage:
- Decide on some test data.
- Suggest any problems with the system that you think may arise.

Getting on with others

Most people get on together and can work well in a team. If you *are* having problems, whether it's your fault or someone else's then try to think of
- what advantage there is to your opposite number in behaving as they do or saying what they do
- something that you can do to make the situation easier – you cannot change the other person's behaviour, but you can change yours.

Figure 7.8 In spite of trying your best to talk to Charlie, he won't listen to anyone else, won't stop talking and tells everyone else what to do. Is Charlie behaving like this because he feels that no one else in the group is coming up with any ideas?

Look at the problem in Figure 7.8. Perhaps you could make Charlie act as observer for a team meeting where you decide and allocate tasks Don't forget to allocate a task to Charlie – and it should be one that he would like to do and will do well. The rest of the team can then get on with their tasks – but they have to do them or prove that Charlie was right all along!

Activity 7.6

1 Which two people in the class would you like to work with best? Give two reasons for each.
2 Which two people in the class would you like to work with least? Give one reason for each.
3 What could you do to make it easier to work with these people?

Building a computer system

The stages in building a computer system are shown in Figure 7.9.

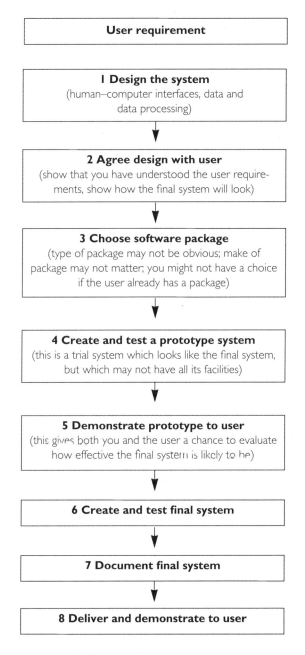

Figure 7.9 Building a computer system from user requirements

User requirements

The user is your customer. He or she will tell you what they require. These are the **user requirements**. The user requirements should include:

- The purpose of the system – the person building the system must know what they are aiming at.
- The constraints of the system – those factors which you *have* to include. For instance, the user may have a maximum cost for the system, or might insist on using existing hardware or software.
- The output – the information required from the system. It might be a general requirement such as 'an analysis of the data', or an exact requirement such as 'a pie chart showing …'.
- The input – what data the user is to start with.

It is the responsibility of the system developers to make sure that they understand the requirements. If the user has been vague, the developers have the choice of deciding for themselves how to do it, or of asking the user to clarify what they want.

Understanding the user requirements You need to make sure that you have understood the requirements properly. One way of doing this is to pretend to present your design to the user and show them what will happen when they use your computer system. They will be able to see immediately whether you have understood exactly what they require.

Designing the system

1 Obtain some test data. If the user has not given you any, you will need to invent some plausible data. If the user has not given you enough information to do this, you will have to go back to them.

2 Using the test data, work by hand (or better with your brain as well as your hand) from input through to output, making sure that you understand what must be done with the data. Record the processing required. Record any problems in your understanding of what is required. Also record any problems which you think may occur if you computerise your processing.

3 Design the output screens and printouts. These will give the user the information required by the system. Record any problems that occur at all stages. You might find at this stage that the output data you have been asked to list may be too long to fit on one line of a printed page.

4 Design the input screens and/or any other way of inputting. Problems could occur with data capture forms currently in use.

5 Decide on the data that must be stored and input in order to arrive at the output data. Record any problems – e.g. how would you list data that is too long to fit on one line?

Presenting the system design to the user

You will need:

- examples of input screens, which may be produced by computer or hand
- sample output screens or reports (computer produced or hand produced)
- data storage diagrams
- data processing diagrams.

Present your design in a way that shows how your final system will work. Do not go into technical details – just show

- how the data will be input (input screens, on-line help during input, how it can be accessed from current data capture forms) – at this stage you must check with the user that you have understood the data capture correctly

- the data files that need to be stored on the computer – this will check that you have understood the data requirements correctly
- the data processing that will be carried out (show examples of test processing) – this will demonstrate that you have understood the processing required
- sample outputs.

At each stage you must describe any problems that you have in understanding the requirements, any assumptions that you have made (especially if you invented the test data) and any problems that you think the system won't be able cope with. The user should now be happy that you have understood the requirements – if not he or she must explain further.

Case study

Part one

Nik is the assistant manager of a fast food restaurant chain selling pasta and pizzas. There is also a salad bar where customers can help themselves, and a choice of desserts. The owner wishes to find out what the customers think of the restaurants, so she asks the managers to give questionnaires to all the customers to discover their opinions of the food and service. The manager has asked Nik to head the committee in charge of this project. Nik puts up a notice to staff (see Figure 7.10) with the agenda of a meeting he intends to call.

Customer Care Committee

Leader: Nik
Secretary: Jo
Members: Ray, Lee, Tiny

Agenda
1. Questionnaire to ask customers about how they like us.
2. How to get customers to answer
3. Can we computerise it?

3.00pm in my office today.

Be there, and bring your brains !

Figure 7.10

The minutes of this meeting are shown below:

```
Minutes of Customer Care Committee
3.00 p.m. Monday 23 September in Nik's office
People present: Nik, Jo (secretary), Ray, Lee, Tiny
1 Questionnaire about the restaurant          Action by
  It was decided to ask six questions:
  1. Have you been to this restaurant before?    Yes/No
     Then four questions where they tick one of four boxes.
     The boxes to be headed:
              Excellent     Good     Not bad     Awful
  2. What did you think of the food?
  3. What did you think of the service?
  4. What did you think of the staff friendliness?
```

```
5. What did you think of the toilets?
6. Will you come to this restaurant again? Yes/No
Name:
Address:
How many people in your group?

There should be space for the initials of the waiter/waitress.
```

2 How to get customers to answer

```
We have customers' names and addresses, so we could have a monthly
raffle. The manager should be asked about possible prizes. Print it
on the back of the bill, so we can see what the customers have
eaten, and what they like best. We can also find out if larger
groups have more expensive meals, for instance.        Nik
```

3 Computerisation of questionnaire

```
Design format of questionnaire and data entry screen together so
they look the same                                      Jo
  Questions 2-4 should be analysed separately (i.e. compare number
of people who thought the food excellent with number who thought
it good with number who thought it not bad and the number who
thought it awful). Decide how to show this graphically    Ray and
                                                           Lee

  Questions 1 and 6 should be analysed together to compare number
of new customers to number of repeat customers        Ray and Lee
  Compare number of people coming in different group sizes. Graph
                                                       Ray and Lee
  Comparisons of questions 3, 4 and 6 can be used in staff
appraisal. Work out how                                Nik
  Design report                                        Tiny
  Design data file                                     Tiny
  Description of processing - basically selecting some data and
performing statistics on it. People designing output reports can
describe the processing needed for their reports     Ray, Lee, Tiny
  Test data needed - 20 filled in forms                Jo, Nik
  File with equivalent of 100 filled in forms. We can use random
number generator                                       Tiny
```

4 Next meeting

```
Same time next week. All work to be completed by then.
Meeting ended at 3.45.
```

Giving a presentation

The user is your customer. You want to impress the customer, so dress smartly, start punctually and sort out the administration tasks (i.e. who is responsible for making sure that presentation aids such as overhead projectors and transparencies etc. are set up ready?) well in advance. You should rehearse your team before making the presentation: who will say what? what diagrams or computer screens will they use? The user may ask questions at any stage, so the presenter should be ready to answer any questions.

Speak clearly and slowly, even if you are nervous. Look at the people you are speaking to and don't fidget. Listen to any questions and answer them if you can. If you can't, then either ask a colleague to answer it or say that you do not know. If you have not understood the question, ask the questioner to explain it. Do not interrupt another speaker, even if you think they have got it wrong.

If you have not understood the user requirements, the fault may actually lie with the user for giving vague requirements. Do not blame the users but do not feel guilty about getting it wrong – make sure you get it right now.

Case study

Part two

```
Minutes of Customer Care Committee
3.00 p.m., Monday 30 September, Nik's office
People present: Nik, Jo (sec.), Ray, Tiny
Apologies: Lee
```

1 Minutes and matters arising   **Action by**

The minutes were agreed as accurate. Nik thanked all members for completing the work on time, especially Ray who had also done Lee's share.

Nik had seen the manager, who agreed to offer a voucher for a free meal for four for the raffle winner every week.

The manager also asked for a presentation of how the computer system would look.

2 Presentation

Questionnaire and data entry screen   **Jo**

Printouts for reports put on OHT – Each to do the outputs they have planned plus description of processing, i.e.

Questions 2–4   **Ray and Lee**

Questions 1 and 6

Group sizes   **Nik, Tiny**

Staff appraisal

OHT for design of data file   **Tiny**

All examples to use test data provided by Jo and Tiny.

3 Next meeting

Same time next week. All work to be completed by then. Agenda:

1. How to make a presentation
2. How to give the presentation with the visual aids that we have
                                                                     Nik
3. Who will say what, in what order
4. Run through of presentation
5. Allocate administrative tasks for presentation   **Nik**
6. Date of presentation

Meeting ended at 3.45.

Test questions

I At a team meeting, describe the job of
   a the chairman
   b the secretary
   c a team member.

> **2** What information should a user give to a system developer in the way of user requirements?
>
> **3** Explain how a system developer could demonstrate to a user that he or she has understood their requirements.
>
> **4** List the tasks to be done in building the design for a computer system.
>
> **5** List the tasks to be done in preparing for a presentation.

Element 7.2: Implement a prototype of the system design individually

Software packages

Software packages are becoming more and more versatile. Packages originally designed for one purpose can now also be used for other purposes. For instance:

- in a word processor you might be able to
  - do simple arithmetic, in some cases even creating graphs from the figures
  - perform simple filing of data, particularly names and addresses, and searching, sorting and selection of this data
  - sort lines of text into alphabetical order
  - set up data entry screens
  - draw simple diagrams
- a spreadsheet may have facilities to
  - do some word processing (such as formatting text)
  - create graphs
  - do simple database work such as sorting, searching and selection
  - set up data entry screens
- with a database package you may be able to
  - do some fairly complicated mathematics
  - do some word processing such as mailmerges
  - produce graphics.

Integrated packages automatically share data between a word processor, a spreadsheet, a database and possibly other facilities such as a graphics package.

There are also packages which are designed for special purposes, for instance

- statistical packages allow data analysis to be done more simply than on a spreadsheet
- accounts packages can produce accounting reports more easily than a spreadsheet or database
- questionnaire analysis programs can produce and analyse questionnaires with less work than a spreadsheet, database or word processor
- packages exist to find biblical quotations, write timetables, keep track of hospital or student records, calculate examination results, work out forces on bending beams – and almost anything else that's needed.

Anyone who writes their own program, or adapts a package to a purpose which they think may have uses to other people in their profession, is likely to try to market it. Sometimes these special-purpose packages are excellent but sometimes, although they allow standard processes to be done quickly and easily, they cannot be used for less common processes.

Availability of software packages

Software can be expensive, and a company may buy only one package for a user. It often happens that the user is then asked to set up some fairly complicated systems on that package. The user becomes expert on this system and starts to use it for purposes other than its original use.

In real life you cannot always have the best package for the job. A secretary who is expert on a modern and sophisticated word processor sometimes keeps quite complicated records and does quite complicated accounts on it. The secretary claims that reports look best when word processed, and this is important enough to make it worth the extra ingenuity and work needed to use the word processor rather than a database or spreadsheet. An engineer who is expert on a spreadsheet also uses it for word processing and filing information. This allows easy access to calculating facilities, saves the cost of buying another package and prevents the engineer from having to learn to use another package.

Case study

Part three

```
Minutes of Customer Care Committee
3.00 p.m. Monday 14 October, Nik's office
People present: Nik (team leader), Jo (sec), Ray, Tiny, Lee
```

1 Minutes and matters arising.   **Action by**

The minutes were agreed as accurate. Nik thanked all members for the presentation. The manager was impressed.

2 Building a prototype – which package?

There was some disagreement over the package to use for the implementation, so it was agreed to prototype a number of different methods.

Jo said that if she was going to have to run the system, it would have to be in the word processing package on the secretarial computer. It already has an entry screen and it is possible to do tables and graphs   **Jo**

Nik felt the same way about the spreadsheet package on the management computer   **Nik**

Tiny claimed that a database package would be best for the job   **Tiny**

Ray suggested we compromise on an integrated package   **Ray**

Lee suggested a specialised package called 'Answers' which is written to analyse questionnaires   **Lee**

3 Facilities needed

Before going ahead with a prototype, we need to agree on facilities needed to build the system. However there is no time now. Tiny offered to list the facilities that he thought would be necessary   **Tiny**

4 Next meeting

Tomorrow, same time and place.

Meeting ended at 3.45.

Activity 7.7

Work in the team you were allocated to in Assignment A7.1. Keep minutes while you complete the tasks below.

1 Using computer magazines, Shareware catalogues and any other means, try to find

any software that might have been specially designed to work for your project. Find out if any such software is available for your use at your educational establishment.

2 List all the software packages available which you might be able to use for setting up the system you have designed.

3 Allocate a software package to each team member for prototyping the system. You should use at least two different types of package, and as far as possible allocate different packages.

Matching facilities needed to those offered

Input facilities:
- making the screen look like the data capture form
- inputting data into a field which can be validated by
  - type checks
  - range checks
  - checking against a list
  - checking against a file
  - check digits
- inputting data into fixed length fields
- inputting data of any length
- inputting formatted data, such as text formats and graphics.

Output facilities:
- choose screen layouts for text or graphics
- choose print layouts for text, graphics or tables
- lay out reports, labels, mailmerge
- produce sound.

Processing facilities:
- calculations
- comparisons
- searches
- sorts.

Data storage:
- text and numeric constants
- variable data which can be processed
- lists or tables of data
- data on
  - text files
  - data files with a record structure
  - databases.

Learning how to use a package

Eighty percent of computer users use less than 20% of the facilities. With a GNVQ in information technology, you should not be a member of the 80%/20% club.
- Read the screen. If you have menus in your package, take some time to find out what all the different options are.
- Use the on-line help. Always find the easiest way to do anything. It may take longer the first time, but in the long run it will speed you up. Assume that you can do something until you prove that you can't.

- Use on-line or written tutorials. Even if you think you know the package check through the tutorial quickly to see if you have left anything out.
- Read the manuals – they very often have information which is not on the on-line help screens. Use the index.
- Read books about the package. The more advanced of these often contain information that is not in the manual (some features of a package were not originally planned) and they are also often easier to understand than the original manual. These books can be very long, but look through the list of contents – you may learn about facilities that you didn't know even existed.
- Share information. Show off what you know to your friends. Learn from them. You may learn from students in other groups, from technicians, from shop assistants in computer stores, from telephone help lines – and even, sometimes, from your tutors. Don't be afraid to ask.

Case study

Part four

Minutes of Customer Care Committee
3.00 p.m. Tuesday 15 October in Nik's office
People present: Nik (team leader), Jo (secretary), Ray, Tiny, Lee

1 Minutes and matters arising

    The minutes were agreed as accurate.

2 Facilities needed compared to facilities in package

	Word processing	Spreadsheet	Database	Integrated package	Special package
Input					
Screen same as form	✓	?	Can choose from a list, rather than have a tick box	✓	?
Validation	Choose to put a I in a box	?	✓	✓ ✓	
Output					
Tables	✓	✓	?	✓	✓
Graphs	✓	✓	?	✓	?
Processing					
Calculations	✓	✓	✓	✓	✓
Searches	No, but I can copy parts of the table into another table	✓	✓	✓	✓
Data storage	Any data storage will do				
Text file	✓	No	No	✓	?
Data file	No	✓	✓	✓	?

Key: ✓ = yes, ? = probably, but need to find out

3 Next meeting

    Monday 28 October, 2.00 p.m., same place. Demonstrate prototypes
Meeting ended at 3.45

Activity 7.8

I List the facilities that you will need to create your system under the headings
  a input facilities required
  b output facilities required
  c data storage facilities required
  d data processing facilities required.

2 For each facility listed make notes explaining how it can be done in your chosen package. If it is not possible, explain how you will need to adapt the original design.

Creating a prototype

You will need to create the following.

1 Input processes, to include:
  • data capture forms
  • data input screens
  • data validation, if possible, or a data verification process for the operator.

2 Output processes, to include:
  • screen layouts
  • printed report layouts
  • any other output, such as sound.

3 Data stores, such as:
  • constant data that you will use (including perhaps the name of the firm at the head of every page)
  • variables that you may need for data processing
  • lists or tables of data
  • data files
  • databases.

4 Internal data processing, to include:
  • calculations
  • comparisons
  • searches
  • sorts
  • combinations of these processes.

A prototype system is the original system from which the final system will be developed. Most of it should work – certainly enough to give the general flavour. If, however, you run out of time, you can get by in a prototype by explaining what will happen eventually when you demonstrate the system.

Testing your system

Test each part of the system as you set it up. Also test the complete system. You should have test data from Assignment 7.1 – if not, invent some now. If some of the tests fail (perhaps not all the validations work), then you will need to explain how you intend to make them work when you demonstrate the final system.

You should keep a test log, containing details of:
• test data
• expected results
• actual results (which *should* be the same as the expected results – if they are not you must explain why).

User documentation

You must explain to the user how to use your system. The documentation you provide should be good enough for the user work your system from. It should include

- instructions for loading
- instructions for using
- notes on how to deal with errors.

Test questions

1 What sort of input facilities (hardware, data input screen, validation) would you use for:
   a inputting a number between 1 and 4
   b inputting text of unknown length
   c choosing a name from a list of names
   d inputting a self checking number, i.e. one containing a check digit?

2 What sort of output facility (hardware, type of application software) would you require for:
   a printing text in a variety of fonts
   b showing a pie chart on a screen
   c printing a table
   d printing 50 form letters separately addressed to different people
   e addressing envelopes.

3 What sort of processing facilities (calculation, search, selection, sort, validation) do you require for:
   a printing form letters to people with a Peterborough postcode only
   b printing out all the names in a list in alphabetical order
   c printing out the average price for a list of houses.

4 Explain how to keep a test log.

5 What do you need in user documentation?

Element 7.3: Evaluate the prototype implementations as a team

Evaluation of the prototype

At this stage the team comes together to decide on the prototype they will recommend to the user. Because the team will have to build the eventual system they will need to consider three factors:

1 How suitable the software package is for the purpose.
2 How easy it is to use the software package to develop the prototype further.
3 How easy the finished system will be to use.

Suitability of the software package

The software package can be judged by asking the following questions.

- How automatic is the processing? Must the user (your customer) make the processes happen or can the system developer (you) make it happen for them? If the system developer can make it work for the user, how easy can it be made for the user? Will the user, for instance, have to choose from a menu, use one or more key presses or will the processing be totally automatic?

- How easy is the input process? Will the user have to move the cursor between fields, or will it move automatically? Will validations be automatic or must the user verify the inputs? Can you easily add prompts and help messages?
- How easy is it for the user to produce reports? Are they generated automatically or must the user set them up? How well produced are the reports? Can they look word processed?
- How closely does the prototype look like the agreed design?

Ease of development of the system

This is another judge of the software package. It is important because systems that are more difficult to develop will be more expensive to develop and will cost more whenever the user needs modification. Ease of development can be judged by asking the following questions:

- How long does it take to set up the system?
- How good are the package's help facilities? How easy is it to do something that you have never done before on the package? How easy is the manual to understand?
- How much expert assistance did you need to learn the package?
- How much expert assistance did you need to use the package?

Ease of use of the prototype

This must be the major factor in making a recommendation to the user.

- How long will it take the user to learn to use the system? If the user is familiar with the package used, they will learn quite complex things more quickly than they will learn simple things on an unfamiliar package.
- How much training is required to use the system? Will the user need more help than is available in the user documentation?
- What happens if the user does something really stupid? Will the final system prevent this? Will the users be able to sort themselves out if they go wrong?
- How easy will it be for the user to modify the system themselves?

Recommend a system

Select the system that you recommend by asking the following questions in order.

1 Does it meet user requirements?
2 Is it easy to use?
3 How easy is it to develop?

Case study

Part five

```
Minutes of Customer Care Committee
2.00 p.m. Monday 28 October, Nik's office
People present: Nik (team leader), Jo (secretary), Ray, Tiny, Lee
```

1 Minutes and matters arising   **Action by**

   The minutes were agreed as accurate.

2 Demonstrations

   Word processor: Entered data into a table. Table had two columns each for possible answers to questions 1 and 6, four columns each for questions 2 25, one column for question 7 and one column for waiter no. Started a new table for each day. Entered a 1 for a tick and nothing otherwise. Could sum each column and make graphs from these sums. Easy to use if familiar with word processing package. Quite hard to develop **Jo**

Spreadsheet: Very smart input screen. We could see why Nik is an assistant manager – must have read whole manual! Input 1 for a tick (like Jo's system). Added a field for date, default taken from computer date so data could be chosen over a required period of time. Smart reports and graphs using function keys. Easy to use. Spreadsheet quite hard to learn, specially the twiddly bits. Needed some help understanding the manual and on-line help. Used help line at one stage. Now felt confident if questionnaire were to change **Nik**

Database: Smart input screen. Chose Yes or No (questions 1,6) and from four choices (questions 2-5) from a list, waiter's initials from list. Suggested control totals every 20 forms for checking data. Reports could be chosen from menu. Had not had time to work out how graphs could be added. Easy to use. Control totals a pain, but they would be necessary for checking that data entered correctly. This would be true for all the packages. Perhaps we should suggest a mark reader for the company? Database just as hard to learn as spreadsheet, but once learnt, changes could be made fairly easily. Inbuilt validations easier than making own on spreadsheet **Tiny**

Integrated package: Input Y or N (questions 1,6), 1-4 (questions 2-5). Reports and graphs chosen from menus, Had the best of facilities for word processing, spreadsheet and database. Did not go as deep as the specialist packages, which made it easier to learn, although some facilities were missing. Could change questionnaire fairly easily **Ray**

Specialised package: Input screens supplied and validated by package. Not as smart as Nik's or Tiny's. Reports and graphs supplied by package, Again, not as smart as the others, but very easy to produce. Very easy to use. Very easy to learn. Very easy to make alterations. Impossible if you wanted to do something not thought about already by package writers **Lee**

3 Recommendation

Word processor was most convoluted to amend. Also could not see how to validate. Spreadsheet, database, integrated package all produced smart and purpose-built reports and input screens. If company wanted to use a package already available in all branches then go for spreadsheet. These packages were all quite difficult to learn – the integrated package being easier than the other two, although the other two had more facilities. Specialised package reports and graphics were the least impressive, but exceedingly easy to learn, set up and amend.

Suggest choose *spreadsheet* if happy with this questionnaire, or *special package* if questionnaire needed altering.

4 Summing up

Nik thanked the team. Will take recommendations to area manager. Watch notice board for developments. **Nik**

Meeting finished 4.15 p.m.

Assignment A7.1
Design a computerised system

This assignment provides portfolio evidence for Element 7.1 and also for the following key skills:

Application of number Element 2.2:	Tackle patterns
Application of number Element 2.3:	Interpret and present data
Communication Element 2.1:	Take part in discussions
Communication Element 2.2:	Produce written material
Communication Element 2.3:	Use images

GNVQ Projects are working on:
1 Scenario 1 (see Activity 7.2).
2 Scenario 2 (see Activity 7.5).
3 A computer system to record interim grades and calculate final grades for each GNVQ student. It should be able to print out at any time:
  a the grades so far
  b the grades needed by each student to achieve
    • distinction (if possible)
    • merit (if possible).
4 A computer system to record where students go after they leave a course at that educational establishment. It should be able to store the information in categories:
  a further education at the current educational establishment
  b further education at another educational establishment
  c a job
  d other
and should be able to report the findings in useful ways.
5 Other systems suggested by your tutor.

Your line manager (your tutor) will put you into project teams of 3–6 students and allocate your team a system to design.
1 Organise your team. Minutes must be taken of all meetings showing
  a participation of team members
  b agreement on the meaning of user requirements
  c allocation of tasks between team members.
2 Design the system.
3 Organise the presentation.
4 Give the presentation.

Assignment A7.2
Implementing a prototype system

This assignment provides portfolio evidence for Element 7.2 and also for the following key skill elements:

Application of number 2.1:	Collect and record data

Application of number 2.2:	Tackle problems
Application of number 2.3:	Interpret and present data
Communication 2.1:	Take part in discussions
Communication 2.2:	Produce written material
Communication 2.3:	Use images
Communication 2.4:	Read and respond to written material

1 Create and test the system designed in Assignment A7.1 on the package allocated to you in Activity 7.7.
2 Demonstrate the system to your tutor.
3 Write user documentation.

Assignment A7.3
Evaluate the prototypes and select one for the user

This assignment provides evidence for Element 7.3 and also the following key skills:
Communication element 2.1:   Take part in discussions

Hold a minuted meeting to evaluate the prototype and select one to recommend to the user. Your tutor will either observe the meeting or appoint an observer to check how well members of the team participate in the meeting. During the meeting the team will:
1 Evaluate the software packages used for suitability.
2 Evaluate the software packages for ease of development.
3 Evaluate the implementations for ease of use.
4 Select one of the systems for the user, giving reasons for the selection.

CHAPTER 8

Presenting information using application software packages (intermediate)

What is covered in this chapter

- Presentation of numerical information
- Presentation of information as text and pictures
- Presentation of information as audio visual aids
- Benefits of a house style
- Designing a house style
- Creating documents in a house style
- Creating a guide to a house style
- Presenting numerical information graphically
- Presenting a report
- Creating promotional literature
- Creating audio-visual aids

Resources you will need for your Organisations and Information Technology file:

- Your written answers to the activities in this chapter
- Your written answers to the questions at the end of the chapter
- Your completed assignments A8.1, A8.2 and A8.3

Introduction

One very important use of IT is in presenting information. This unit investigates the use in information presentation of commonly available IT packages.

Word processors allow written information to be presented clearly and attractively. **Graphics** packages allow pictures and diagrams to be produced easily, and these can be added to text. **Desktop publishing** (DTP) packages allow text and graphics to be put together on a page easily, and the layout altered at the touch of a few keys or mouse movements. **Business graphics** packages and spreadsheets allow graphical presentation of numerical data. **Presentation** packages can be used to produce visual aids and complete presentations. **Multimedia** packages, which are becoming affordable and therefore more common, also allow sound and animation to be added. **Hypertext** packages pull together 'computer pages' to make interactive computer presentations and allow cross-referencing between computer pages and other presentations written with hypertext. Hypertext is used for pages on the Internet and allows cross-referencing to other Internet sites across the world.

Computerised production of text and graphics, together with high-speed copying techniques have changed the printing industry completely. Pages used to be set in lead – lead letters for text and pictures engraved on lead blocks in a lead foundry. Changing the layout of a page involved serious work. Nowadays page layout can be altered on a computer in minutes.

Element 8.1: Investigate the use of software packages to present information

Presenting numerical information

Numerical information means any information involving numbers. This will include measurements such as length and weight, and quantities such as numbers and values.

Numbers may be shown written anyhow . . . . . .

Production figures for past three years			
Quarter	1994	1995	1996
Jan – Mar	23000	24500	26000
Apr – Jun	25000	26200	26300
Jul – Sep	23450	28200	26500
Oct – Dec	32100	34500	35400

in a table . . . . .

or

shown in a graph

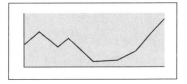

Figure 8.1 Presenting numerical information

Graphs

We can sometimes make numerical information easier to understand by putting the information in a table or in a graph.

Line graphs On a line graph you join points with straight lines. It is possible to draw more than one line on a graph. This is useful if you want to compare two different sets of numbers. Drawing two lines that have nothing to do with each other is unhelpful. Some examples are shown in Figure 8.2.

Bar charts In a bar chart the length of a bar is used to show the size of a number. Bars may be vertical or horizontal. They can also be used to show proportion. Figure 8.3 shows the data in Figure 8.2 as a bar chart. Which do you think is more effective?

Pie charts Pie charts are useful to show proportion, or how a quantity is shared. An example of a pie chart is shown in Figure 8.4. Newer versions of integrated packages, dedicated spreadsheets and dedicated business graphics packages are likely to have more graph drawing facilities than these.

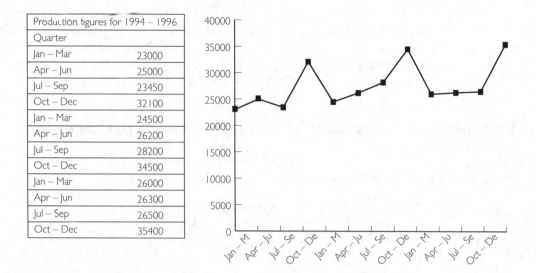

Production figures for 1994 – 1996	
Quarter	
Jan – Mar	23000
Apr – Jun	25000
Jul – Sep	23450
Oct – Dec	32100
Jan – Mar	24500
Apr – Jun	26200
Jul – Sep	28200
Oct – Dec	34500
Jan – Mar	26000
Apr – Jun	26300
Jul – Sep	26500
Oct – Dec	35400

This shows that production seems generally to be going up, but with odd peaks. Let us regroup the data...

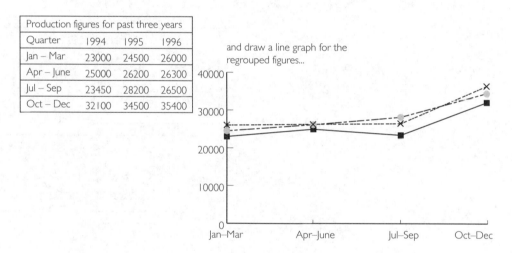

Production figures for past three years			
Quarter	1994	1995	1996
Jan – Mar	23000	24500	26000
Apr – June	25000	26200	26300
Jul – Sep	23450	28200	26500
Oct – Dec	32100	34500	35400

and draw a line graph for the regrouped figures...

This shows us that production peaks in October to December, (perhaps due to Christmas?). We can also see that sales for the third quarter for 1996 were below the third quarter for 1995.

Figure 8.2 Drawing line graphs from data

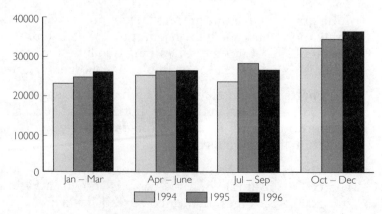

Figure 8.3 Bar chart from the data shown in Figure 8.2

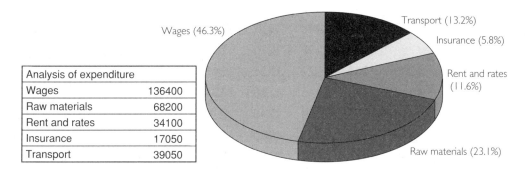

Analysis of expenditure	
Wages	136400
Raw materials	68200
Rent and rates	34100
Insurance	17050
Transport	39050

Figure 8.4 Expressing data as a pie chart. The spreadsheet package drew the graph as well as calculating the percentages.

Activity 8.1

May produce evidence for communications element 2.3 and application of number 2.3.

A record company wants to write to its shareholders giving them the following information:

- The sales in the second half of the year have gone up by 1.6% to £1 467 800 000.
- The pre-tax profits have gone up by 37.4% to £146 200 000.
- Shareholders' dividends will go up to 8p per share, which is 12.6% more than they received in the first half of the year.
- The operating profit came geographically:

£11.7 million	from the UK
£67.1 million	from the rest of Europe
£7.8 million	from North America
£24.9 million	from Asia
£8.3 million	from the rest of the world.

1 Using your spreadsheet show these figures in as many different ways you can.
2 Which graphs would you use to give this information to the shareholders?

Numerical data

A set of numbers may be unrelated data items or tables of data. Unrelated data items have nothing to do with each other. For instance, if I say that I am 1.68 m tall, own two cats and yesterday I bought 2.5 kg of carrots, the numbers 1.68, 2 and 2.5 have no relation at all to each other. I cannot do any useful analysis on these numbers. Tables of data, on the other hand, will contain numbers that are in some way related to each other. The fact that they have been put in a table already shows that some analysis can be made.

Activity 8.2

May produce evidence for application of number 2.2 and 2.3.

A washing powder manufacturer weighed a random sample of their 1.2 kg packets and found the weight of powder (in grams) to be:

1222	1196	1247	1219	1196	1196	1262	1212	1191	1260
1255	1207	1208	1232	1197	1234	1190	1216	1212	1191
1204	1238	1239	1215	1217	1236	1261	1215	1214	1213
1266	1250	1222	1226	1217	1212	1207	1201	1232	1249
1242	1223	1215	1216	1251	1247	1217	1217	1253	1249
1214	1203	1254	1240	1229	1215	1220	1256	1212	1194
1210	1220	1201	1260	1199	1232	1201	1227	1218	1233
1245	1221	1232	1195	1233	1216	1228	1214	1196	1237
1202	1248	1272	1257	1198	1214	1219	1217	1222	1225
1244	1285	1237	1254	1204	1192	1211	1244	1186	1217

1 Use the data to complete this table:

Weight of washing powder in boxes

Underweight	Not more than 1% overweight	1% or over but under 2% overweight	2% or over but under 5% overweight	5% or more overweight

2 To make sure that no boxes would be underweight, which would be illegal, the filling machine is reset to give an extra 10 g. Assuming that the variation in the amount of powder in the boxes stays the same (i.e. each box would have 10 g more of soap powder than before), how would the table look?

3 Draw a suitable graph to show the two sets of figures.

Types of numerical data

Discrete data

Data which can only have certain values is called discrete data. All digital data is discrete because it can only have whole number values. Examples of discrete data are number of children in a family (there must be a whole number), or British shoe sizes, which go up in halves.

Continuous

Continuous data can have any value at all – for example a person's height does not jump from 1.60 m to 1.61 m, but goes through all the in-between values, even if we cannot measure them exactly. Related continuous data can be converted using a line graph, as shown, for example, in Figure 8.5.

Activity 8.3

May produce evidence for application of number 2.2.

1 Draw a graph to convert temperature between degrees Fahrenheit and degrees Celsius, given that:

- the freezing point of water = 0°C   32°F
- the boiling point of water = 100°C   212°F.

2 Why wouldn't this method work for converting between age and school year?

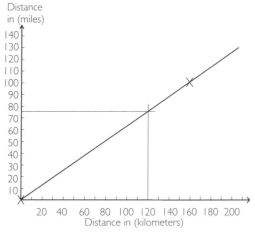

To convert between miles and kilometres
We know that:

Miles	Kilometres
0	0
100	160

Draw a graph with miles marked along one axis and kilometres along the other.
Mark and number a convenient scale on each axis.
Plot the points from the table above (2 points).
Join them with a ruler to make a straight-line graph.

Figure 8.5 Drawing a graph from a set of continuous data

Proportions

As we have seen, pie charts are very useful way of showing proportions. Another way is to use a proportional bar chart.

Compare the chart in Figure 8.6 with the pie chart in Figure 8.4. Which is more clear? The bar chart can be much more effective than a pie chart when comparing sets of proportions. Figure 8.7 shows a set of proportional bar charts for the data given in Figure 8.2.

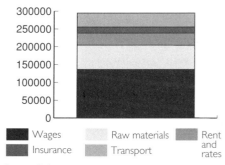

Figure 8.6

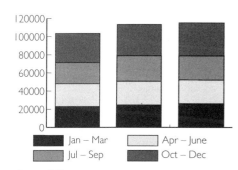

Figure 8.7

Activity 8.4

May produce evidence for application of number 2.1, 2.2 and 2.3.

1 Look up advertisements for property in your local newspaper. Make a table showing the numbers of properties in different price ranges. Choose your price ranges according to the prices in the paper.

2 Use a suitable graph to compare the number of houses for sale in the different price ranges.

3 Repeat this exercise over several weeks. Use suitable graphs to compare
   a number of houses for sale over this period
   b trends in house prices.

Amounts of data

The amount of data to show will have some bearing on how you show it. For instance, a pie chart becomes too muddled if it is split into more than eight or ten slices. The sizes of ranges can make a difference.

Activity 8.5

May produce evidence for application of number 2.1, 2.2 and 2.3.
Compare different students' answers to Activity 8.4.

Desktop publishing

A DTP package is there to do the work of a publisher. It takes text (from a word processing package) and illustrations (from a graphics or painting package) and allows the publisher to move them around to produce a clear, informative layout. The DTP package may have limited word processing and/or graphic processing facilities itself, but its main job is not to write or draw. Equally, nowadays many word processing packages and graphics packages include some DTP facilities, but page layout this is not their main job.

Desktop publishing is used to lay out a page or pages of a larger publication such as a book, magazine or newsletter. The package should allow you to set up individual pages, and also to set up master pages to hold the layout for individual pages. Many modern DTP packages have ready-made master pages that you can choose from as well as letting you tailor your own.

The facilities that you should master in desktop publishing are page layout, paragraph layout and graphics layout.

Page layout

You should be able to set the following in a DTP package:

- The size of a page. Your package will usually give you a choice of standard sizes – A4, A5, US letter – and will also allow you make up your own page size in imperial measure (inches), metric measure (cm), point sizes (there are 72 points to an inch) or picas (there are six of these to an inch).
- The orientation of a page – a portrait page is longer than it is wide, landscape is wider than it is long.
- Separate text areas and picture areas, and the way text behaves at pictures – how close to the picture can it go, whether it flows round the picture, whether pictures and texts be printed above each other.
- Text to be printed in columns if required, and the size of each column.

Paragraph layout

This will include the following:

- Font, size and colour of text. The word font comes from the boxes (similar in shape to fonts in churches holding holy water for christenings) which held the lead type letters.
- Whether paragraphs are framed, shaded or left plain.
- Spacing between lines and letters and between paragraph. The spacing between lines is called leading, because it was once produced by putting a strip of lead between the rows of lead letters.
- Indentation of paragraphs – whether they are indented at the beginning, whether they are indented after the first line (these are called hanging indents), or no indentation used.

- Whether the letters of text are kerned – whether they overlap or whether each letter is separate so that a vertical line can be drawn between them (Figure 8.8).

Figure 8.8 The letters on the right have been kerned – they overlap. The letters on the left have no kerning between them

Graphic layout
The graphic layout should include:
- putting frames around pictures if required
- choosing the shape and size of the pictures.

Importing text and pictures
A DTP package should allow you to import text from most word processors and text editors, and graphics from most graphic packages and graphic formats.

Graphics images can come from a number of sources:
- Libraries of pictures – most DTP and graphics packages will have their own libraries and it is possible to buy libraries of pictures.
- From a specialised drawing package, such as CorelDraw, ClarisDraw.
- It is possible to scan photographs and line images using a flatbed scanner or a hand scanner, and then use a specialist graphic package to process them. There are many such packages available – processing for instance Micrographix, Ofoto.

Text is generally entered into a computer using a word processor, but it is possible to scan text and use a package such as Calera Wordscan or OmniPage to turn it into word processed text. If you have access to a scanner and the appropriate software you should practice scanning pictures and text at some stage in your activities or assignments.

Activity 8.6

May produce evidence for communication element 2.2, 2.3 and 2.4.

You are asked to edit a newsletter for sending to shareholders of British Music Recording Company, a large record company. The newsletter is to be A5. It will be made up of a sheet of A4 folded in half and will therefore contain four A5 pages. The first page will consist of the chairman's report, which will be about 250 words. This report will be accompanied by a picture of the chairman, with a suitable caption. The heading should just be 'Chairman's Report'. You will be expected to add a subheading once you have read the report. The cover of the newsletter will also have the company's and name logo. Remember that this is a newsletter for shareholders when you decide the layout.

I Design the layout of the cover page, printing out Greek rubbish text and a picture which could of be the chairman. (Using Greek letters is known in the printing trade as **greeking**. By using Greek letters, the eye is unlikely to be distracted into reading the text rather than judging the layout. Symbol is a Greek alphabet font. Another foreign alphabet could as easily be used.)

2 The back page will contain the statistical information given in Activity 8.1. Design and produce this page.

3 Inside, page 2 will hold an article about the company's best selling artist or artists. As editor you have total control over this page (Choose your favourite artists or invent some). However, remember your readership is more likely to be impressed by the money these artists make for the company than their sex lives.

4 Page 3 is about the new facilities for artists who design the covers for CDs; these are described in Activity 8.7. Your job as Newsletter Editor is to write and illustrate a short article for the shareholders about these facilities. You will need to research computer-aided art hardware and software in computer or graphic art journals.

Making a presentation

When you write a report and give it to someone to read, they can read it more than once, study it carefully and look back if they have forgotten something. When you make a **presentation** you talk to an audience. Once you have said something, it is gone – you cannot be 'rewound'. And a member of the audience may well lose attention for a short while. When making a presentation you use **audio-visual aids** to:

- Give the audience a visual focus to what you are saying. This helps to keep their attention.
- Explain a point using a picture, diagram or graph to illustrate what you are saying.
- Remind the audience what you are talking about to keep their attention from wandering.

Planning a presentation

If you have to make a presentation you might find the following checklist useful.

1 Plan what you want to say.
  a Write down the main points.
  b Write down sub-headings for the main points, or even sub-headings to your headings.

2 For each point (and sub-point) write down
  a exactly what you want to say – that way you won't forget anything
  b how you will illustrate this point:
    • with a visual aid
    • with a joke or anecdote
    • or whatever.

3 Prepare the visual aids.

4 Remember that your audience cannot go back and listen again, so:
  a tell them what you are going to say – give them a 'contents' for your talk using a visual aid
  b make your presentation using such visual aids as you think necessary
  c summarise what you have said – giving them an opportunity to ask questions.

5 People look at overhead transparencies from quite far away, so they should be
  a bold
  b in large print
  c fairly simple.

If possible, give the audience copies of your transparencies because not everyone has perfect eyesight.

6 When you put a visual aid up give the audience time to read it before continuing to talk

7 Rehearse, and time, your presentation.

Presentation packages

Presentation packages are designed to help you with the complete presentation. The best known presentation package is probably Microsoft's Powerpoint. With Powerpoint you can create your own visual aids. Providing you have the right output devices you can print out transparencies, 35 mm slides or create a computer presentation to project directly. The package offers a large number of formats with pictures and text including the sort of text formats, such as bullet points, often used for overhead transparencies. It also allows master slides to be made – so that all the transparencies can come up with the company logo, for instance. The package is also likely to include a large library of graphic images. As well as creating visual aids, Powerpoint allows you to create notes to go with the aids, handouts for the audience and an outline of the presentation. Later versions also give you help with organising the presentation. You pick the type of presentation you want from a menu and the package will suggest points that you may want to make. There are several slide layouts to choose from; these include spaces for graphs, tables, charts and graphics. It is possible to create patterns from text, such as wavy or sideways text, to add pretty extras like stars or balloons to the background, and if giving a computer presentation there are smart ways of moving between slides (like cross-fading, for instance). The package even contains a facility for timing how long you spend on each slide when you rehearse your presentation. As you would expect with a package this sophisticated it also comes with comprehensive help facilities.

Activity 8.7

May produce evidence for communication element 2.2, 2.3 and 2.4.

British Music Recording Company has hired you to be in charge of public relations. You have persuaded the art department to buy new graphics equipment which will enable them to produce new, exciting covers for the recordings, which can be printed in different languages for different countries. This is one of the factors in the success of the company this year – the sales of existing recordings that were given new covers increased by an average of 7.2%.

1 Use the help facilities on your presentation package to create a short presentation introducing yourself to the shareholders and explaining the new technology and how it has increased sales.

Test questions

1 Name two types of graph which might be used
   a to show proportions
   b to show change in income over a period of time.
2 What two criteria would you use to choose a suitable graph type?
3 Describe the difference between
   a discrete data items and tables of data
   b continuous and discrete changes.

4 Name a software package that you use for drawing tables and graphs of numerical data. Explain how you
  a change the graph type
  b change the graph size
  c name the axes
  d change the paper orientation.
5 Name a desktop publishing package that you have used. Explain for how you can
  a set up a page format with text area and picture area
  b import text
  c import a picture
  d make a headline
  e put a border round a picture.
6 Name a package that you have used to present information as an audio-visual aid. Describe one aid that you have created, and explain how you made it.

Element 8.2: Create a house style for presentation of information

Trade marks

A commercial company wants to be recognised by the public, and wants its customers to think of them at every opportunity. So it tries to use some sort of design or colour which makes you think of them and which you recognise immediately.

Figure 8.9 Producing a company image

These trade marks are so important to the companies that they can be registered by law, and anyone else using them, or something similar to them, may be sued.

Activity 8.13

Make a collage of about ten trademarks that you find memorable. Can you include some colours that make you think of a particular product?

House style

Companies then create a company style – this is known as a **house style**. They decide on a **logo** that represents them, on a colour or set of colours, even on a particular font to use in their literature. (Times Roman was invented by the publishers of *The Times* newspaper). They paint their vehicles in company colours, dress manual staff in the company colours, have ties with company logos, and produce all their stationery with the company logo.

So that all communications from the company look similar, they produce rules for the layout of letters and other external communications. These are called **company standards**.

Benefits of having a house style

1 The company can create an image. This has benefits:
   - Externally, in that customers and potential customers get to know that the company exists. Hopefully this is a good image, which makes people feel kindly disposed to the company.
   - Internally, by making staff feel a part of the company. This can build up company loyalty, and a feeling of belonging. If employees feel proud of their company, they will work better and will also advertise the company to their friends and acquaintances.
2 At the same time they can improve the quality of communications in the company. They can ensure that all communications, both inside and outside the company, conform to a set pattern.
   - Externally this will be of benefit in that all documents will look neat, dynamic and businesslike.
   - Internally the rules will make it easy to read information quickly as the layout of the documents will be in a standard format.
3 The company can set standards that all its staff must stick to. These are instructions on layouts, text styles and numerical styles.

Company stationery

Company stationery is printed in the sizes the company chooses to use, with the company's logo printed in a set position in the company colours and in the correct size for the page. Depending on the use for the stationery, the company's address, phone, fax and e-mail numbers, VAT number and directors' names will be printed in the correct colour and the correct place. For internal communications, such as memos and telephone messages, much simpler stationery, without a logo and in only one colour (probably black) print might be used.

Outlines for memos to be sent by e-mail through the company's LAN or WAN should be held on computer, as should fax front sheets. It is possible for outlines of all company stationery to be held on computer, and the whole letter, logo and all, to be printed on white paper, but it is usually cheaper to print the stationery separately. This is because colour printing of the logo will wear out one of the colours on a colour printer more than the others. Also companies often use special, expensive, paper for its external letters, and people will waste this if it is used for internal mail.

Outlines of text to be printed on headed paper need to take into account the spaces needed for headers and footers when setting the margins.

Figure 8.10 This company writes database software. They chose the name for the software to have the image of fitting the right piece of data into the right place – where it fits. At the same time, they thought an image of a square peg in a square hole was a good idea. Hence the name, Datafit, and the logo. They chose the colour, orange, for brightness

It is not unusual for organisations to change their name if they feel the old name has the 'wrong' image. The name, the logo and the image should all fit together. Many logos are made from the organisation's initials. Often an organisation will have rules about when a logo can be used and what size it should be.

Activity 8.14

In your new job as public relations director to British Music Recording Company you need to think of the company's image. Design a logo for the company and decide when it should be used, what size it should be and its colour. You may change the name of the company if you think it necessary.

Text styles

Letters

Letters are important means of communication for a company. In Europe the page size used is A4, or sometimes A5 (half the size of A4). Some organisations use only A4 for letters, others use A5 for short letters. Not all computer printers can handle A5, so you should consider this when deciding on letter size.

The logo, address, telephone, fax and e-mail numbers will be printed on the letterhead. Other information is sometimes printed on the letterhead, or sometimes on a footer. This information may include:

- details of any parent organisation
- directors' names and qualifications
- trade associations
- registration numbers
- VAT number.

The type font and size may be company standard, as may the letter's layout. The layout will tell the employees where to position the following on the page:

- references, if the are not printed
- the date and its format
- the greeting (Dear ...)
- the beginning of the letter – whether to have a heading for the letter and if so whether it should be enhanced (bold, italic and/or underlined)
- subsequent paragraphs
- the salutation (Yours faithfully for letters starting Dear Sir, or Yours sincerely for letters naming the recipient)
- the space for the signature, and how to type the name and position in the firm of the signer
- the address of the recipient
- who copies are sent to.

Compliment slips

Compliment slips are usually about a third or a quarter the size of the printed letter paper, and contain similar information. They usually show the header and footer of the letter paper, with enough room in the middle for a printed message ('with the compliments of') and a short hand-written message. They are used to insert with a communication other than a letter, such as a copy of a report or an example of the organisation's output. If, for instance, you wrote to a wallpaper manufacturer for some samples, or you sent back a faulty product which was being replaced free of charge, the samples, or new product might be sent back to you with a compliment slip.

Figure 8.11 A company's standard letter paper

Figure 8.12 Datafit's compliments slip

Reports

Reports are formal communications written for a purpose. The purpose of a report is usually known as its terms of reference and explain what the report is about and why you are writing it.

A short report is usually made up of:

- terms of reference
- investigation procedure – i.e. how you collected the information
- findings – what information you found
- conclusions – what this information tells you
- recommendations, if required by the terms of reference.

A long report will need more structure to make it easier to read. You will need the following:

- a title page with report title, name(s) of author(s), date of writing, perhaps the name of the person or people who asked for the report
- a table of contents to make it easy to find what you want in the report

- a summary of the report
- the main report – which is the same as the short report (terms of reference, investigation procedure, findings, conclusions, recommendations)
- acknowledgements, which is a list of people who helped you with the report, and list of source material (such as books) you used
- appendices – these will contain the raw data which you discuss in the report.

Memos

Memos are for internal use only. There is no need for the organisation's address and there is usually no need for greetings or salutations. There should be space for:

- the date – can be automatically inserted by computer
- the name(s) of the sender(s)
- the name(s) of the recipient(s)
- a heading
- the message.

STANLEY THORNES

MEMORANDUM

To: From: Date:

Re:

Figure 8.13 The stationery for internal memos might look like this

Note pads

Pads for telephone messages should be put by the telephones. They need space for:

- date of telephone call
- time of telephone call
- caller's name and phone number
- the message
- name of the person taking the message.

Some organisations print these on two-part paper, so that a copy of the message remains in the message pad. The person being called has to say when the call was returned.

Fax front sheets

Fax messages usually have a front sheet, giving:

- who the fax is to – company and individual and fax number
- who is sending the fax – individual as well as company information

- the number of pages (this is usually added automatically by software sending the fax)
- date
- company name and logo, fax number and address
- other relevant information about the company.
  The fax front sheet that Datafit use is shown in Figure 8.14.

Figure 8.14 Datafit's fax front sheet

Number style

Many people find numerical information harder to understand than textual information. It helps to send numerical information in an agreed format. An example in a college might be lecturer returns of student attendance to Management Information, or monthly figures sent from the finance section to heads of departments detailing items purchased and money still available in the departmental budget.

Related numbers are always easier to understand if the relations are obvious. They should therefore always be displayed in relevant tables. If the numerical information is being sent to anyone who may not be used to dealing with numbers it should be shown graphically to help the recipient.

To summarise, use tables whenever numbers are related, and the recipient is not a mathematician or accountant. Use graphs when pictorial form will aid understanding – line graphs for statistics over a period of time (such as sales and profits, birth and death rates, weather), bar graphs for comparing similar statistics over a period of time (e.g. relative sales of CDs, tapes and vinyl records over a period), pie charts for showing proportions of a total.

Presentation styles

Overhead transparencies are used to illustrate a spoken presentation, but can also be used to keep the name of the company in mind while the presentation is taking place. For instance, the company logo could be present discreetly on all transparencies, or the background could be in the company colours. The

The secret of a good presentation is

PANIC

Be sure of your	**P**urpose
Gear it to the	**A**udience
What is the	**N**eed for the presentation
Collect your	**I**nformation
Prepare the	**C**ommunication

Figure 8.15

organisation may also produce standards for any outside presentations – such as

- slide 1 should *always* introduce the organisation (and may even be a standard transparency)
- slide 2 should introduce yourself – in standard format (and may even be produced for each individual by a central department)
- slide 3 should outline the presentation, and the style of bullet points to be used may be standardised
- slides showing equipment or goods produced by the company could be standard within the organisation
- always take a company's laptop and projector to an out-of-house presentation in case their equipment does not work.

Leaflets are written presentations. As such they are often in a standard format to promote the organisation and its image. They may

- be of standard size – this could be a fairly complicated standard and could vary with the number of pages in the leaflet and how the leaflet is to be distributed. Leaflets that are usually sent by post should be a convenient size for putting in an envelope, while leaflets left for taking in a library should maybe be larger and more eye-catching
- be a standard colour – this could also be a complicated standard. A further education college, for instance, might use a different colour and front picture for each faculty so that potential students can pick up the one they are interested in quickly and so that the cover of, say, the engineering faculty leaflets is more likely to catch the eyes of students interested in engineering
- include the company logo
- be correctly spelt and grammatical.

Posters are used to attract attention. Their message must be put across using as few words as possible, but at the same time they must tell readers all they need to know. Standards for posters might include an instruction such as 'all posters must be produced with the help of the publicity department'.

Test questions

1 List the benefits of having a house style.
2 List the attributes which may be specified for a house style.
3 List information which should go into a guide on house style.

Element 8.3: Present information using house style

Promotional literature

Promotional literature sells an idea or product. Advertising is a sort of promotional literature, but so is a memo to your boss in which you try to persuade her to agree to one of your ideas. People reading promotional literature might not agree with what you say, at least to start with. The job of this literature is to persuade, so:

- keep it short
- keep to the point
- be positive, but truthful
- make your main point first
- make it interesting
- once you have got the attention of the reader, you can make further points
- pictures can help, but should be chosen to make a point of their own.

Activity 8.13

1 Choose three of your favourite advertisements.
   a Why do you like them?
   b What points are they making?
   c Do they make you want to buy the product?
2 Choose the advertisement you hate most, and analyse why you dislike it. Has it stopped you buying the product?
3 How can you persuade the rest of your class to accept your logo for British Music Recording Company?

Audio-visual material for presentation

Very often in a presentation you are promoting an idea or product. The audience have not always chosen to be present.

Start a promotional presentation with its purpose.
- What do you want to persuade your audience about?
- Why do they need something new?
- What is your answer to that need?
- What are the benefits to your audience of your answer to the need?
- Summarise your points.
- How can your audience support you with your answer?

Visual aids

People see these from a long way away, so keep words, diagrams, graphs and pictures large and clear.
- Keep any writing on a visual aid short – five or six lines only. Make them as large as possible.
- Would a picture help?
- Whenever possible, show numerical data as a graph and label your graphs clearly. Keep all writing horizontal, even on vertical axes of a graph. Large scales on vertical axes against small scales on horizontal axes emphasises ups and downs. Write labels outside any colouring or shading.

Assignment A8.1
Investigate the use of software packages to present information

This assignment provides portfolio coverage for Element 8.1.

head of public relations to British Music Recording Company you were amazed by how little technology is used in the offices of the company, especially as they all have access to a variety of software over the company network. Write a report to be circulated to office staff on using software packages to present information. The report should include the following points.

1 The suitability of graph types for the illustration of numerical data.
2 The capabilities of a spreadsheet to present numerical information as graphs.
3 The use of desktop publishing to present information as text and pictures.
4 The use of software packages to present information as visual aids.

Assignment A8.2
Create a house style for presentation of information

This assignment provides portfolio coverage for Element 8.2.

In your position in the public relations department for the British Music Recording Company you wish to build on your success with the new artwork by making the whole image of the company more dynamic. Your new logo (produced in Activity 8.7) has been accepted by the board, and your next job is to produce a total house style guide for the company.

1 Design the following:
 a the total house style including
  • logos (position, size, colours)
  • text styles (letter layout, report layout, memo, telephone messages, fax messages)
  • numerical style (tables, graphs)
 b documents, which should include
  • internal documents (memos, reports, message pads)
  • external documents (letters, reports, letter heads, compliment slips, fax sheets)
  • presentation (overheads, posters, leaflets)
2 Produce
 a samples of documents in the house style
 b instructions for the production of each document, including both written instructions and computer templates where relevant. Any computer templates should come complete with instructions on how to use them
 c a guide to production of documents to be sent to the staff of the Company, which should include
  • a description of the benefits of the house style
  • the designs
  • the samples and instructions.

Assignment A8.3
Present information using the house style

This assignment provides portfolio coverage for Element 8.3 and also for the following key skill elements:

Communication 2.1:   Take part in discussions
Communication 2.2:   Produce written material
Communication 2.3:   Use images

The American subsidiary of the British Music Recording Company has adopted your house style, but there is some opposition in the UK offices. You have done some market research into the company image in the USA and the UK and have obtained the following figures:

Feature	Yes	No	Don't know
Recognised the company logo			
USA	90%	10%	
UK	42%	58%	
Could name a company product correctly			
USA	87%	13%	
UK	39%	61%	
The company name is a guarantee of good quality			
USA	78%	12%	10%
UK	32%	23%	45%
The company is dynamic and knows what we want			
USA	82%	12%	6%
UK	34%	23%	43%
The company has signed up most of the best groups			
USA	80%	14%	6%
UK	34%	20%	45%

Company sales have increased in the USA by 13% last year, while decreasing in UK by 1.4% over the same period (in line with overall figures in the music trade in the UK).

1 Design suitable promotional literature (in the house style) to persuade the staff in the UK to accept your ideas.
2 Design an audio-visual presentation (in the house style) to persuade the staff in the UK to accept your ideas.
3 Write a report to the British board of directors
   a showing the results of your market research
   b tying it to sales figures in the UK
   c suggesting that they let you promote your ideas to themselves and the staff in general using the literature and presentation designed above.

Glossary

Accuracy check	A check to make sure that data entered into the computer is accurate. It includes **validation** checks, **verification** checks, **correctness** checks.
Analogue data	Analogue data is represented by another quantity proportional to it. For example, a temperature sensor produces an analogue reading – more temperature, more voltage. See **digital data**.
Attribute	A characteristic or property of something. One of a person's attributes is their date of birth. In a database an attribute is equivalent to a field.
Audio-visual aids	Slide-show, animation, overhead transparencies, multimedia.
Backup	A second copy of something to be used if there is a problem with the first. Backup copies of important **files** should be kept.
Bar chart	Diagram showing data as a bar or line, whose length is in proportion to the size of the data being represented.
Batch processing	Dealing with a whole set of transactions in one operation, rather than individually. Electricity bills are normally produced in a batch. The alternative is interactive **on-line** processing.
Bit	A binary digit – a 1 or a 0.
Boot	'Booting' happens when a computer starts up, or is reset. A bootstrap program is run, and this loads the operating system from disk into memory and starts it running. The boot program is stored in **ROM**, so it is not lost when the computer is switched off.
Bug	A fault in a computer program causing it to work incorrectly.
CD-ROM	Stands for compact disc read-only memory. Looks like a music compact disc and is used to store large amounts of information. Much software is now supplied on CD-ROM.
Characters	All the symbols on a keyboard – letters of the alphabet (upper and lower case), digits, punctuation marks and the SPACE character. Different countries use different sets of characters, such as Φ and Ω and Ä. There are also symbols such as ™.
Check digit	A number which has been added to a reference number so that the complete reference number can be tested using an arithmetic formula
Cleaning disks	Removing data from disks.
Clip art	Drawings, diagrams, paintings and photographs stored in computer files. Since most computer users are not very artistic, it is easier for them to choose graphics from large collections of clip art, and paste them into their own documents. Clip art is often kept on **CD-ROM**.
Configuration	How a computer is set up, such as whether it uses a British or American

keyboard, colour monochrome monitor or, whether dates are shown in English or American format, and so on.

Constraints	Limits or restrictions, or some rule to be followed. An information system might have a constraint that it had to use no more than 10 MB of disk space.
Consumables	The items that are 'consumed' by computer users – floppy disks, printer paper, mouse mats, etc.
Continuous numerical data	Any values within a certain range, e.g. length, temperature.
Copyright	The owner of data and the manufacturer of software owns the copyright on the data and software. Anyone using the data or software without permission is breaking the law
Correctness check	Checking data at **input** by looking at it and deciding if it is meaningful. Data can be verified and validated and still be meaningless.
CPU	Stands for central processing unit. This is the part of the computer which contains memory and can carry out program instructions.
Data	Data can be in the form of text, numbers, graphics, sounds, and so on. It is **input** into a computer, stored, **processed** and **output**.
Data capture	Entering data into a computer system. May be by using a barcode reader, keyboard, magnetic medium reader, mouse or a sensor.
Data file	Files stored with a record structure.
Data handling systems	Computer systems for particular purposes.
Data process	Process carried out on data – calculating, searching, selecting, sorting or validating.
Data source	Way of finding data – perhaps using documents, electronic files, interviewing people, sending questionnaires or barcodes.
Database	Quantity of related data stored in such a way that any data item can be found quickly when required. It is made up of **tables** containing **records** containing **fields**, and the tables are related to each other in some way.
Database component	A field, record, table or relationship.
Database report	A report about information on the database produced by the database.
Default	A default is what you get unless you change it. A default value is the normal, usual thing, and if you want it differently you must alter it. For example in a word processor the default page size is usually A4, and if you are using different paper you would have to alter it from this.
Design	To design something means to plan it, work out how it will operate, choose what it will look like, find a way of achieving something. Graphic design means deciding on the appearance of something, such as its colour.
Design task	A task which is part of designing the system.

Digital data   Data is represented on a computer by sequences of ones and zeroes. The alternative is **analogue representation**.

Digits   The numbers 0 to 9. Digits are combined to make other numbers.

Directories   Ways of storing files so they can be found easily. Directories are often split into **sub-directories**.

Discrete numerical data   Data that can only have certain separate values – e.g. number of people on a bus (must be a whole number).

Disk management   Organising files into suitable directories, backing up at sensible intervals, cleaning off files no longer required. If several people use the same disk data must also be stored so that the right people only have access to each file.

Document   Printed or written material. Often used as source of data.

Documentation   This means written material about something. For example, your portfolio is very important documentation about your progress through this course.

DTP format   Attributes of a desktop published page

Editing a database   Amending (altering), appending (adding to) or deleting a record in a database table.

Error reporting   Identifying and recording errors.

Event log   See **fault event log**.

Fault event log   Diary recording problems dealt with on computer systems. It should include date, time and by whom the problem is reported, what the fault is and what action has been taken.

Fault logging system   Procedures for recording problems with computers and recording how they were dealt with.

Field   One item of data within a record on a database.

Files   A collection of information, stored on disk or tape. This includes word processed documents, spreadsheets, graphics and programs. Paper-based files are stored in filing cabinets.

Floating point numbers   Numbers that are not **integers** (e.g. 4.76).

Form   A form is used to collect information. It contains blank places to be filled in, and 'prompts' to tell the user what is needed. Forms can be on paper or on a VDU.

Formatting   Organising a new disk in preparation for storing files on it. Formatting a disk deletes any data already on it.

Graph   Way of showing numerical data in diagrammatic form – usual forms are pie charts, bar charts or line graphs.

GUI   Stands for graphical user interface. The user has a mouse, and on the screen there are windows, a pointer and icons. The user can use the mouse to click, double-click and drag to tell the computer what to do. Most people find a GUI easier to use than other user interfaces. Also known as a WIMP (windows, icons, menus, pointer).

Hardware	The physical components of a computer system – the CPU, screen, keyboard and **peripherals**.
House style	Rules for presentation of information in an organisation which will present an image of the organisation to the world.
Housekeeping	Performing the following duties: backing up files, storing media, handling consumables, managing disks, cleaning hardware and disks, ensuring printer works, keeping manuals available.
Housekeeping log	A diary of housekeeping activities.
Housekeeping schedule	Timetable for housekeeping activities.
Human–computer interface	How a person uses a computer.
Hypothesis testing	Computers are used to test whether a hypothesis might be correct by calculating what will happen according to a numerical model, often on a spreadsheet.
Icons	A picture which has an important meaning. An icon in a GUI is a small graphic which when clicked will start a program running or do something useful. The icon should show what will happen, so the user does not have to learn complicated commands.
Implementation	To implement something means to actually do it.
Implementation task	A task which is part of building a computer system.
Importing	Bringing data from a file into another document. For example, clip art might be imported into a word processed document.
Index key	Field used as an index for selecting or sorting.
Input	Putting data onto a computer system. Input devices include the keyboard, mouse, scanner, sensors.
Integers	Whole numbers with no decimal parts, such as 23 or -14. Numbers which are not integers (like 3.12) are called **real numbers** or **floating point** numbers.
Integrated package	Computer program that contains word processor, spreadsheet and database all together. Data is shared between all parts of the program.
Interface	An interface is where two things or people meet and information passes between them. At a hardware interface two pieces of equipment join together. A user interface is the link between the person and the computer, usually through a VDU.
Invoice	This is used by a company supplying goods or services to tell the customer how much to pay and when to pay it.
Key field	Field which is unique for each record in a given table.
Line graph	Represents data as a dot in a position measured along two axes at right angles to each other. The dots are joined by lines.
Loading software	Installing software according to instructions (usually by running an

	installation program) and setting it up for the hardware and the **user requirements**.
Logical operator	These are AND, OR and NOT. These are used in spreadsheet work, database searches and programming. For example we might search a database for all caravans that are blue AND cost less than £2000
Logo	An emblem used to represent an organisation.
Magnetic strip	A small strip of magnetic material in which data can be stored. Found on credit cards, cash cards, railway tickets etc.
Mailmerge	A word processed letter is merged with a database, producing a batch of personalised letters.
Mainframe	This is a very large and powerful computer, usually used by many users at the same time.
Maintenance	Doing what is needed to keep something working. Maintaining a laser printer probably involves changing the toner cartridge and cleaning it when it is needed. Most computer hardware needs little routine maintenance. Maintaining software means fixing minor bugs as they are found, and making small alterations to keep the program doing what is needed.
Manual	Book supplied with hardware or software explaining how to use it and what it does.
Media	Paper, disks and tapes used to store data.
Modem	Stands for *mo*dulator-*dem*odulator. Needed to connect a computer to a telephone line. The modem converts the digital signals from a PC into analogue signals that go along the phone line, and another modem converts them back at the other end. Some modems are on printed circuit boards fitted inside the computer, while others are in small separate cases with their own power supplies.
Monochrome	Monochrome means literally 'one colour'. This is the alternative to full colour, usually in the context of VDUs. The term black and white should not be used, since many monitors are green and black, or amber and black.
Numerical data	Information described in numbers.
Numerical style	Rules explaining how numerical information should be presented.
On-line	The user is connected to a computer and works interactively with it, getting immediate responses.
Operations information	Information needed for running an organisation.
Order forms	Used when one business buys goods or services from another business. The order form specifies what is required and the quantity.
Organisation	A group of people working together in a formal way for a common purpose.
Output	The information that comes from the computer system, and the form it takes (on screen, on paper sound, etc.).
PC	Stands for personal computer, a small computer used on a desktop by

one person. Other types of computer are mid-range systems and **mainframes**, which are much larger and are used by several people at the same time.

Peripheral	Devices used for the input and output of data. A keyboard is an input peripheral, while a printer is an output peripheral.
Pie chart	Diagram showing data as wedge-shaped pieces of a round pie. The size of each piece is in proportion to the size of the data being represented.
Pixel	Derived from the words 'picture element', one of the tiny dots which make up a computer image. Pixels are arranged in rows and columns on a screen.
Presentation	Spoken report. A formal communication.
Presentation task	A task which is part of a presentation which might be talking or making a visual aid or a demonstration.
Printer driver	A program that runs the printer.
Procedure	A set way of doing something. It is a set of rules to be followed to achieve some goal. Large programs contain many small procedures. Each procedure is like a small program in itself, and does one small thing, such as delete a file or draw a line.
Process	See **data process**.
Programming	The process of creating software.
Programming language	The language used to write the instructions which make up a computer program.
Proofreading	Checking a **document** for errors.
Prototype	A trial or first attempt.
Quality control	Making sure a process produces products with acceptable characteristics.
Range check	Validation check to test that data entered is within a given range.
Real numbers	Numbers that are not whole numbers (like 3.25). Also called **floating point** numbers.
Record	All the data items needed to give information about one object.
Relationship	The relation between two tables on a database.
Report	Formal communication giving details of a researched topic.
ROM	Stands for read-only memory. Dtata stored in ROM can only be read – it can't be altered or saved to.
Scanner	A device which can read printed information, such as pages of text or photographs into a computer.
Schedule	A schedule is used when a task involves doing several things. The schedule shows when things need to be done and in what order. Sometimes several things can be done at the same time in parallel, by a team of people.
Scheduling task	A task deciding when to do what, such as making a timetable.
Search	Finding all the information in a database which agrees with given criteria.
Secondary key	A field in a record which is a key field in another record.

Security check A procedure to try to make sure that data is not lost and is not used by unauthorised users.

Selection choosing the fields to be shown in a search, and choosing the records to be used.

Sequence A special order of things. In IT sequences are important – for example you have to load a spreadsheet before you can print it out.

Simulation Software is used to imitate or represent something else, according to a mathematical model. An example is a flight simulator.

Software The general term used to describe programs or groups of programs. Software is distinct from **hardware**.

Software facilities Things that software will let you do, such as emboldening text or validating inputs.

Sort Ordering data in alphabetical, numerical or date order of a chosen field or fields.

Sorting Arranging data in order, alphabetically or numerically.

Specialised package Computer program written for a particular purpose, such as accounting or analysing questionnaires.

Specification A set of rules describing what something must be like.

Spooling Putting files into a queue for processing.

Spreadsheet Computerised squared paper for doing arithmetic.

Stored data Data saved to a file.

Sub-directory A directory within a directory for storing data. Acts like a drawer in a filing cabinet.

Table A collection of records about the same type of object. A database file.

Task A job which is part of a bigger job.

Team A group of people working together for a purpose.

Template A layout or design which is used as the basis for many similar items. Templates are used in word processing and spreadsheets.

Test data Data used for testing a system.

Test log A diary kept while testing a system, describing what happens.

Text file File stored as text which can be read by a word processor or desktop publisher.

Text style Font, text size and layout for company documents.

Transaction processing The processing of a single data item. Financial transactions include depositing money into an account or withdrawing money out of it. Transactions can be processed **on-line** or by **batch processing**

Type check Validation check testing that data is of the correct type – letters, numbers or dates.

User requirements What the user wants in the way of a computer system.

User support Helping users – includes identifying the user's problem and putting it right.

Utilities	Small programs which carry out common useful housekeeping tasks. Examples are **formatting** a new disk or copying a file.
Validation	Checking data input to test that data is allowable. Validation checks include **type checks**, **range checks**, **check digits**.
Verification	Checking the correctness of data or a command by requiring some kind of repetition. For example when a user changes their password, they will be asked to enter it twice to confirm it.
Virus	A small program intended to interfere with the normal operation of a system. Viruses are designed to copy themselves undetected from one computer to another. Anti-virus scanners are **utilities** intended to detect and remove viruses.
Volatile	Memory which loses data stored in it when power is switched off.

Index